MIDWEST UNREST

JUSTICE, POWER, AND POLITICS

Heather Ann Thompson and Rhonda Y. Williams, editors

EDITORIAL ADVISORY BOARD

Dan Berger
Peniel E. Joseph
Daryl Maeda

Barbara Ransby
Vicki L. Ruiz
Marc Stein

The Justice, Power, and Politics series publishes new works in history that explore the myriad struggles for justice, battles for power, and shifts in politics that have shaped the United States over time. Through the lenses of justice, power, and politics, the series seeks to broaden scholarly debates about America's past as well as to inform public discussions about its future.

A complete list of books published in Justice, Power, and Politics is available at https://uncpress.org/series/justice-power-politics.

MIDWEST UNREST

1960s Urban Rebellions
and the
Black Freedom
Movement

ASHLEY HOWARD

THE UNIVERSITY OF NORTH CAROLINA PRESS

Chapel Hill

© 2025 Ashley M. Howard

All rights reserved

Designed by Jamison Cockerham
Set in Scala, Payson, and Huntley
by codeMantra

Cover art: National Guard roadblock, 1967. Photo by William Gielow and Dan Wesolowski, Milwaukee Police Historical Society, Wisconsin.

Excerpt from "One-Way Ticket" by Langston Hughes used by permission of the Estate of Langston Hughes and International Literary Properties LLC.

Manufactured in the United States of America

LIBRARY OF CONGRESS CATALOGING-IN-PUBLICATION DATA

Names: Howard, Ashley (Ashley M.), author.
Title: Midwest unrest : 1960s urban rebellions and the Black freedom movement / by Ashley Howard.
Description: Chapel Hill : The University of North Carolina Press, [2025] | Includes bibliographical references and index.
Identifiers: LCCN 2024045140 | ISBN 9781469684857 (cloth) | ISBN 9781469684864 (paperback) | ISBN 9781469684871 (epub) | ISBN 9781469687315 (pdf)
Subjects: LCSH: Civil rights movements—Middle West—History—20th century. | African Americans—Civil rights—History—20th century. | Race riots—Middle West—History—20th century. | Racism against Black people—Middle West—History—20th century. | BISAC: HISTORY / United States / State & Local / Midwest (IA, IL, IN, KS, MI, MN, MO, ND, NE, OH, SD, WI) | SOCIAL SCIENCE / Gender Studies
Classification: LCC E185.915 .H69 | DDC 323.0977/0904—dc23/eng/20241209
LC record available at https://lccn.loc.gov/2024045140

This book was made possible with generous support from the University of Iowa's Office of the Vice President for Research and College of Liberal Arts and Sciences.

For product safety concerns under the European Union's General Product Safety Regulation (EU GPSR), please contact gpsr@mare-nostrum.co.uk or write to the University of North Carolina Press and Mare Nostrum Group B.V., Mauritskade 21D, 1091 GC Amsterdam, The Netherlands.

For my children

CONTENTS

List of Illustrations ix

Acknowledgments xi

Introduction This Ain't No Riot 1

1 Midwestern Myth, Midwestern Realities 21

2 This Can't Be the Parade 43

3 A Creative War 63

4 It's Time to Stop Asking and Start Taking 87

5 Black Men (and Women), Are You Ready? 109

6 The Changing Same 133

Conclusion Revenant Revolt 159

Notes 171

Bibliography 207

Index 227

ILLUSTRATIONS

20 Protestors at George Wallace's 1968 Omaha rally

37 De Porres Club flyer

52 NAACP picketers in front of Cincinnati City Hall

70 Lomark drugstore engulfed in flames

84 Wisconsin National Guard marching down the street

95 *Dundee and West Omaha Sun* political cartoon

101 Community leaders in front of a burned-out building

126 Women stopped and searched at a National Guard roadblock in Milwaukee

141 Children walking past a burned-out building

154 Students running down the street

ACKNOWLEDGMENTS

Writing a book is a solitary, tedious experience, a considerable undertaking that requires you to show up day after day and do the work. For me that load has been lightened considerably by the colleagues and community that have supported me intellectually, professionally, socially, and emotionally.

Although I did not connect the dots until several years later, my deep love of history began with my fifth-grade teacher, Mrs. Dora Gommerman. In her classroom I learned to take pride in my schoolwork and that the ugliest chapters in history occurred because good people looked away. Perhaps the most lasting lesson was one day after school when she asked me to stay behind; she took out of her teacher's closet a piece of the Berlin Wall. Holding this graffiti-tagged concrete in my hands indelibly marked that history was not some distant, stuffy thing in textbooks but tangible and happening in our own lives. I have had exceptional teachers along the way and especially appreciate the guidance of Jerold Simmons, Richard Breaux, Mary Lyons-Carmona, and Robert Chrisman, then faculty at the University of Nebraska at Omaha who encouraged my development as a scholar, offered professional advice, and read the earliest iterations of what would ultimately become this book.

It was Professor Chrisman who recommended that I apply to the University of Illinois. The history department scheduled my recruitment visit for the Black Power Conference sponsored by the African American Studies Department. The organizers scheduled an all-star lineup, and I spent much of the weekend in awe. The magic continued when I matriculated to the university in the fall. To put it simply, my six years there were charmed. Working with scholars like Jim Barrett, Antoinette Burton, Cheryl Greenberg, Clarence

Lang, Mark Leff, Bruce Levine, Erik McDuffie, and Kathy Oberdeck helped me deepen my historical practice. The cohort I entered with was exceptional. Intensely brilliant, but even more collaborative, they exemplified how graduate students can support one another. My experiences at Illinois taught me so much about how to show up at your job and for each other.

My first job out of graduate school was at Loyola University New Orleans. Lightning struck twice, and I found myself joining a dynamic community flush with new hires. Over Monday's red beans or Friday's fried fish, we would chat about research, class prep, and Mardi Gras costumes in the faculty dining room. The kindness and support offered by my history department colleagues during many major life milestones will always be appreciated. Thanks to Sara Butler and Dean Maria Calzada for your professional guidance and encouragement. Many thanks to Rosanne Adderly, Mark Fernandez, Guadalupe García, Justin Nystrom, and Angel Parham for offering feedback on early chapters and to the Anna Julia Cooper Project reading group.

These previous institutions also generously supported my research through travel grants, fellowships, and course releases. A big thank you to Loyola's Documentary and Oral History Studio, now the Digital Humanities Studio, for providing student workers Natalie Wuest, Ayesha Saldanha, and Shawn Kelly to transcribe my oral history interviews. My sincere appreciation to the Moody Foundation for awarding a research grant, which allowed me to spend a month at the Lyndon Baines Johnson Presidential Library in Austin, Texas. I deeply appreciate the many librarians and archivists who eagerly and ably assisted me in this research. To Dawn Durante and the entire staff at UNC Press, your belief and support for this book has been unmatched and I am forever indebted. Thank you to the Black Midwest Initiative for providing such a warm and generative community. Thank you to the radio disc jockeys, public access TV show hosts, and community institutions who welcomed me. Your willingness to spread the word about my project provided me with access I could never have obtained on my own. I offer my most sincere appreciation to the many individuals who shared their personal experiences of the uprisings with me. You offered profound insight, candor, and complexity to a historical era deeply in need of your perspectives. Thank you for trusting me with your stories. Thank you also to the Adams Park Community Center in Omaha, the *Cincinnati Herald*, and the Wisconsin Black Historical Society/Museum for allowing me to use your offices for my interviews.

Community is the bedrock of this project. From inception to research methods to target audience, local people are who matter most in this book.

Throughout this process, my own community has been a constant support. The words that follow are but a small token of my love and gratitude.

When I came to Illinois, I had no idea that the people I would meet there would become my lifelong friends. To Dave Bates, Meg Bates, Heidi Dodson, Stephanie Seawell Fortado, Kerry Pimblott, and Alonzo Ward: whether watching the game at Esquire, organizing with the GEO, and now as grown folks with partners and kids and Weber grills, there is still a beautiful earnestness to our discussions filled with hope, solidarity, and irreverence. Illinois also brought academic siblings into my life, Edward Onaci and Augustus Wood. Edward helped me navigate being ABD (all but dissertation), and his gentle inquiries about my progress helped me to get this book done. Augustus's careful eye for detail and ability to weave narrative and hard-hitting data in an accessible way is downright inspiring.

Our adviser, or perhaps "their" adviser, depending on the day, has been a guiding light. I first met Sundiata Cha-Jua at the Association for the Study of African American Life and History in 2005. I introduced myself per Chrisman's instructions, and Sundiata invited me to sit down and join the conversation he was having with other senior academics. He saw me not as an acolyte or even a newbie but an emerging scholar with something valuable to contribute to the conversation. From day one as his student, I knew not only that my scholarship mattered but that I did too.

In every place I have called home, I have been fortunate enough to find my people early on. To my New Orleans krewe, thank you for go-drinks and your enthusiastic dancing in the streets. To my Iowa folks, thank you for plant starts and long, lingering meals. Thank you to Ari Ariel, Christian Bolden, Tara Bynum, Nikki Eggers, Hillary Eklund, Natalie Fixmer-Oraiz, V Fixmer-Oraiz, Mary Hernandez, Donika Kelly, Greg Larsen, Carol Ann MacGregor, Guillermo Morales, Archana Parajuli, Jessica Peterson, Jonathan Peterson, Yasmin Ramadan, Victor Ray, Sanjog Rupakheti, Louise Seamster, Rae Taylor, Rian Thum, and Derek Yeadon.

Three people have provided sage advice and encouragement at critical junctures. Simon Balto, my dear midwestern brother, encouraged me to reach out to UNC Press and offered chapter feedback and research leads. Lina-Maria Murillo, my writing bestie, helped me hone my arguments in real time and always looked fabulous doing it. Laura Murphy provided invaluable guidance in how to shape the dissertation into a book, push through setbacks, and celebrate every step in the process. For a decade she has done this labor with immeasurable grace and unparalleled generosity. Not only have these three individuals directly impacted this book's completion, they remind me daily that we are not just our work but full, vibrant people. Thank you for sharing your brilliance and friendship with me.

Thank you to my parents, Hilary and Jeanne, who fostered a love of reading and Black people and the Midwest. Your own recollections of the uprisings and their aftermath are the inspiration from which this book grew. To my favorite sister and her family, your encouragement keeps me going. Thank you for your steadfast love and support. I had no idea all those years ago at Rock the Bells that chatting up some guy from Jersey about the Plainfield '67 uprising would lead to my own beautiful family. To my husband Chris, you have been with this project as long as I have. Thank you for reading countless drafts and being parent number one while I worked on this book. You're a real one. While I continue to encourage our children to build their cursive-reading skills so they can be my research assistants, I already have so much to thank them for. Thank you for being kind and hopeful and funny and curious. I love being a historian, but being your mom is the best thing in the world.

MIDWEST UNREST

INTRODUCTION

This Ain't No Riot

For those happily residing a red line away, the images of raging fires, glittering broken glass, and National Guard convoys broadcast on their nightly news seemed irreconcilable. By all accounts, African Americans were on the move. President Lyndon Johnson's Great Society programs delivered increased economic opportunity and stability. The 1964 Civil Rights Act outlawed discrimination in public accommodations and the workplace. That same year, Sidney Poitier won an Academy Award for his role in *Lilies of the Field*, becoming the first African American to receive the prize.[1] Motown Records provided the soundtrack to the nation, integrating popular music.[2] Following the passage of the 1965 Voting Rights Act, the number of Black elected officials grew exponentially, blossoming from 300 to 1,469 by 1970.[3] In 1967 Johnson appointed civil rights attorney and Black icon Thurgood Marshall to the Supreme Court. Yet, despite these seemingly progressive events, American cities continued to ignite, burned at the hands of angry and frustrated Black citizens every year between 1963 and 1972.[4]

Amid these upheavals, the white American public grappled to understand "the Black mood."[5] Mainstream news magazines devoted whole covers to the topic of "Negro revolt," pairing their copy with images of destruction, fire,

Black suffering, and supposed criminality.6 The federal government also took notice, establishing a National Advisory Committee on Civil Disorders led by then–Illinois governor Otto Kerner to investigate the root causes of the uprisings. After an eight-month investigation, the Kerner Commission articulated what Black Americans already knew and could never forget: "Our nation is moving toward two societies, one Black, one white—separate and unequal."7 The broad, sweeping changes that the southern civil rights movement, subsequent federal civil rights legislation, and evolving social norms brought about had done little to remedy the inequities that routinely shaped Black life above the Mason–Dixon line.

In few places was this truer than in the Midwest—the nation's so-called heartland—where racism was subtler than in other parts of the nation but often more insidious. With the exceptions of the major metropolises of Chicago and Detroit, Black midwestern life and political struggle has sat at the extreme margins of African American historiography. In the past decade, scholarship on African Americans in Milwaukee, St. Louis, and Cleveland has brought more attention to the region as a Black space, but given the sheer numbers of African Americans in the Midwest, the lack of historical attention to their experiences remains surprising.8 Even in large, edited volumes on the Black Freedom Movement outside of the South, like Jeanne Theoharis and Komozi Woodard's *Freedom North* and *The Strange Careers of the Jim Crow North* (also edited by Theoharis and Woodard, with Brian Purnell), the Northeast and West dominate.9 When midwestern cities are included in such studies, Chicago and Detroit are the most common sites of inquiry.

Black midwesterners faced inequity in all aspects of their lives, especially in midsized cities like Omaha, Cincinnati, and Milwaukee. I focus my regional study on the "urban Midwest," foregrounding the African American experience in a region unified by cultural, industrial, social, and economic conditions. Historian John C. Teaford asserts that although "Kansas City, Omaha, Minneapolis, and Des Moines were the sites of many mills and factories . . . they were not Detroits, Milwaukees, or Garys"—in other words, industrial powerhouses. Rather, his "industrial Midwest" is defined as cities within the Old Northwest region, including St. Louis. By considering industries of scale, however, midsized metropolises are just as vital to understanding the role of the "industrial Midwest" in the Black experience. Here industry began to decline as early as the 1960s, and African American workers were more likely to be unemployed than both their northeastern racial and their white regional counterparts.10 Besides facing major layoffs in the industrial sphere, discriminatory hiring practices by trade unions severely restricted African Americans' access to these jobs as well as to higher wages and increased job security. In their day-to-day lives, African Americans endured inferior housing and recreational opportunities, underfunded schools, rampant police brutality, and city and state governments uninterested in ameliorating these issues. Given the levels of racial inequity in the Midwest, it is not surprising that when Black communities across America went up in flames, midwestern cities were among those most likely to burn. In 1967 alone, the region experienced fifty-five uprisings in places as widespread as Peoria, Illinois; Waterloo, Iowa; and Minneapolis, Minnesota.[11]

Midwest Unrest explores these 1960s Midwest rebellions, with particular attention to the ways that region, race, class, and gender all played critical and often overlapping roles in shaping Black people's resistance to racialized oppression. Focusing on the uprisings in three midsize midwestern cities—Cincinnati, Ohio; Omaha, Nebraska; and Milwaukee, Wisconsin—*Midwest Unrest* shows how these men and women engaged in the uprisings informed by their multiple, intersecting identities. These characteristics also influenced how authorities read, journalists represented, and scholars interpreted the rebels' actions.

As such, this book is in part a necessary excavation of rebellions in an understudied region, but it is also much more than that. By explicating the roles that region, class, and gender played in the 1960s urban rebellions, in addition to race, the contours of the Black Freedom Movement come into sharper and more complicated relief. The revolts reveal intraracial class tensions that often divided Black communities. They highlight the disagreements Black activists had over tactics and strategy and showcase how violent forms of protest functioned concurrently with nonviolent direct action. In these ways *Midwest Unrest* challenges the prevailing portrait of a homogeneous North and documents the complexity of Black politics and struggle through the urban rebellions.

Midwest Unrest asserts that the Black urban rebellions that swept both the Midwest and the nation must be understood as complex, deliberate political actions.[12] After years of agitation proved to be unfruitful, the oppressed amplified their demands through effective mobilization of violence. This tactic was but just one tool in an arsenal of strategies used to defend people and communities against structurally violent social hierarchies. Far from being unfocused acts of violence, the revolts constituted a calculated strategy to articulate grievances. Nor were these isolated incidents of limited consequence.

The rebellions transformed African Americans' consciousness, the strategic vision of Black liberation movements, and the relationships between Black people, their white neighbors, municipalities, and the state.

NAMING AND FRAMING UNREST

Following the summer of 2020 upheaval, the *Associated Press Stylebook* put out a series of tweets calling for journalists to "use care in deciding which term best applies" when covering the mass demonstrations following George Floyd's murder, given media's historical role in stigmatizing protesters.[13] Their definitions of "unrest," "revolt," "uprising," and "protest" ignored the great fluidity with which collective behavior occurs. That "unrest" was somehow "milder and less emotional" and that "revolts" and "uprisings" with their "broader political dimensions" were distinct from "protests and demonstrations [as] actions meant to register dissent" misses the point.[14] Media's assessment that collective action can be identified as discrete, stand-alone categories that do not run a tactical spectrum (legal to illegal, organized to spontaneous, peaceful to violent) is absurd. Naming, particularly when viewing contentious incidents, is an inherently political act. As such, the discourse on what to call these mass demonstrations is as contested as the events themselves.

While the terms "civil disorder" and "disturbance" are largely deployed to assert an "ostensibly neutral" stance, it is all but impossible to take a neutral stance on uprisings, even in their broadest conceptualizations.[15] Point of view, description, and whose narratives are amplified alert audiences to the author's perspective of the event, even when neutral language is used. Scholars who sought to depict these actions as being motivated by "concrete and politically sophisticated goals" employed the term "rebellion."[16] H. Rap Brown echoed this sentiment, telling a Cambridge, Maryland, crowd, "This ain't no riot, brother. This is a rebellion and we got 400 years of reason to tear this town down."[17] Others wrote about these disturbances as riots, as they believed participants "lacked direction and were undisciplined."[18] Thomas Sugrue argues that "uprising," although infrequently used, best captured the political intent absent "a full-fledged revolutionary act." Sugrue defines rebellion as "a deliberate insurgency against an illegitimate regime, an act of political resistance with the intent of destabilizing or overturning the status quo."[19] This is an important distinction. As I demonstrate in subsequent chapters, the uprisings sought to bring attention to community grievances to achieve greater inclusion and equality, not to dismantle extant structures.

These terminological distinctions signpost the scholarly frame but do not augment the analytical specificity with which to understand these events. I use "uprisings," "revolts," and "rebellions" interchangeably to describe "a collective act of violence intended not only to bring attention to long-standing injustices and abuses suffered by those who are convinced, based on past disappointments, that seeking redress through conventional channels is an exercise in futility, but a collective retaliatory strike against those who the revelers believe are responsible for their oppression."[20] Correspondingly, I refer to participants in these struggles as "rebels," as they are individuals who are pushing back in opposition against established class, gender, and racial hierarchies. Recognizing that there are many ways to participate in uprisings, I have reserved the use of "rebels" for those engaging in activities deemed criminal by the state with the intent of destabilizing the extant order. Those supporting the revolts as lookouts, recipients of goods, or cheerleaders, as well as those acting to maintain the dominant order, will be acknowledged as such.

The task of identifying these events is just as important, if not more so, than naming them, so researchers must focus on both equally. Contemporary definitions vary widely. The Kerner Commission, the most authoritative available source, focused its research primarily on twenty-six cities that exploded in 1967. Casting their net wide, investigators gathered information from the Department of Justice's Criminal Division, the Federal Bureau of Investigation, the US Commission on Civil Rights, Brandeis University's Lemberg Center for the Study of Violence, and the September 8, 1967, *Congressional Quarterly* to collate the civil disorders that occurred that year.[21] That the aforementioned organizations' tabulated lists ranged from 51 to 217 separate incidents reveals the considerable variation in applied criteria.[22] The commission culled the list to 164 uprisings that took place in the first nine months of the year, ranking each as major, serious, and minor.[23] These designations were based on three criteria: the degree and duration of violence, the number of active participants, and the level of law enforcement response. The commission classified the 1966 Omaha disorder as serious and Milwaukee's and Cincinnati's 1967 uprisings as major.[24] Contrary to popular and historical memories of the "long hot summer," 75 percent of the uprisings that year were categorized as minor, with the commission concluding that these events "would not have been regarded as nationally-newsworthy 'riots' in prior years."[25]

Second in importance in documenting civil unrest is the Lemberg Center for the Study of Violence at Brandeis University. At its height the center retained thirty employees, and due to their research methods, their findings provide the broadest collection of disturbances. Specifically, upon the center's creation in 1966, it was tasked with "analyzing the causes of civic disturbances, charting their numbers, and advising community leaders on ways of handling and preventing them."[26] The center entered into a contract with Luce Press Clippings service to identify civil disorders for their data collection using a broadly defined criteria so as not to exclude potentially pertinent events.[27] The Lemberg Center's expansive definition of civil disorder encompasses actions that, on their own, would not typically be recognized as urban rebellions.

> We have defined civil disorders as events involving crowd behavior, characterized by either damage to persons or property, or defiance of civil authority, or aggressive disruptions which violate the civil law (such as building seizures). Crowd behavior refers to the activities of four or more persons acting in concert. Our criteria for the number of persons involved were kept extremely small in number in order to maximize the number of events identified for at least the preliminary stages of analysis. Defiance of civil authority is characterized by one or more of the following types of behavior: 1) disobedience of the orders of civil authorities such as local, state, and federal officials and 2) physical attacks upon such authorities and/or their symbolic equivalents such as police cars, police stations, etc.[28]

Because the center's principal purpose was to act as a clearinghouse, these records lack the granular depth of the Kerner study but are essential for a more complete accounting of the frequency with which civil disorders occurred.

After Luce Press Clippings forwarded their research, the Lemberg Center staff reviewed each event, writing a summary and publishing this information in the Riot Data Review. To qualify for inclusion, each uprising had to be reported in at least one local paper in 1968 and 1969, resulting in 1,114 identified race-related disorders in these years.[29] As the clipping service combed local newspapers, Lemberg researchers captured events that Kerner investigators asserted would not have been nationally noteworthy.

The aggregated events provided by the Lemberg Center are vital to ensure a more complete and thoughtful accounting of this under-told history; however, we must be careful not to equate the raging, weeklong fires along Detroit's Twelfth Street with the Black Student Union's September 1968 occupation of the Illini Union in Urbana, Illinois, or a shootout between the New Orleans Police Department and the Black Panther Party in the

Desire housing projects, or a white student protest in Lincoln, Nebraska.[30] All examples shared by Luce Press Clippings with the Lemberg researchers.

Scholars must decenter the state as the sole arbiters of what a "civil disturbance" is, especially given that both the Kerner Commission and the Lemberg Center recognized that the national fixation on uprisings uncovered more events than would have been previously recognized. As Lemberg researchers wrote:

> It is unlikely that the *real* increase in the occurrence and intensity of civil disorders between 1967 and 1968 is as severe as the figures in Table I-1 seem to indicate. To an unknown degree, the increase is a result of the change in the nature of media reporting. Owing to the severe, large-scale riots in the summer of 1967 and the subsequent appointment of the Kerner Commission, plus the assassination of Martin Luther King, Jr., in April, the press in 1968 was much more attentive to racial disturbance than in previous years. Almost any violent event with racial overtones was reported as a "race riot." Accounts of such events tended to appear on the front page rather than hidden away in the back pages, if reported at all. This development clearly contributed to the increased recording of the absolute number of events identified as race-related for 1968 and 1969.[31]

Although media reporting is not solely responsible for the entire increase, it is important to consider the accuracy of the sources from which most uprising aggregating came. Additionally, a staggering 49 percent of the Lemberg Center documented events did not feature Black people or included them along with other racial groups. The center acknowledged that its figures likely overstated the disorders proportionally attributed to Blacks due to the inherent bias of media: "In fact, our sources were such that we were more likely to obtain information on specific types of events if they involved members of minority groups as participants. This was particularly true for small-scale events characterized by short term attacks on persons and private property."[32] Thus, the Lemberg Center's research model, by design, netted smaller, less damaging unrest, particularly if the main participants were people of color.

The violence that racked the nation in the 1960s was read, interpreted, and remembered as exclusively Black events. Race drove the national media coverage as mainstream outlets associated Blackness with violence, overreporting these incidents. As Daniel J. Myers and Beth Schaefer Caniglia demonstrate in their analysis of the *New York Times* and *Washington Post* coverage, "Inner-city civil disorders in which Black participants destroy property and loot stores are 'culturally resonant' for whites, illustrating, highlighting, and reinforcing prior suspicions and stereotypes about Blacks, and thereby providing a well-fitting news 'peg' for white audiences."[33] Consequently, African Americans faced increased extralegal violence, racial profiling, and policing due to their perceived predilection toward violence. The uptick in reporting these events was not accidental but tied to a broader "law and order" agenda, allowing the state to dictate what violence is and who are the perpetrators.

When reflecting on what is and is not considered collective violence during the Black Freedom Movement, a great number of incidents are left out of the story. Only certain episodes seem to register in the mainstream discourse as violence. Not when white New Orleans parents stormed the school board meeting after Ruby Bridges integrated her elementary school. Not when a Cicero mob threatened open housing marchers. Not when armed carloads of white people drove to Black neighborhoods during the uprisings. Whether we choose to recognize it, civil unrest is a potent fixture of American life, a fundamental cornerstone of this country's history. Violence "opened" the frontier through the murder and displacement of the Indigenous nations who lived there. Violence maintained systems of racial enslavement and xenophobia at home and abroad. Violence suppressed labor disputes and terrorized those on gender and sexual margins to maintain patriarchal control. Yet this nation forgets the omnipresence of violence, "its extraordinary frequency, its sheer commonplaceness in our history."[34] The relationships with, and perceptions of, violent protest are fraught and deeply steeped in American national mythology.[35]

This misremembering is an acute problem in the post-2020 landscape. While the opening decades of the twenty-first century resurrected the shadow of widespread revolt from unsubstantiated fear to painful reality, the meanings of these events have been distorted. The Armed Conflict Location and Event Data project found that between May 24 and August 22, 2020, fully 93 percent of American demonstrations that took place after the murder of George Floyd were nonviolent.[36] Nevertheless, as one poll captured, 42 percent of respondents believed that "most protesters" affiliated with the Black Lives Matter movement are "trying to incite violence or destroy property."[37] This is not an innocent misinterpretation but a strategic frame employed to undermine the protests' efficacy. Between June 2020 and September 2020 white support for Black Lives Matter declined by 12 percent, and Republican support—while not high to begin with—fell by 21 percent.[38] As criminologist

Tim Newburn writes, when we consider how collective violence is framed, we "recognize that the influence of the reactions to rioting—what politicians, journalists, and others have to say—often continues long beyond the period of rioting itself."[39] The imperative to center participants has far-reaching effects.

To only see "riots" is to inevitably see like the state, which has a vested interest in suppressing challenges to the status quo. People rarely, if ever, go out to "riot"; rather, street demonstrations escalate into violent encounters. The police and courts, using punishment as a mechanism for social control, are driven to broadly define revolts and immediately repress them. The US Criminal Code defines a riot as "a public disturbance involving (1) an act or acts of violence by one or more persons part of an assemblage of three or more persons, which act or acts shall constitute a clear and present danger of, or shall result in, damage or injury to the property of any other person or to the person of any other individual or (2) a threat or threats of the commission of an act or acts of violence."[40]

By setting interpretative parameters of what a riot is, the state easily categorizes and dismisses these events, effectively neutralizing protesters' power by attributing what are deliberate political actions to Black people's allegedly violent nature. Through this carceral logic, reading any small gathering as a riot or potential riot is quite convenient for policing's designed purpose. In shifting terminology and analytical frames, this project captures the experiences of community members through first-person narratives, moving the discourse of Black resistance from the powerful and retaliatory gaze of the state to those seeking liberation.

Due to intentionally broad definitions as well as timeline inconsistencies, it is difficult to determine how many uprisings occurred throughout the Black Freedom Movement.[41] Moreover, as the number of uprisings increase in any given dataset, a greater distortion between popular memory and historical portraits emerges. This shift is particularly stark when looking at the unrest that took place between 1968 and 1972. According to the University of Michigan's Radical Information Project, 55.3 percent of uprisings in this period involved Black people, 36.2 percent involved white people, and 4.9 percent involved Latinx individuals.[42] Additionally, 45 percent of these uprisings took place in an educational setting (32 percent in K–12; 13 percent at universities) and only 25 percent in the streets.[43] As indicated by this statistical portrait, post-1967 unrest featured multiracial participants and frequently took place at schools, a significant shift from how the popular memory of the events are evoked.

It is also important to consider the latter clashes in terms of scope and damage. Of the 16,766 incidents cataloged, half reported no injuries, 55 percent reported no arrests, and 95.7 percent reported no deaths. In fact, 41 percent of these events reported no property damage, and in the remaining events, the majority involved either a very slight or minor level of damage.44 Finally, over one-third of the urban disturbances that took place between 1968 and 1972 featured groups with fewer than fifteen participants.45

Do numbers matter? Yes. As sociologist Michael Biggs argues in his analysis on rebellion size, "Whether we treat protest as an effect and seek its causes or treat protest as a cause and seek its effects, we need to differentiate less protest from more."46 While many of these events may very likely fall into the category of contentious politics, without a careful investigation of participants' motives and objectives in these smaller disturbances, we risk replicating the repressive frames the state employs. Additional research on crowd size, damage, and location will provide scholars with deeper insight to the many kinds of revolts that took place in the "long sixties." But because the published histories of the uprisings are woefully few, this study focuses on serious disorders that received national coverage as they "have greater power to construct and distort social reality than those that languish in their local newspapers."47

UPRISINGS IN THE MIDWEST

The Midwest provides a dynamic case study of the Black freedom struggle—one that both clarifies and moves beyond standard narratives that distill the twentieth-century African American experience to a discussion of either the rural South or northern megametropolises.48 Indeed, the Black American experience is just as much a story of the prairie as it is Lenox Avenue and the Mississippi Delta. Black midwesterners waged constant campaigns against racial oppression, often preludes to more celebrated moments in movement history. In 1951, four years prior to the Montgomery campaign, Black Omahans successfully boycotted the local trolley company. In 1958 members of the National Association for the Advancement of Colored People (NAACP) Youth Council in Wichita, Kansas, organized a sit-in at the local drug store counter in protest over its segregationist practices—two years before the famous sit-in movements among college students originated in Greensboro, North Carolina.49 In Milwaukee, Black youth engaged in heated confrontations with abusive police for years before that city and hundreds of others exploded in rebellion.50 As Matthew Lassiter and Joseph Crespino ask, "Why do Americans remember Little Rock but not Levittown?"[51] While many works have come out in the past decade focusing on the civil rights movement beyond the South, they either do so as a singular urban study or as the North writ large. Nuance must be at the center of these analyses.

In narrating stories of civil rights activism in the Midwest, it is essential not only to undertake the economic, political, and social impetus for agitation but also to insert region as a critical analytical lens. Historian Clarence Lang encourages scholars not to "reduce the 'North' simply to any place that was not *the* South," in effect flattening the history of places as diverse as Boston, Detroit, and Los Angeles.[52] Disproportionately, the bulk of scholarship on the rebellions have documented uprisings in Watts, Newark, and Detroit, but, as Elizabeth Hinton has argued, the geographic and temporal breadth of the rebellions is far greater.[53] Similarly, historian Gretchen Cassel Eick calls for more comparative studies in locales outside of the South before we can characterize the midwestern movement.[54] This study focuses not only on a regional analysis of midwestern cities but also on midsized locales, demonstrating the ubiquity of collective violence as a protest tactic as well as paying close attention to local conditions and people. By offering this specific focus on the particularities of the Midwest, I highlight not only the material differences that African Americans would later protest but also how their calls for change remained unheeded due to white midwesterners' commitment to a false meritocracy. As case studies in Omaha, Cincinnati, and Milwaukee demonstrate, a region "is more than simply an area marked by common geographic features, accidents of history and cultural values also defined it."[55] These cities share a strong manufacturing base that provided industrial jobs for Black residents, a history of organized protest by African Americans, municipal initiatives to address race problems, police incidents as uprising catalysts, and a presentation of explicit grievances during the unrest.[56]

Omaha's first urban rebellion occurred over the Fourth of July weekend in 1966. Late Saturday evening, a neighborhood woman called the police on a large group of teenagers who had gathered in a parking lot.[57] After a brief confrontation between the youths and officers, violence began at 1:00 a.m. as rumors of police brutality circulated throughout the community. Over the course of two days, twenty businesses reported broken windows, and police arrested 122 people.[58] Youth leaders provided Mayor A. V. Sorensen with a list of demands, including more educational training facilities, more recreational outlets, the immediate end to police brutality and abuses, more jobs, and the release of youths jailed in the disturbance.[59] While previous protests made little headway, the uprising in Omaha brought drastic and rapid changes. The most glaring example of this occurred in the relocation of a state employment office to the Near North Side. What had taken "respectable" entities two years of unsuccessful lobbying, a group of teenage rebels accomplished in a weekend.

Like many other urban locales, Cincinnati, Ohio, in 1967 was experiencing a tense racial climate. For the previous two years, an unknown assailant had been assaulting middle-aged women. In 1966, jazz musician Posteal Laskey was convicted of one of the murders and sentenced to death. Many African Americans believed he received an unfair trial, including Peter Frakes, who protested his cousin's conviction by carrying a sign that read "Cincinnati Guilty—Laskey Innocent!" In response to Frakes's defiance, police arrested him, and the Black community took to the streets in protest of continual police harassment, burning down over 100 businesses in the process.[60] The uprising lasted from June 12 to 17, and during this time Mayor Walton H. Bachrach met on multiple occasions with African American leaders and participants. Despite the initial hopefulness of such meetings, efforts such as increasing police–community relations personnel fell short.[61]

Milwaukee's rebellion began on July 30, 1967, and lasted until August 6. Although it is difficult to pinpoint a specific incident that began the uprising, residents cited continuous police harassment as the instigating factor. Four people died in the uprising, and nearly 2,000 people were arrested during the weeklong rebellion.[62] Mayor Henry Maier imposed a citywide curfew and deployed 43 percent of Wisconsin's National Guard forces to quell the uprising. In the aftermath, numerous community organizations became increasingly politicized. Liberal, radical, religious, and secular groups—including the Young Commandos that, although affiliated with the NAACP, advocated Black Power—collaborated to bring open housing to Milwaukee.[63] However, due to Maier's belief that outside agitation led to the uprising, he was reluctant to implement change.[64]

Omaha's, Cincinnati's, and Milwaukee's uprisings, although individually unique, demonstrate broader trends of rebellions throughout the United States, creating the context for studying the gendered and working-class nature of the uprisings. The anger witnessed in these disturbances grew organically from midwestern soil. These rebellions were not mere instances of metropolitan mimicry in which Black midwesterners saw news stories about their counterparts in places like Watts or Harlem rebelling and decided to do the same. Rather, these were authentic responses to local conditions. As a Black Omaha newspaper reporter concluded in 1965, "the Negro in the Midwest feels injustice and discrimination no less painfully because he is a thousand miles from Harlem."⁶⁵ Racial discrimination in the Midwest was not typically the "Whites Only" posted notices and rampant anti-Black violence of the South, but it could be. While no less painful, discrimination in the Midwest is certainly distinct, principally in that it is a racism grounded in the erasure and invisibility of people whose experiences deviate from an expected "norm." In comparing their own racial virtue, white midwesterners imagined the region as absent discrimination; consequently, "Blacks became to whites in the Midwest the epitome of people who failed to realize the potential of the Midwest because they failed to inculcate its central values of self-discipline and industry."⁶⁶

INTRARACIAL CLASS STRUGGLES IN THE UPRISINGS

The regional and class aspects of Black identity are intimately entwined in the Midwest's urban rebellions. Sociologist Janet Abu-Lughod notes that the uprisings occurred in an "economic recession whose effects appeared first in Black areas but subsequently spread to the wider US economy. It was almost as if Blacks were the 'canaries in the mines' signaling economic retrenchments."⁶⁷ The midcentury decline of the Midwest as an industrial powerhouse more acutely affected African Americans than it did their white neighbors, as Blacks disproportionally suffered the effects of the economic crisis due to rampant racial discrimination.⁶⁸ The repression of union organizing and the systematic exclusion of African American laborers from certain job categories left many working-class Blacks in a vulnerable position.⁶⁹ Intersectional oppression closed off the Black working class from traditional outlets for class protest such as unionizing, while many with whom they shared a racial identity felt that their lots were improving. While the middle class–led civil rights movement achieved important victories, working-class African Americans found themselves in increasingly dire financial straits with little political recourse.⁷⁰ In such a context, violent protest became a viable and effective method for articulating Black working-class grievances.

Using theories of labor violence, *Midwest Unrest* isolates five characteristics within Black urban rebellions that mark them as working-class activism. Numerous studies conducted following the uprisings have documented the first characteristic of working-class rebellions. The Kerner Commission describes the "average" rebellion participant as better educated than the typical inner-city Black resident, and as likely to be "working in a menial or low status job as an unskilled laborer" who faced frequent bouts of unemployment.⁷¹ Second, and despite their economic marginalization, working-class

Blacks rebelled more frequently in the Midwest than the South because midwestern Blacks had long been politically enfranchised but had seen the ineffectiveness of electoral politics to respond to their needs.[72]

As African Americans felt more politically marginalized, they sought out outlets and alternative forms of protest to make their grievances heard. Evident in the employment and recreational concessions made in Omaha and Cincinnati following the uprisings compared to the mayoral co-optation of the events in Milwaukee, the local political climate and prior organizing determined the utility of violence. As political scientist James Upton remarked, "Rioting as a form of violence is conceived as an anger directed at the inadequacy of the political system to process demands, and to make political and economic allocations in a responsive, equitable manner."[73] The average uprising participant's stance relative to electoral politics was skepticism with a deep distrust of the political system and its leaders.[74] When municipal governments responded to the violence by acknowledging and attempting to ameliorate the grievances put forth, rebels gained a newfound sense of political efficacy.

The third and fourth characteristics, collective interest and tangible gain, are difficult to quantify, but qualitative analysis of quotes and author-conducted interviews taken from rebelling neighborhoods are telling. Collective interest, or issues deemed important by virtue of being a group member, cannot be simply defined in racial terms. For African Americans in the United States, collective interest often divided along class lines. Sociologist Jeffrey Paige, who studied uprising participants in Newark and Detroit, found that "those who felt negatively about middle-class Negroes were more likely to have participated in the riot . . . despite the fact that rioters are strongly identified with other Negroes, they are more likely to agree that rich Negroes are just as bad as white people."[75] As one activist opined in August 1967, "I know that there is a lot of feeling in the community now—not only in Detroit but all over the country—that middle-class folk have not done as much as they can for the brethren. I'm sure that you've heard the expression many times that 'When he [middle-class Blacks] gets into the system he becomes whiter than Whitey.'"[76]

The Kerner report highlighted these intraracial class antagonisms on a national level, too, noting that the average participant "is extremely hostile to whites but his hostility is more apt to be a product of social and economic class than of race; he is almost equally hostile toward middle-class Negroes."[77] Furthermore, counter-rioters, those telling the demonstrators to "cool it," were often significantly better educated and more affluent than the average inner-city dweller. One working-class Black man captured the widespread distrust, arguing that middle-class African Americans "have obtained a certain amount of power and they don't want to rock the boat. They don't want to alienate the so-called white liberal. They don't support us anyway."[78] Combined with apathy toward formal politics and the perceived abandonment by the middle class, the urban Black working class had to organize for their own collective interest.

Black working-class residents' feelings of abandonment by the Black middle class increased the collective stakes in the uprisings. Participants realized not only that their actions represented their own class interests but also that, contrary to their engagement with formal politics, something would result from their rising up. Thus, tangible gain in this context was not more empty promises but impactful community changes. Rebels' comments reflect this immediacy. Sterling Tucker, director of field service for the National Urban League, recounted at a congressional hearing what one young man told him, "You're always in the newspaper and we know that you're fighting hard to bring about some changes in the condition the brother faces. But who listens, Mr. Tucker, who listens? Why, with one match I can bring about more change tonight than with all the talking you can ever do."[79] The participant's acknowledgment of his own individual political power is key to understanding the changing consciousness of young African Americans. During the revolts, rebels became "cognitively liberated," realizing their own potential as individual and collective agents of change.[80]

The final characteristic of the Black urban rebellions was that these actions were frequently directed at outsiders. Social historian Charles Tilly and other Marxist scholars believed that violence occurred when important collective interests hung in the balance.[81] The working-class mob, whatever the objective or ideology, always directed its actions against the rich and powerful. The Kerner Commission found that rebels frequently targeted white-owned businesses known for price gouging.[82] In the Omaha 1969 uprising, rebels torched twenty buildings, most owned by white entrepreneurs, yet Black community institutions such as advocacy groups and the Black-owned *Omaha Star* newspaper remained untouched.[83]

THE ROLE OF GENDER IN THE UPRISINGS

Gender has been a fundamental, although not always explicit, discursive framework in the urban rebellions as racial ideologies are "closely linked with notions of manhood and womanhood."[84] Nationwide, incidents of men protecting women were catalysts for rebellion, most notably in Harlem (1943), Chicago (1965), Watts (1965), and Omaha (1969). In each of these cases, a police attack on Black women or girls mobilized Black men into the streets.[85] While most accounts cite the drunk-driving arrest of Marquette Frye as the tipping point for the Watts rebellion, it was the police harassment of Frye's mother, Rena Price, and a woman presumed to be pregnant that incited the crowd.[86] In addition to protecting Black women, male rebels asserted their masculinity in several ways, inverting power relationships by asserting control over their lives, rallying supporters on the imperative of being manly, and taunting police officers using gendered language.

The rebellions, however, should not be interpreted solely as exercises in Black masculinity. Women also fully engaged in the rebellions. Although often erased from the official accounts, women were central to the uprisings' efficacy. Women participated in the urban uprisings, protesting their racial, class, and gender discrimination.[87] Many women patched up those hurt in the uprisings, provided food and shelter to those whose homes were destroyed, and sustained the community during and after the revolts. In specifically identifying women's actions, broader definitions of uprising participation beyond those activities codified as criminal have become apparent. This shift portrays the uprisings beyond false depictions of rampant criminality, offering insight into how community members themselves understood these events and their own participation. In so doing, the uprisings and their significance are no longer understood through the state's punitive lens but through the people's freedom dreams.

MIDWEST UNREST

The urban rebellions constituted pivotal crises that marshaled a new social and political order. These incidents directly related to local politics and circumstances, highlighting the unique regional conditions of the urban Midwest. Not only did these occasions hold significance for the people who participated in and witnessed these uprisings, they also reshaped America. *Midwest Unrest* shows how the uprisings altered relationships and consciousness, leaving a social context markedly different from before the uprisings. The urban revolts signal a shift in tactics and strategies in the Black Freedom Movement while also revealing the end of a liberal Black–white détente in the Midwest.

This book is structured chronologically, highlighting the continuity of grievances, protests, officials' failure to respond, and, finally, violence as one point on a longer political continuum. Because the uprisings themselves were fluid, reflecting a range of articulated complaints, rationales, and often-conflicting ideological views, these core arguments are woven throughout the narrative. Similarly, by using the rebellions as a lens to view the African American experience, the transition between civil rights and Black Power is made apparent. In emphasizing the historicity of violent protest, this work challenges lingering notions pathologizing violent protest.

Midwest Unrest's seven chapters can be subdivided into *precipitating events* (chapters 1–2), *uprisings and participants* (chapters 3–5), and *aftermath* (chapter 6, conclusion). Chapter 1 distinguishes the specific cultural, social, racial, and class characteristics of the urban Midwest in the 1960s, framing them as the catalyzing factors of the revolts. These attributes include declining principal industries, Black and white income disparities, limited political power for African Americans, and what I identify as the "midwestern myth," or the imagining of the region as an exclusively white space and the naturalizing of racial disparities. Through this myth, white midwesterners remained indifferent to the legal, political, and economic barriers that prevented African Americans from achieving equal status. This ideology, combined with the three aforementioned factors, created a distinct regional context to which the urban uprisings were specific responses.

In the urban Midwest, economic and race oppressions acted as co-conspirators. By focusing narrowly on race as the impetus of the rebellions, scholars ignore the equally salient contributing factor of class in shaping these events.[88] The 1960s revolts amplified long-standing concerns about class, tactics, and militancy in the civil rights struggle and thus precipitated strategic transformation in the Black Freedom Movement. Chapter 2 argues that three significant factors contributed to this shift: Black working-class disillusionment with middle-class leadership, a growing sense of Black pride, and dissatisfaction with the pace of traditional civil rights protests. The structural conditions of midwestern Black life laid the foundation for the uprisings, but frustration with elite-driven civil rights actions led working-class Blacks to view violent protest as a viable and necessary option.

After providing a narrative sketch of each uprising, chapter 3 analyzes the actions of the rebels through a political lens, focusing careful attention on the grievances they presented. I also assess the state's tactical responses, which not only disrupted the uprisings' momentum but also co-opted the revolts to advance their own goals. In this way, I highlight the paradox at the center of violent protest: every rebellion was an act of diminishing political return, with each subsequent uprising garnering fewer and fewer tangible gains.

Drawing from classical theories on the crowd and violence, I position the urban rebellions as working-class revolts. Whereas previous chapters establish the precipitating factors driving working-class people to seek out alternative protest methods, chapter 4 outlines how individuals acted in the uprisings informed by their class identities. Although dominated by Black working-class rebels, white working-class and Black middle-class people also participated in the rebellions. White working-class males, angered by recent civil rights victories, invaded Black neighborhoods looking for physical confrontations. Black middle-class midwesterners mobilized community resources to support those affected, with some undertaking the role of "counter-rioters," encouraging participants to return home. Each group partook in the revolt using drastically different actions informed by their race, class, and gender position, marking the uprisings as much more than just a working-class African American matter.

In 1965, contemporaneously with the first wave of uprisings, the US government published the infamous Moynihan report that claimed that Black matriarchy "imposed a crushing burden on the Negro male."[89] Chapter 5 argues that gender has played a central role in the function and discourse of the urban insurrections. Undertaking a variety of roles—defender, spectator, beneficiary, and catalyst—women participated in collective violent action not as African Americans or women or workers but as Black working-class women. Gender, however, cannot be distilled solely to discussions of "lady rebels." In the Midwest, political disenfranchisement, combined with crushing poverty, routinely impeded Black men from fully expressing their masculinity as patriarchs and breadwinners. By undermining patterns of racial control in the rebellions, male participants engaged the power structure as equals demanding (and often winning) grievances that restored their masculinity. Rebels and municipal officials, however, depoliticized female arrestees' participation, painting them as accidental actors without their own grievances.

Chapter 6 examines the significance of post-rebellion transformations of both white and Black midwesterners. African Americans emboldened by the uprisings created new organizations and waged sustained campaigns. Although the uprisings opened space for increased Black political agency, this ultimately led to the retrenchment of white political power. As cities developed programs to allay claims of police brutality, they simultaneously mobilized a more forceful law enforcement presence in Black neighborhoods.[90] White midwesterners interpreted the uprisings and new militancy as overt attacks on white people, sparking the growth of vigilante groups. Coupled with these changes, the persistence of the midwestern myth ensured that long-standing systemic inequalities remained, only to become exacerbated in subsequent decades.

The 1960s urban rebellions continue to haunt perceptions of activism and political discourse. Black America's dissatisfaction did not end in the era of dashikis and naturals. Collective racial violence has been resurrected in many forms in the new millennium, including rumors of unrest, so-called flash mobs, and full-scale insurrection. However, the seeming similarities connecting the 1960s uprisings and the discontent of the new millennium must be contextualized. Centered on the 2020 uprisings, the conclusion argues that both individual and collective recognition of systemic oppression as well as a political vocabulary to articulate this knowledge were the necessary conditions to foment a twenty-first-century revolt. These factors, in conjunction with race, class, gender, and region, illuminate why there has been a relatively muted response to racialized oppression in the past few decades. This intersectional framework provides a lens to understand modern uprisings, identifying catalysts and regional conditions and analyzing rebels' actions to combat oppression. By understanding the texture of modern rebellions, activists, elected officials, and policymakers can begin to find meaningful solutions beyond the failed attempts of the 1960s.

Community advocate Ernie Chambers predicted in a December 1965 *Omaha Star* article that "if Black men are Frankensteins, white men made them such. And as with the original 'monster' the mechanism for controlling us is rapidly failing."[91] Chambers's prophetic assertion acknowledged that the mainstream civil rights reforms did not effectively address many of the issues within the Black community. *Midwest Unrest* investigates the role of working-class Black activism and gender in racial uprisings and in so doing establishes the Midwest as a specific analytic landscape within the Black Freedom Movement. *Midwest Unrest* shifts the urban disturbances from deviant acts of violence to historically contingent acts of resistance, highlighting the coeval nature of organized protest and violent outbursts. The 1960s Black revolts must be seen in a more complex manner beyond shattered glass and dreams, beyond broken bones and promises, to demonstrate the ways in which desperate people seek political recourse.

Chaperones sit in the balcony of the Omaha Civic Auditorium during George Wallace's 1968 rally. Minutes later, young protestors sitting on the floor were run out of the venue.
Omaha World-Herald.

ONE

Midwestern Myth, Midwestern Realities

On March 4, 1968, presidential candidate George Wallace strode into a University of Omaha political science classroom and shared his feelings on the "pseudo-intellectuals" protesting outside the building, "If I get to be president and one of these anarchists lays down in front of my car, it will be the last one he lays under."[1] Boisterous applause followed. The Alabama governor, known for such escapades as his infamous "Segregation today, Segregation tomorrow, Segregation forever!" admonition, frequently goaded protesters into confrontations, painting them as uncivilized and un-American.[2] Audiences enthusiastically embraced this rhetoric, as he captured white midwestern unease, capitalizing on the racial, economic, and gendered anxieties of the region.[3] That night voters helped Wallace form a third political party in the state, with Laurel, Mississippi, mayor Henry Bucklew declaring, "In seven and a half minutes Nebraska has placed the name of George Wallace on the ballot!"[4] What happened next can only be described as a "police-induced riot."[5]

Officers dressed in black shirts led high school protesters marching outside the venue to a reserved section immediately adjacent to the stage where Wallace was scheduled to speak. When the adult marchers came to the entrance, the police directed the chaperones to sit in the balcony. The students, sandwiched between the pro-Wallace crowd and Wallace's "goon squad" composed of plainclothes Omaha police officers, were like sitting ducks.[6] When Wallace gave the signal, "it is people like you," and pointed down at the youths, the melee began.[7] The police forced the protesters to run a gauntlet from the front of the auditorium down the center aisle and across the back to a rear side exit. Witnesses recount a Black girl being kicked by two white men, a Black boy on his hands and knees being hit with a steel chair by an older man, and a Wallace supporter holding a young Black man while a police officer struck him.[8] The Wallace-initiated violence trickled out into the streets as aggrieved protesters broke windows, damaged cars, and set fires along North Twenty-Fourth Street.

Although grave disparities in employment, housing, recreation, and police treatment characterized the African American experience throughout the United States, the pervasiveness of the midwestern myth in the 1960s exacerbated and reinforced these dynamics. White people often possessed deeply misinformed ideas regarding the opportunities for African Americans in the Midwest. In the aftermath of the 1968 Wallace-stoked uprising, Omaha newspaper reporters zigzagged from the north side's smashed windows and charred buildings to West Omaha's manicured lawns and racial covenants, documenting exactly this. The wife of a railroad worker and mother of six admitted she was sympathetic to the plight of Black people, "but they're not willing to work for it. They want handouts without working for anything. If you give them a nickel, they want a dime." A thirty-two-year-old truck driver echoed similar sentiments, "I've got nothing against the colored people as long as they know their place and stay in it. . . . 90% of them just don't want to work."[9] Another housewife offered, "Why don't they do what every minority did? Why don't they pick themselves up by their bootstraps?" When a second reporter repeated such perspectives to a Black laborer, the man offered this counterpoint, "They tell me to pick myself up by my bootstraps. Why, hell, they've taken away my boots."[10] These average white midwesterners came to their conclusions about Black opportunity and employment from a place of detached and stereotyped observation, not understanding. They recognized that African Americans were often unemployed but did not acknowledge the social, political, and labor influences preventing Black midwesterners from obtaining gainful employment. As a Black Cincinnatian offered when he was asked why African Americans could not get ahead like other ethnic minorities, "These are very unfair questions, only the pathetically naïve or the inwardly dishonest would even attempt to compare the prejudice and discrimination that the American Negro faces with that faced by the Irish, Italians, Germans, and Poles."[11] This chasm between myth and divergent racial realities provides the central context for the 1960s urban rebellions that tormented the region.

In the violent year of 1967 alone, roughly half of all urban disorders unfolded in the Midwest.[12] The region's nominal commitment to equality seen through the lens of the midwestern myth heightened these tensions. The midwestern myth knots numerous threads to create a distorted regional self-perception and to justify oppressive conditions. This tangle integrates several contradictory assertions to naturalize unequal conditions and obscure the actions of those who set it in motion.[13] The first of these is that, in the Midwest, hard work is rewarded with prosperity and security: the American Dream.[14] Second, popular imagination situates the region as an exclusively white space; as such, there can be no racism or racial problems. Finally, and contradictorily, if any racial inequities *do* exist, they are the fault of the affected people, as those individuals have not taken advantage of regional opportunities. In this vision, African Americans' personal shortcomings—not entrenched structural discrimination—are to blame for the yawning gaps between Black and white life on every socioeconomic measure. Mass civil disorder forced those veiled by the midwestern myth to open their eyes, even if just for a moment. Black unrest in the Midwest, then, is hardly peripheral; like its geographic situation, it is central to the region's mythology, history, and self-identity.

MIDWEST MYTHS

Through the dispossession of Indigenous nations, white settlers established the region's foundational identity as it is known today—a framework born from violence, removal, and racialized exclusion.[15] Even a cursory exploration of the Midwest's professed commitment to "the ideals of equality, freedom of opportunity, [and] faith in the common man" reveals that such principles were strictly for whites only.[16] The normalizing of the Midwest as an exclusively white, male, cisgender, heterosexual, and Christian place remains endemic in both popular conception and much of the scholarly discourse.[17] The region's prominence in the broader American imagination makes these assertions all the more troubling. Envisioning the Midwest as not only the quintessential American region but also a place absent racial discord and sustained by hard work provides cover for a national legacy of white supremacy, capitalism, and paternalism. The midwestern myth was not created in a vacuum; it was (and is) a response to protest from the very people regional and national mythologies seek to erase.

This book wrests midwestern history away from unreliable narrators. The presidential candidates who evoke "heartland values" and serve hotdish.[18] The filmmakers who capture on screen a nostalgic America that never actually existed.[19] The scholars who fortify the construction of the "mild frontier," silencing the stories of people who shaped a more complex regional identity.[20] By reconceptualizing the region through the perspectives of Black midwesterners, I argue that the region's very identity is constructed not as a place of racial homogeneity but in direct opposition to the "other."[21] That is to say, the Midwest has always been a multiracial space, but its history has been whitewashed in service of its own mythology.

National stakeholders came to imagine and promote the Midwest as a place of safety, stability, and homogeneity.[22] Tamara Winfrey-Harris offers, "The so-called flyover states have long been an avatar for the real America—small towns, country music, conservatism, casseroles and amber waves of grain. Whiteness. It is that mythologized heartland that pundits seem to think will engender empathy."[23] But ignoring the region's most diverse parts is essential to this false framing. As Tobias Higbie contends, "to put it bluntly, what people usually mean by the heartland is the Midwest without Detroit, Chicago, St. Louis, and the kinds of people who live in those big cities, without Native American reservations, and without rural poverty."[24] This need for a symbolic heartland requires that people reimagine the very parameters of the Midwest: carefully excising urban areas, erasing populations of color, and shifting regional boundaries to include only what former Alaska governor Sarah Palin referred to as the "real America."[25]

The concept of a "heartland," in and of itself, is a construction. The British geographer Halford Mackinder first used the term in 1904 in reference to central Eurasia. The term, however, did not gain broad traction until Nazi propagandists employed the concept to justify their expansion into eastern Europe. Political scientist Paul Taggart argues that a lost "heartland" is a central framing component in populist politics because "it assumes or asserts that there was a good life before the corruptions and distortions of the present." He continues, "Heartlands are something that are felt rather than reasoned, and something that is shrouded in imprecision."[26] The very malleability of the term allows the people who benefit from its imagining (read: white, male, middle class) to define the concept, fortifying their position in racial, gendered, and classed hierarchies. The Midwest as heartland, then, underwrites core American populist beliefs, asserting who is and is not a part of the polity.

It is no coincidence that politicians, journalists, and white citizens fashioned the Midwest as "heartland" in the 1950s and 1960s, an era wrought with great uncertainty, angst, and progressive social change. Frozen in the past, albeit one dissociated from any actual historical reality, the Midwest "serves a national need for a living memory of a unified and unifying past." Through a mythic entanglement of race and region, the Midwest morphs into a "museum-piece" constructed in the popular imagination as an entire region inhabited by *Leave It to Beaver* and *Happy Days* extras.[27] In this vision, residents know and ably perform proscribed gender roles; families have secure, middle-class lifestyles complete with comfortable homes, verdant lawns, and backyard cookouts; and since everyone is white, there are no pesky "race issues."

Through Midwest unrest, this book disrupts that vision. Narratives of resistance and representation at the intersection of race, class, gender, and region dislodge the fallacy of a pastoral meritocracy. The midcentury Midwest mythologies arose contemporaneously as—and, indeed, *because of*—activists' challenges to those very narratives as they attempted to dismantle regional intersectional oppression. The creation of the Midwest mythology should be seen as a white defense mechanism. By falsifying a golden era of meritocracy absent conflict, white midwesterners mobilized this mythology at the expense of others' equality. To understand the Midwest is to understand how the nation sees itself, a white nation for white people, despite ample evidence to the contrary. In detailing a broader, more complete history of the Midwest, scholars and the public alike can engage with the region's tangled history of race, oppression, and resistance. In so doing, scholars decenter standpoints that only comprehend discrimination as a past phenomenon, a southern problem, or the actions of a few rogue agents to see the ways racism has snaked through the entirety of this nation's long history with significant geographical reach.

The uprisings laid bare an incontrovertible truth: structural inequality could not be ignored or explained away with the midwestern myth. What follows is an account of the specific conditions that Black Milwaukeeans, Cincinnatians, and Omahans endured as antecedents to their cities' uprisings. By investigating racial disparities in employment, housing, education, recreation, and police violence—the issues most grieved in the rebellions—the quantitative and qualitative differences between white and Black midwestern life becomes evident. Despite the ways many midwesterners sought to discredit claims of racism, the 1960s rebellions should be read as undeniable acts of resistance against constant regional erasure.

MIDWEST REALITIES

The Midwest promised opportunity but failed to deliver. Blacks optimistically arrived in the region eager for economic and social equality but with each passing decade found those opportunities dramatically diminished. By actively ignoring the structural quality of exclusion, as well as comparing themselves favorably to parts of the country assumed to be more blatantly racist, white midwesterners wrote off Black grievances as unfounded. In this conceptualization, the significant disparities between Black and white life were accidental, preserving white innocence. In offering a specific focus on the political economies of the urban Midwest, I highlight not only the material inequalities that African Americans protested but also how their protests went unheeded due to the denial of racism and false belief that Black indolence led to inequality.

With the onset of decentralization and mechanization in the 1960s, "the cities of America's industrial heartland were the bellwethers of economic change."[28] With industrial opportunities dwindling, an increasingly stark division of employment occurred.[29] When emerging fields of growth developed, these opportunities remained out of reach for Black workers, and economic instability grew. By the 1970s the Midwest lost more in employment, manufacturing, and population out-migration than both the New England and the mid-Atlantic regions.[30] The Midwest's moment as an industrial powerhouse—making the beds Americans awoke in; producing the bacon, eggs, and cereal they ate for breakfast; and building the cars they drove to work—largely benefited only a single generation of laborers.[31] For Black midwesterners, economic catastrophe loomed large.

As major industries declined, the stability offered by once-coveted positions evaporated for African Americans. Beginning in 1967 Omaha's "Big Four" meat-packing companies abandoned the city, resulting in 10,000 lost jobs.[32] Black workers were disproportionately among those who were let go.[33] In 1966, of Cincinnati's 8,000 Procter and Gamble employees, only 129 were Black, and they were primarily in hourly positions.[34] James Abernathy, the chair of the labor and industry committee for the NAACP, outlined the stakes of such discriminatory hiring, "Those federal officials who do not enforce anti-discrimination statutes and contractual provisions are, at the very least, as guilty of breaking the law as the person who throws 'Molotov cocktails' during disturbances in the ghetto."[35] Although many labor officials comprehended the direct correlation between unemployment and civil unrest, municipal officials, union representatives, and captains of industry refused to alleviate the problems.

The trade unions' lackluster attempts to recruit or protect employed African Americans in meaningful ways demonstrated the duplicity between word and deed. By using these methods, industrialists were able to attribute a supposed unwillingness on the part of African Americans to take advantage of available labor opportunities while overlooking the ways these programs were systemically and structurally flawed. The Journeyman Union Manpower Program, or JUMP, a locally based, federally funded pilot, was one such initiative. Nominally designed to help Black Cincinnatians qualify for craft union positions in the building trades, the program was embroiled in controversy for its six short months of existence. Funders eventually shut the program down, citing difficulties in recruiting candidates, a lack of successful graduates, and the high program overhead. Others, however, attributed the program's failure to internal racism, accusing JUMP directors of rejecting trainees capriciously. White unionized instructors refused to teach Black trainees the skills needed to pass the journeymen exam. When critics charged that unions were unwilling to accept Black apprentices, union officials claimed that the program sent them insufficiently trained applicants. This circular blaming concealed acts of intentional discrimination and placed the program's failure on the individuals it was charged with assisting.[36]

Municipal initiatives to mitigate Black unemployment also fell short due to institutional and structural racism. Milwaukee mayor Henry Maier claimed to be "baffled" by the request for new training programs, feeling that the city was doing everything it could to provide jobs. While bragging that Milwaukee's vocational training program was the largest in the country with 42,000 participants, Maier acknowledged that the program struggled to recruit African Americans. Structural discrimination such as racial redlining and inadequate public transportation were to blame.[37] The Milwaukee unemployment office was located on 124th Street, fifteen miles away from the city's Inner Core. Anyone relying on public transportation, as many unemployed working-class African Americans did, would have to walk twenty-eight blocks from the nearest bus stop on 96th Street.[38] This embedded racism and disregard previews the ways that the midwestern myth not only exacerbated African American problems but ignored the reasons those problems existed in the first place.

These employment woes augmented African Americans' embitterment with the midwestern myth that hard work is rewarded. Yet the middle-aged men who had migrated to the Midwest as children during the first and second waves of the Great Migration did not represent the most destitute. African American teenagers and young adults, the second and third generations, held both the highest expectations for opportunities open to them and the most acute feelings of deprivation. Like their parents, young workers' employment opportunities quickly diminished.[39] In 1967 the Milwaukee Neighborhood Youth Corps and Youth Council Operation had 7,000 job applications on file but only 100 job openings, which the director regarded as "social dynamite."[40] In sad vindication, it was this population who most frequently and actively participated in the uprisings. The grievances put forth by young participants unanimously articulated the need for increased employment opportunities that delivered.

Economic instability directly correlated with access to quality housing and education. At the local level, racial covenants severely restricted Black midwesterners' ability to reside outside of designated African American enclaves. The Housing and Urban Development Act of 1965 provided impoverished citizens with the opportunity to renovate substandard housing at affordable rates.[41] But many of these initiatives—what Keeanga-Yamahtta Taylor terms policies of "predatory inclusion"—as well as a lack of adequate housing helped create the inequities that led to the rebellions of the 1960s.[42] Elaine Davis, who worked at a Cincinnati real estate office, recalled the discriminatory counseling to potential Black buyers, "You couldn't call it that [redlining], you couldn't call it steering, you couldn't call it what it was actually, but it was very subtle. . . . 'Oh you don't want to look in that neighborhood, you want to look over here.'"[43] Tejumola Ologboni recalls that his mother "could talk white" and would call landlords in Milwaukee to see if a property was available. Upon arriving at the listed dwelling, however, the agent would lie, offering "Oh no, somebody just rented it. And I'd like to rent it to you, but look here on this piece of paper it says right here on the clause when they built the house, on the deed it says 'No Negroes can own, rent, or live in this property.'"[44] The Omaha Real Estate Board refused to end racial covenants until 1969. Consequently, in 1963, of the 25,000 new homes on the market, only 50 were allotted for Blacks.[45] African Americans' inability to purchase or rent homes where they wished demonstrated that white midwesterners did not need to brazenly display "Whites Only" signs to achieve an identical effect.

Most Black students in the Midwest attended segregated schools with very few Black teachers and even less funding. Milwaukee boasted about their highly integrated K–12 schools, stating that of the thirty junior high schools in the city, twenty-nine had a biracial student population. The school board disingenuously employed these statistics, however, qualifying any school as "biracial" if it enrolled even a single student of a different race. One such school had 1,500 Black students and 5 white ones. Another registered 1,900 white students and only 2 Black.[46] Within these discriminatory systems, a high school student's race often determined his or her educational trajectory. High schools with a balanced racial demographic like Cincinnati's Hughes, ensured that white students populated the college preparatory courses while administrators tracked Black students into industrial courses.[47] Solutions to overcrowding reflected the same structurally racist intentions that course schedules did. Milwaukee Public Schools devised a program called "intact busing," where Black students transported to white schools would remain as a unit, or intact, in separate classrooms and lunch hours. Even more absurdly, Black students frequently boarded buses back to their own schools to eat during the noon hour.[48] From their earliest moments, racial disparities complicated Black midwestern children's lives, at work and at play.

In the years leading up to the rebellions, Black teenagers identified adequate access to recreation as a critical issue.[49] Municipal governments' weak response to demands for playgrounds, fields, and summer programming demonstrated their persistent and willful cluelessness to Black needs. City budgets for recreational expenditures illustrated the limited interest in remedying the situation. When African Americans protested these matters, they were chastised for not following arbitrary rules. Black Cincinnatians agitated vigorously to have a portion of the 1967 Department of Recreation's $1.6 million budget directed toward their neighborhoods. On April 29 more than 200 Blacks, led by local activist Clyde Vinegar, appeared in the council chambers to seek more recreational facilities. This unscheduled and unannounced appearance resulted in the council scolding the protesters. Vinegar, incensed at the treatment the group received, declared, "I would rather they [African American youths] expressed themselves here [than] in the streets. Council should not be ruled by technicalities that are raising frustrations a Council may not be able to control. Now the only way I am to get heard is to throw a rock at a policeman."[50] Although African Americans made local governments aware of the critical need for better recreational facilities, city officials deflected to meet budgetary concerns over the requests of its residents.[51]

Police abuse was perhaps the most ubiquitous grievance in Black communities in the 1960s. Police disproportionally arrested, juries more frequently convicted, and bodily harm was meted out against Black midwesterners at rates unmatched by their white counterparts. Omaha police officer Marvin McClarty captured the impunity with which police operated in Black neighborhoods, "If you were to ask any city police officer where they would rather work . . . they would say the inner [city] because in the suburb [residents] tell him what to do, [in] the inner city he tells those people what to do, that's the difference."[52] Police leadership ignored and often encouraged the terrorizing of Black citizens by officers. Col. Stanley Schrotel, the Cincinnati Police Department head, outlined a procedural change he touted as progressive but in fact penalized victims. In his protocol, a supervising officer would bring any person injured by a police officer into headquarters to be questioned, intimidating individuals who brought forward charges of police brutality. Schrotel created this policy because he believed that "the true victims of police abuse were not those individuals against whom the abuse was directed but rather the police themselves." In his scholarly article outlining this practice, he closed with a blaze of self-congratulation, noting that in the six months since the program began, not a single individual had filed a formal complaint of excessive force.[53]

Black midwesterners, overpoliced in their own communities, had little recourse to address issues of police brutality. Responding to criticism of unnecessary policing at an event in Cincinnati for activist Stokely Carmichael, the police glibly stated, "On that occasion, accusations were made that police attire (riot gear and helmets) offended the dignity of the Negro community."[54] Citizen protest did not elicit meaningful changes. As Simon Balto writes, "for black people to have their rights to equitable, fair, and nonracist policing undermined . . . was not simply another form of racism. It was the social compact, undone. It was a derogation of their very rights as citizens."[55] Incidents involving police brutality served not only as catalyzing events precipitating the urban uprisings in each city but also as a continual complaint in both the immediate aftermath and the decades following the revolts.[56]

Throughout the postwar years, the police departments in Omaha, Cincinnati, and Milwaukee remained disproportionally white, despite police officials' assurances that they were recruiting officers of color. Kerner Commission investigators noted that declining numbers of African Americans in the Cincinnati Police Department resulted from systematic exclusion by personal interviews and subjective evaluations.[57] Moreover, the culture within these predominantly white police forces made it a difficult work environment for Black officers. The Omaha police union representative, William Bloom, voted against open housing. Local activist Ernie Chambers editorialized that Bloom's 1967 vote was yet another slight in Black officers' long list of grievances: "Negro officers are made painfully aware that they are to be cannon fodder in the event of 'racial disturbances.' At the same time, they are publicly told by a paid representative of their union that they are unfit to purchase a decent home for their family.... An impossible situation is forced upon the Negro officers because they are asked to help 'put down' a racial disturbance which they might feel like joining."[58] This affront, coupled with other daily degradations, caused most of the Black officers on the Omaha force to resign from the Local 531 by the fall of that year.[59] African Americans, whether civilians or on the force, faced continual brutality, hostilities, and indignity at the hands of law enforcement officials.

WHEN REALITY MEETS MYTH

Black protest against police brutality, inferior housing, and uneven labor opportunities clearly delineated the limits of equality along the color line in the Midwest. The midwestern myth—that anyone who lived there would be rewarded equitably for the fruits of their labors—functioned to discredit the realities that Black midwesterners faced daily. Historian Richard Pierce argues that in Indiana, for example, "white civic leaders set an agenda to marginalize African Americans in the public domain while maintaining harmonious, peaceful race relations."[60] Through that prism, Black grievances did not have to be taken seriously, and token efforts could be mobilized to placate people but not enact actual, meaningful change.

Black community members across the region recognized this farce for what it was. The NAACP disparaged the much-extolled 1963 Executive Code of Fair Practices as "window dressing" and a mere restatement of an 1884 Ohio law. Moreover, the organization took Governor Jim Rhodes to task for cutting the budget of the civil rights commission and for his passivity on fair housing laws.[61] Kerner Commission investigators noted that, in Milwaukee, "Mayor [Henry] Maier appears to be an energetic, hard-working 'liberal' in the traditional sense. As do most white liberals, he appears to resent the fact that his best efforts have not been rewarded by content among Negroes."[62] By celebrating moments where they addressed the "needs" of Black citizens, politicians undermined meaningful understandings of inequality, buttressing midwestern myths of change through hard work and appropriate channels, when in fact those initiatives neither represented the authentic desires of the Black community nor brought about meaningful change. Those who did not praise city and state officials for their benevolence were characterized as ungrateful.[63]

White midwesterners ignored actual Black grievances and lived experiences, citing what they believed to be Blacks' ample opportunities to get ahead. This denial of systemic problems in the region can be seen in public opinion surveys conducted in Milwaukee after the city's rebellion. The majority of African Americans polled, regardless of their uprising participation, cited glaring racial disparities as the catalyst. Whites, on the other hand, attributed the revolt to outside agitation, rebellious youths, and a lack of parental discipline.[64] Solutions offered by Black and white midwesterners also varied greatly, with 84 percent of Black respondents recommending more jobs to reduce the likelihood of future disturbances, while only 35 percent of suburban whites responded similarly. Over half of central city whites advocated for increased police presence—specifically, the use of stop and frisk—to end uprisings.[65] As Omaha civil rights advocate Fr. Jack McCaslin reflected of his own father, "My dad was a saint but he had all of these years of accumulated ignorance and bad information about Black people. And that was what white people were afflicted with, I was afflicted with it to a certain extent. And you had to get it washed out of your system."[66] The midwestern mentality shielded even well-meaning whites from understanding the ongoing structural racism that pervaded the region. By ignoring it, white midwesterners could blame Black midwesterners for racialized inequality and their unwillingness to use appropriate avenues for change.

One of the lingering fallacies of twentieth-century history is that the right to vote directly led to political power. In 1967 over five million African Americans resided in the nation's ten largest cities, excluding Washington, DC. Despite the masses of African Americans living in locations where they had both the constitutional right and the opportunity to vote, only twenty-nine Blacks served on the city councils of these cities.[67] Narrowing the focus to solely midwestern cities, these figures become bleaker. Clarence Lang notes, "Protected in their right to vote, black Midwesterners experienced electoral manipulation and domination, rather than outright voter exclusion, as the norm."[68] In 1966 no Black members sat on the Omaha City Council and only one of the forty-nine members of Nebraska's unicameral legislature was African American.[69] In 1967 only two out of the twenty-one-member Milwaukee County Board of Supervisors were African Americans, and no Blacks sat on the county welfare board or on the five-member fire and police board. The scarcity of elected and appointed Black officials was so notable that

Milwaukee CORE director Cecil Brown joked that if "more than fifty Negroes can be found working in City Hall," he would "roll down Wisconsin Avenue in a barrel without any clothes on."[70] The confidence of Brown's quip was a testament to the paucity of Black representation in the city power structure.

Without a seat at the table, Black residents found it difficult to have the needs of their community heard. In Cincinnati one researcher surmised that the city administration was "fundamentally committed to maintain[ing] the status quo, lacking the 'will' to act on behalf of the Negro community."[71] As a Black resident vividly put it, "If whitey wants something, he gets it. If he wants a toy on the riverfront to play in [a new football stadium], the mayor and the governor and a convoy of PR men will rush down to Florida to court the National Football League. . . . Whitey only has to want to do something and he raises thirty-six million dollars to do it. Well, it's sure as hell apparent they don't want to do something about us!"[72]

Electing Black officials who could "want to do something" was not as easy as running a viable candidate. Municipal stakeholders enacted institutional structures that ensured African Americans would not have equal representation, then deflected blame by ignoring the intentional decisions that led to that inequity. For instance, every two years Cincinnatians would elect a nine-person council on a proportional representation basis, effectively enabling Blacks to select at least two council members each term. The council would then appoint a city manager and nominate from their own ranks a mayor, often the individual with the largest number of votes for council. In the 1955 election this person was Theodore Berry, an African American. Instead of receiving the ceremonial honor of mayor, council instead named him vice-mayor. The mere *possibility* of a Black mayor so unnerved politicians that in 1959 the council passed a charter amendment changing the election of councilpersons to an at-large vote. An African American candidate would have to win not only his or her district but the entire city at large.[73]

Like Cincinnati, Milwaukee held at-large elections that undercut the geographically based power of racial and ethnic minorities. Milwaukee's Common Council, composed of nineteen members, had been nonpartisan as early as 1910, when reformers attempted to end corruption through party politics.[74] Half a century later that dynamic was gone. As an unnamed Marquette University professor recounted to the Kerner Commission, "governing the city often boils down to a power struggle between the Mayor and Council: each looking for publicity and credit, each sidestepping blame for the failures."[75] Within the political realm of Milwaukee, nobody collaborated, and due to the weak-mayor system and the absence of council party affiliations, there were few uniting factors to push through broad, sweeping policy changes.

In addition to having a weak-mayor system, many people interviewed for the Kerner report attested to Milwaukee mayor Henry Maier's great personal flaws. One respondent described Mayor Maier "at best as extremely sensitive to criticism and at worst as paranoiac." The most critical observer stated that he was an "egomaniac with delusions of grandeur . . . [who] considers himself one of the top-ranking mayors in the country, on par with [Mayor John] Lindsay [of New York City], and that he also regards himself as one of the country's foremost urban experts."[76] This final assessment of Maier, although harsh, best encapsulates how Milwaukee's city government worked against the interests of African Americans. Maier sincerely believed that he understood Black people and urban problems. Due to this, he was reluctant to seek the opinion of African Americans apart from select advisers from the Black elite who cosigned his initiatives.

Even in places with greater mayoral power, the dynamic still held. In 1956 Omaha adopted a charter reinstituting a strong-mayor form of government away from the previous commission model. The original charter drafters, including future mayor A. V. Sorensen, desired to establish a more professional, educated city council. Initially, this may have seemed devastating to Omaha's African Americans, who were disproportionally blue-collar workers. But by allowing the mayor to appoint professionally qualified candidates without the approval of the city council, this actually allowed for more progressively minded mayors, such as Sorensen, to appoint African American department heads.[77] City council elections remained at-large, however, resulting in no African Americans elected to the city council or to the Douglas County Board of Commissioners until 1981, when legislation was passed to make elections by district. If Black Omahans wanted their problems addressed in council, they had no African American representation to introduce legislation and needed to resort to alternative methods, most frequently direct action.

Across the Midwest, politicians prided themselves—even in the face of potential rebellion—on their earnestly implemented but ultimately worthless human rights commissions, revealing the depth of frustration caused by the midwestern myth. On October 22, 1964, Reverends Rudolph McNair and Kelsey Jones, founders of Citizens Coordinating Committee for Civil Liberties (4CL), engaged in an act of civil disobedience. Like Clyde Vinegar's stand in Cincinnati, the Omaha City Council refused to put the men on the speaker's list to express their support of open housing. Despite considerable public attention to the issue, none of the seven city council members were willing to introduce the open housing ordinance, claiming they were waiting for the mayor's Bi-Racial Committee to propose it. The council, fully aware that the mayor's fifty-eight-person committee would not put forth such a proposition, remained safely shielded behind procedural red tape. As Reverend McNair sagely noted, the "Bi-Racial Committee is too large to be effective. . . . If you want to kill something, just appoint a lot of people so it will bog down."[78] Mrs. Thomas Hayes, vice-chair of the board, said, "I don't think the majority of the board members are in sympathy with civil rights problems. . . . Any time anything gets hot, they start tiptoeing out." Lawrence McVoy, president of the Omaha chapter of the NAACP and member of the biracial board, stated that Blacks "bought a mess of pottage" when they accepted the creation of the board.[79] By establishing human relations or civil rights committees within city structures, mayors and city councils could sidestep the protest of African Americans, deflecting these issues to committees to address the problem. These groups, however, were too large, too unfocused, and often too unwilling to bring about actual change.

Many smaller-sized midwestern cities felt that urban troubles were a major metropolitan problem. Civil rights activist Rev. Harold Hunt, who had agitated in New York City before moving to Ohio stated, "I think Cincinnati is basically very provincial in its outlook, having a tendency to say that they don't have problems, as stated by even many of the officials. They don't have any ghetto problems. It depends on who's defining the term."[80] Nelson C. Jackson, the associate executive director for the National Urban League, said, "Things are bound to move at a slower pace in Omaha and other Midwestern cities than on the East and West Coasts. But I think Omaha is moving without the trauma of some more thickly-populated areas."[81] This feeling that race relations were better managed in the Midwest helped to assuage fears of urban unrest. In addition to this reassurance of midwestern cities' own superiority to other major metropolitan areas' racial friction, midwesterners took great pride that they did not have the racial strife of the South.

Midwestern cities often held the South's racial antagonisms up as a mirror to their own superior dealings with African Americans. In 1963, by a unanimous vote, the Omaha City Council adopted a resolution that rejected all recommendations for an open housing ordinance. One advocate of open housing, Mrs. Warren Schrempp, spoke to the body, "The name of Omaha will start to ring with the ugly sound of some other cities, like Birmingham and Little Rock."[82] Although Omaha rejected an open housing bill and had a greater level of residential segregation than Birmingham in 1965, this civil rights activist was remiss to definitively compare Omaha with more well-known racist cities.[83] Similarly, during hearings on the Craft–Orme–Danner bill to abolish Nebraska's law banning interracial marriage, African American state senator Edward Danner remarked, "It is astonishing, when you come to think of it—and really quite scandalous—that a supposedly civilized state could live with such an uncivilized law for over a century. This is not Mississippi, after all; this is Nebraska."[84] David Stahmer, a member of the Educational Advisory Committee of the Human Relations Board, said that in Omaha "at least we have a possibility of solving civil rights problems. This isn't so in the South."[85] Fifty years later, newspaper publisher Marjorie Parham described Cincinnati as "a town on this side of the Mason–Dixon line with a very southern flavor," as if somehow racism could be regionalized.[86] The pride that the Midwest felt, despite its own shortcomings, was superior to the South led elected officials to think "it's not that bad" in comparison. What they neglected to understand was that for protesting African Americans, their feelings of relative deprivation were not in comparison to their southern counterparts but rather their white regional peers.

In Cincinnati, a Kerner Commission investigator observed while writing his report that the acting executive director of the Human Relations Council, Clint Reynolds, proudly displayed a Peanut's cartoon in his office. The image featured Charlie Brown on the pitcher's mound with the caption, "We don't win many ball games, but we have some interesting discussions!" When questioned about the significance of this cartoon, Reynolds told him that it was a "singularly apt epigram" for Reynold's position and the council as a whole.[87] African American leader William Bowen remarked that the city governing body is "completely insulated from and unaffected by the desire and needs of the Negro population."[88] As these stories suggest, most of these commissions contented themselves with discussion in lieu of deeds because to act would undermine the midwestern myth and force them to address the actual root causes of structural inequality in their communities.

Milwaukee mayor Frank Zeidler, fearing that racial unrest was imminent after a skirmish between Black teenagers and police in 1959, held an open meeting at city hall so community members could air their grievances. Following this hearing Zeidler created a 1,200-person committee to conduct investigations on the social, economic, and political problems facing African Americans. After seven months the group submitted the *Final Report of the Mayor's Study Committee on Social Problems of the Inner Core Area of the City*. The committee completed the fifty-nine-page recommendation five days before incoming Mayor Henry Maier took office. Maier greatly resented the conclusions presented in the report and considered it an "idea-sack of

Little Rock?
NO
Omaha!

In The Omaha Public School System, No Negro Teachers In High Schools

Negro Teachers Segregated To Near North Side

Of 79 Clerks, Not One Is A Negro

CORRECT THIS

**LET'S MAKE OMAHA REAL?
THE ˅ ALL AMERICAN CITY**

Distributed by THE OMAHA DE PORRES CLUB

De Porres Club flyer, 1959–1960 Omaha Public School campaign.
Creighton University Archives and Special Collections, Omaha, Nebraska.

miscellany, long on description and short on prescription."[89] Underwhelmed by the specific remedies for Milwaukee's north side Inner Core, where most Black people lived, Maier preferred a more comprehensive, citywide approach to Milwaukee's problems, arguing, "You do not solve social problems on a geographical basis. These problems exist in areas of the city besides the near north side."[90] Rather than finding targeted solutions to African Americans' problems, the provisional committee was discontinued.

The lack of political representation, alienation from electoral politics, and the reliance on human relations councils to solve racial problems increased African Americans' feelings of rising expectations and relative deprivation. Blacks were left with few options to address their accumulated grievances in employment, education, recreation, and police brutality. The low pay, political marginalization, and violence that African American migrants sought to escape in the South waited for them in the Midwest. Tejumola Ologboni recalled that when his parents moved to the Midwest, "they had great expectations, but of course they were dashed quickly, because the racism here was not as . . . personal, but it had the same effect."[91] Rosalind Baker, who previously resided in Kentucky and West Virginia before moving to Milwaukee, described racism this way, "It's a different kind of racism in the South than it is in the North. The northern white people [are] phony. They say one thing and they are really doing something else. They're really feeling some other kind of feelings, and with white people down South, we knew. They'd let you know, without a doubt, that you had a certain place and they had a certain place . . . and that's how they treated you."[92] Midwestern racism skulked its way through every institution, leaving treacherous consequences in its wake.

From the perspective of local government and many white citizens, nondiscrimination clauses, the absence of Jim Crow laws, and Black voting rights powerfully demonstrated the region's commitment to racial equality. In turn, the white majority possessed a lack of understanding of their complicity in the oppressive systems that were directly responsible for African Americans' inability to get ahead. In a letter to the editor addressed to the "Negro citizens of Cincinnati," George S. Kopp Sr. stated that his grandfather fought in the Civil War to "free you from slavery and give you the opportunity to live and progress as free American citizens." But

> instead of trying to learn a trade and get an education so that you could take your place in society, you would rather listen to a few bell sheep who are leading you into violence with no respect for the law. . . . Those Negroes who think for themselves are industrious, always

have a job of some kind, get an education and keep their homes spotlessly clean, airy and well-lighted. They want no part of these agitators; they know a Negro has the same opportunity that a white man has. . . . No, don't say the white man doesn't understand you and your needs. Some of us do; but we also know you have to work for what you want. Study, work. And you can have anything, live anywhere.[93]

Besides the assumptions that African Americans were unwilling to work, many white midwesterners felt that they best knew how to solve Blacks' problems, betraying their own racial and class biases. In the wake of Cincinnati's uprising, Eloise Taylor of the Montfort Heights suburb wrote,

We are quite sure the decent Negro citizens of Cincinnati are embarrassed and ashamed of their fellow Negroes. Those of us who happen to be white are embarrassed for them but more than just being embarrassed, we are shocked and puzzled. . . . We know, for a certainty, of the plentiful jobs available. We know without question, of the employers begging for help—but dependable, reliable and honest help—and finding it very hard to locate. If the rock-throwers are doing anything worthwhile by day (even walking the streets looking for work) how do they have so much energy left for rioting by night? None of us could do it. We're too busy and too tired to march, much less riot! Why not put this tremendous energy to work in Uncle Sam's uniform—over in Vietnam, for instance?[94]

From her vantage point, Taylor perceived African Americans' demands for jobs to be unfounded. In her opinion, not only were jobs plentiful but if Black Cincinnatians were genuinely trying to find gainful employment, they would be unable to participate in civil unrest. Kerner Commission researchers heard similar sentiments in their interviews with Francis Demet, deputy director of the Milwaukee Plan-Legal Aid Society and her superior, director Julia Dolan, who offered, "There is a feeling in the deprived Negro community that the world owes me a living." The report writers shared that both Dolan and Demet felt "it was the Negroes who have to come around, not the whites. That the whites are doing just about everything they can possibly do." Researcher Tom Popp handwrote in the margin, "Both these babes are stodgy, self-righteous, narrow, go-slow types. They tend to warp the facts to fit their own preconceptions. I don't think they are vicious—just incredibly out of touch."[95] As Robert Terry noted in his research on residential segregation in Detroit, "racism is couched in quasi-moral terms which command social respectability."96 A social arrangement that blames Blacks as we "are not responsible, so there's nothing we can do about it," enables this viewpoint.97 For these three midwestern women and many others like them, African Americans fell into two distinct and never overlapping categories: those who are "dependable, reliable and honest," the good midwesterners that George Wallace shilled to, and those who are "rock-throwers," effectively ignoring the many reasons why socially marginalized people become violent protesters.

Many midwesterners' commitment to the myth of equality was predicated on the seemingly proactive racial initiatives, southern comparisons, and the accusation that Blacks alone shouldered the responsibility for not taking advantage of opportunities presented to them. As a white fireman offered, "South Omaha whites have never really lived with the Negroes like I have. I went to Kellom School and Tech High and you get to know Negroes and you realized they're not bad at all. In south Omaha, they see the Negro, but they don't really like him. They resent him. They haven't learned that the Negro is a human being in South Omaha."98 Looking back, Mutope Johnson recalled that "the systematic issues that were plaguing Milwaukee at the time were all about that attitude, it's the segregation in the brain, in the head, that becomes policy, or becomes implementation of advantage/disadvantage."99 Due to these reinforcing factors, white and some Black midwesterners read expressions of protest as illegitimate, claiming that numerous opportunities existed to remedy Black grievances. Black midwesterners' lack of political efficacy was not accidental but was the consequence of ineffectual Black political leadership, gerrymandering, and shallow human rights efforts. These elements created an environment in which working for social and economic advancement through traditional channels like electoral politics yielded few results, necessitating a more confrontational form of protest. The insidiousness of the midwestern myth, then, comes full circle as the denial of structural racism forced advocates to engage in violent protest, resulting in a deeper pathologizing of Black midwesterners as un-American and undeserving.

As the 1960s progressed, many felt that the collective commitment to the myth insulated the region from the racial friction sparking fires across the nation. This widespread delusion falsely allayed fears of urban unrest. Newspaper editor Ed Seitz described the identity crisis that many white midwesterners faced: "Sometime this year, Cincinnati awoke to a cold, hard reality: It faced a racial problem. . . . And today, wiping the sleep of a century from its eyes, Cincinnati is asking itself, 'what's wrong? Why are the Negroes protesting? Isn't all that discrimination and segregation the South's worry?' And, more frequently of late: 'What do the Negroes want?'"[100]

Seitz could not comprehend that the region itself, America's most essential core, produced ample kindling. Black midwesterners' point of reference was not their southern counterparts but their white regional peers, a distinction many white midwesterners neglected to make. The mobilization of the midwestern myth in the face of Black rebellion allowed white (and some Black) midwesterners to hold steadfast to arguments of heartland meritocracy, demanding that African Americans work for equal pay, housing, and municipal services while ignoring the structural impediments to them doing so. These narrators refused to center the everyday experiences of Black midwesterners but clung to a tired cliché: that freedom and prosperity came to all those who worked for it.[101] The presence and quantifiably different experience of minorities called this commitment to egalitarianism into question.

Placing African American narratives at the center of the midwestern experience challenges claims of a racially homogeneous meritocracy by demonstrating that some people got ahead *because* others were left out.[102] Although Black Americans have been central protagonists in the region's history, African American inclusion in midwestern accounts aligns with what Vincent Harding describes as "negro history," writing Black actors into white narratives without challenging the fundamental framing of the story.[103] Amplifying a more expansive version of this history and the myths therein exposes the region's deep internal contradictions.[104] If the Midwest is "an avatar of the American spirit," "a weather vane for democracy," or a "conveyor of American values," then opening up this exclusionary history through perspectives of Black midwesterners informs our national discourses.[105] Understanding the ways that this false reality is operationalized sheds light on the significance of the heartland in not only maintaining national nostalgia but also sparking unrest. The midwestern myth, one that promoted the region as a race-neutral meritocracy, naturalized the significant disparities between Black and white citizens. Consequently, Black disenchantment and white resentment combined with explosive results in the form of open revolt.

TWO

This Can't Be the Parade

In the aftermath of the city's first uprising, an *Omaha World-Herald* staff reporter questioned a participant, asking how he felt about traditional civil rights leaders' response to the revolt. The teenager opined that leadership "act[ed] like the old drum major, standing on the corner as the parade came by saying: 'This can't be the parade; I'm not leading it.'"[1] On the opposite edge of the Midwest, Rev. Harold Hunt of Cincinnati remarked two days after the rebellions commenced that there had been increased "dialogue between the leaders and those who think they're leaders." In Hunt's opinion, a recent community meeting revealed that established Black leadership was "out of touch with the man on the street" and that those participating in the uprisings represented new militant leadership in the community.[2] During the urban rebellions something new was at play, something far more complex than solely racial angst stemming from inferior treatment. As Marian Spencer cheekily offered, it was "class, class, and maybe class!"[3] By focusing narrowly on race as the impetus of the rebellions, observers ignored equally significant contributing factors: intraracial class tensions, increasing Black nationalist consciousness, and changing tactical approaches.

The urban rebellions of the 1960s represent a transitional moment within the Black Freedom Movement, amplifying long-standing community concerns. Although the region's racial mythology and socioeconomics created the structural conditions for the uprisings, frustration with movement strategy and tactics caused working-class urban dwellers to view violent protest as attractive, necessary, and viable. Across the Midwest, activists noted the disconnect between established Black leadership and uprising participants expressing the community's new militant sentiment.[4] Urban unrest not only changed the strategic direction of the Black Freedom Movement but highlighted the heterogeneous approaches to change within the Black Midwest.

Contemporary witnesses of the rebellions noted the tension between previous nonviolent, direct-action tactics and more confrontational methods. A Kerner Commission investigator observed that in Cincinnati, "nonviolent protest provided the initial impetus for a growing sense of community self-assertion and race pride. As the effectiveness of non-violent protest . . . tapered off, a twofold movement toward nationalist sentiment and community development began."[5] The relationship between the uprisings and innovations in Black freedom organizing occurred naturally not only in Cincinnati but across the United States. In Los Angeles the 1965 Watts rebellion inspired Maulana Karenga to found the US organization, which held its first annual Unity Day on August 11, 1966, the one-year anniversary of the insurrection.[6] Following multiple revolts in New Jersey, Amiri Baraka organized United Brothers, later the Committee for a United Newark, which helped elect the city's first Black mayor, Kenneth Gibson.[7]

The urban rebellions must be moved from the dark corners of history, where they have been dismissed as marginal anomalies, to their rightful positions on the protest spectrum alongside sit-ins, marches, and boycotts. The uprisings represent a continuation of yearslong struggles reflecting community organizers growing confidence in their ability to challenge the status quo and impatience with the pace of change. Often cutting across class lines, these factors impelled activists to pursue more confrontational tactics to register discontent. In their final report of the June 1967 uprising, the Cincinnati Police Department made an astute summary of the strategic shifts in the Black Freedom Movement and their inherent interconnectedness: "A certain climate is requisite to a community before violence can occur. Our community, therefore, had such a climate. It did not transcend overnight from dignified and intelligent negotiations to breaking windows and setting fires. Like many other cities we first experienced the sit-in, the stand-in, the line-in and freedom marching. Petitions were circulated, committees became organized, and expressions of discontent took as many different forms as there arose new organizations with different ideas."[8] Drawing from long histories of organizing, protesters consciously adapted their tactics to remain effective.

BLACK FREEDOM MOVEMENT APPROACHES

Black midwesterners informed their civic engagement through their intersectional experiences in every era. Through networked institutions such as churches, abolitionist groups, and paramilitary organizations, African Americans throughout the region struggled against slavery and fought for their full rights as citizens. From 1830 through the 1890s, Black people held conventions regionally and within individual states to determine their advocacy agenda.[9] Black women, denied access to the democratic process, built movements for racial uplift that centered their unique midwestern Black cultural experiences.[10] By the twentieth century some of the most potent national movements had deep roots in the region. As Melissa Ford explains in her discussion of Black women's activism during the Great Depression, the Midwest represented "a shared cultural and social space marked by distinctive characteristics of residential segregation, migratory patterns, dependence on Black labor, light and heavy industry, virulent racism, and expansion of radical interracial coalition building."[11] These conditions, coupled with the heightened expectations southern migrants held, encouraged Black people to organize and agitate through a multitude of different organizations. The United Negro Improvement Association fused Black nationalism with midwestern ideals of self-reliance in its advocacy for economic empowerment and institution building.[12] The Detroit Housewives League combined their care work as mothers and wives with economic nationalism to support Black families and businesses.[13] Across every midwestern community, small and large, Black people mobilized through labor unions, fraternal and sororal organizations, and ad hoc committees.[14] As a widespread southern civil rights movement began to take shape, Black midwesterners built on their decades of collective action and autonomous institutions to invigorate this most recent freedom push.

Drawing from Michael Dawson's codification of Black political thought, three dominant organizing strategies—integrationist, militant, and Black nationalist—emerged over the course of the Black Freedom Movement, each responding to changes in the sociopolitical economy and Black consciousness.

From the mid-1940s through the early 1960s, activists in Omaha, Cincinnati, and Milwaukee primarily used integrationist tactics. These activists believed racism to be a "vile ideology that would disappear after vigorous debate and social action" and sought alliances with like-minded activists regardless of race.[15] Beginning in the early 1960s as disillusionment with integrationist approaches grew, organizers developed more militant perspectives interpreting America as "fundamentally racist" and white Americans as too indifferent to be "reliable allies."[16] Under this ideology, activists agitated for "African American autonomy and various degrees of cultural, social, economic, and political separation from white America."[17] This progression toward militancy and nationalism incubated the uprisings.

While Black midwesterners possessed the legal right to vote, political, economic, and legal mechanisms locked working-class African Americans out in many important ways. In the years preceding the urban uprisings, municipal, state, and federal authorities cut off sanctioned avenues for grievances. When Black citizens protested these conditions, either verbally or through nonviolent direct action, state agents ignored, threatened, or jailed activists. In so doing, protest became increasingly ineffective. Malcolm X aptly described this interaction between class and militancy in Black America:

> When you have two different people, one sitting on a hot stove, one sitting on a warm stove, the one sitting on the warm stove thinks progress is being made. He's more patient. But the one who is sitting on the hot stove, you can't let him up fast enough. [Upper-class Black Americans] aren't suffering the extreme pain that the masses of the black people are. And it is the masses of the black people today; I think you'll find, who are the most impatient, the most angry, because they're the ones who are suffering the most.[18]

Black collective interest often bifurcated along class lines. Participants engaged in the rebellions because of their experiences not only with racism but also classism. Barred from legitimate avenues for achievement in political, social, and economic spheres, working-class Blacks sought alternative forms of protest to bring about change and make their grievances heard, argues sociologist Louis Coser.[19] In the prelude to the uprisings, working-class African Americans' belief that violence was a necessary and appropriate response to inadequate political power grew.

By positioning the urban rebellions as a detour in the civil rights movement, the important function of class-based rebellion is obscured. Revolts represented a part of, and response to, the formal civil rights movement. In their pivotal work *Black Power*, Stokely Carmichael and Charles Hamilton dismantle the assumption that a "viable coalition can be effected between the politically and economically secure and the politically and economically insecure," as groups with power "accept the American system and want only—if at all—to make peripheral, marginal reforms in it."[20] Jack Bloom offers that "while the demands of the civil rights movement were of benefit to all in the sense that they were a step toward the recognition of blacks as worthy of human dignity, it was primarily middle-class blacks, who were financially independent of whites, who led the assault and who were able to make use of its victories." As the movement grew and drew in "broad layers of people," lower- and working-class participants began agitating for causes that troubled "middle-class white America."[21] Historian Malcolm McLaughlin similarly states, "To come to terms with the history of the long, hot summers is to confront the failings of the New Deal tradition of liberalism."[22] The rebellions mark a specific and significant tactical change within the Black Freedom Movement. Paralleling a "wildcat strike," the upheavals constituted "a revolt of the ghetto rank and file against an established black leadership which, because of co-optation and other reasons, has failed to deliver the goods, and a form of direct action intended to communicate grievances and apply pressure on the white 'managers' of the ghetto."[23] The motivations catapulting the Black masses into a more violent form of protest originated directly from their marginalization as workers and their corresponding political disillusionment.

THE BLACK MIDDLE CLASS

Class, the relationship one group has to others, to goods, and to labor autonomy, is an especially fluid and imprecise term in the urban Midwest. Glass ceilings, union discrimination, redlining, and impediments to higher education and industrial training severely limited African Americans' opportunities to achieve social and economic success. To tease out the material and ideological differences between the Black working and middle classes, Michael Zweig's assertion that class is "about the power some people have over the lives of others, and the powerlessness most people experience as a result" is instructive.[24] By moving beyond the shop floor, this definition acknowledges that "to be in the working class is to be in a place of relative vulnerability—on the job, in the market, in politics and culture."[25] Although the Black middle and working classes, when placed in the broader American context, experienced similar challenges due to racial discrimination, the Black middle class wielded significant power within Black midwestern communities.

This divide arose from key differences in Black class identity stemming less from markers of wealth and more from attitudes and institutional affiliations. Although both Black working-class and middle-class individuals did not enjoy full access to American citizenship, the Black working class harbored greater distrust of the political system.[26] As Kevin Gaines notes, Black middle-class ideology "cannot be isolated from dominant modes of knowledge and power relations structured by race and racism."[27] A *Chicago Defender* editorial underscored these intraracial class tensions: "The Negro middle-class, which enjoys relative financial independence, entertains a set of values and social concepts that are not identified with the fundamental interests and aspirations of the black masses."[28] Dr. Bruce Green, NAACP chapter president, demonstrated this outward orientation during a television interview in the spring of 1967, when he prematurely reflected on why his community had yet to have an uprising. Green hypothesized that "the Negroes of Cincinnati have adopted the attitudes from German heritage, they preferred a go-slow approach."[29] Green's assertion reflected a two-pronged fallacy that Black middle-class leadership often held about the Black masses. From his middle-class social position, he perceived most African Americans to be content. Additionally, Dr. Green mistakenly assumed that local African Americans had adopted white patterns of political behavior, ignoring the independent racial and class ideologies Black working-class Cincinnatians held. Green's assertion was rooted not only in integrationist ideology but also in the midwestern myth of sustained, hard work begetting progress.

That the Black middle class often centered their feelings of efficacy and possibility within white norms demonstrates their greater confidence in traditional political systems. In a 1967 editorial letter to the *Cincinnati Enquirer*, African American A. Edgar Aub Jr. pontificated with an Abraham Lincoln quote: "Let not him who is houseless pull down the house of another but let him work diligently and build one for himself, thus by example assuring that his own shall be safe from violence when built."[30] Through the avowal of the midwestern myth, Aub blamed African Americans for their inability to overcome the numerous social, political, and structural impediments placed in front of them. In so doing, he acknowledged only the hardship of going without, ignoring the degradation and frustration that accompanied the promise of a better life only half fulfilled.

Political impotency and tokenism contributed to working-class disillusionment as African American leadership provided the illusion of influence but lacked the clout to create lasting changes. Worse yet, some possessed a vested interest in maintaining the current system. Activist Chaney Alexander contended, "The Negro is beginning to see his real political enemies. . . . Cincinnati's Democratic bosses are determined to defeat any Negro for public office who refuses to play the role of Uncle Tom for them." State senator Calvin Johnson, a Democrat and the city's highest-ranking Black office holder, echoed Alexander's comments, "In the past, the sole function of a Negro leader has been to serve the power structure as an informant."[31] Organizer Dan Goodwin Sr. laughingly recalled one Black community leader who participated in the 1963 March for Jobs and Freedom who "wouldn't march here in Omaha, but he's flying 1300 miles to march in Washington!"[32] Long-established civil rights organizations like the NAACP, due to their conservatism, also began to fall out of favor, with a Kerner investigator noting that Cincinnati chapter president Green was "about as welcome in the ghetto as the local police chief."[33]

The divide between the Black community's homegrown desires and local leaders' agendas grew. Leaders frequently employed, "polite protests" such as negotiations, interracial coalitions, and legal challenges believing it "would allow them greater civic and personal freedoms while not antagonizing whites and thereby ensuring additional deprivations."[34] The relationship between class politics and strategy in the Black community echoed an older model where "accommodation became the dominant path for black advancement . . . the custom of acceding to white power, and a leadership that made its way by winning favors from whites."[35] Lawrence W. McVoy presented a report from the White House Conference on Civil Rights to Omaha's Citizens Coordinating Committee for Civil Liberties (4CL), offering, "Our problem is those Negroes who have to eat—they're afraid to do anything for fear they'll lose their jobs and income. Negroes are becoming too middle-class satisfied."[36]

The fissure between Black middle-class and Black working-class individuals was not always insurmountable. Mildred Brown, editor of the *Omaha Star*, linked the common goals of both groups in the aftermath of the 1966 uprisings:

> We cannot commend the methods they [rebels] used to draw attention to the fact that they were frustrated and despaired because they could not feel or see any appreciable betterment of their lot. Likewise, we cannot commend those who have failed over the past three years to listen to the traditional methods of calling attention to the fact that

in Omaha there is discrimination in housing, education, employment, and health and welfare services. . . . We think that less attention should be paid to the methods they used in calling attention to their plight and more to finding some solutions to the causes which brought their actions about.[37]

Middle-class commentators, using both their political and social capital, often framed the rebellions within a broader protest trajectory. In so doing they connected these events to the considerable failures of traditional rights activism and government indifference. These occasions of interclass collaboration aside, Black working-class individuals frequently agitated in their own interest, believing that tangible gain would come from such action.

Although their class position did not insulate them from racial prejudice, middle-class African Americans experienced and fought against racism differently than working-class Blacks. *Cincinnati Herald* newspaper editor Marjorie Parham noted that middle-class Black Cincinnatians "really did not understand that they themselves were being liberated because a lot of Black people were very critical of the people who did the rioting. . . . They had grown up to be complacent. They didn't like what was being done to them, but it would never occur to them to riot."[38] After the 1966 Omaha unrest, Homer C. Floyd, executive secretary of the Human Relations Board, remarked, "We should recognize that their [uprising participants'] actions were a bypass of recognized social order. . . . We should tell them that their actions are not in the standards proscribed by society. But we expect middle class standards from them and now we must find the means to set these standards."[39] Middle-class standards meant speaking in front of city council, voting for political candidates, and engaging in nonviolent civil discourse. Yet in the years prior to the uprisings, these sanctioned means did not elicit the widespread change that working-class African Americans sought. Working-class agitators rightly understood that, to the middle class, Black civility mattered more than Black dignity.

THE BLACK WORKING CLASS

The interwoven relationship between political impotency, organizing in one's interests, and tangible gain all contributed to specific patterns of urban rebellion participation. Black working-class feelings of inefficacy led simultaneously to steadfast determination as well as shame. The Cincinnati Human Relations Committee remarked, "The undereducated white can find jobs, generally excellent ones, while the undereducated Negro generally cannot. The Negro must be able to enter the greater population mass of the blue-collar worker. He must be able to earn a living and support a family and preserve some measure of dignity."[40] While this statement certainly replicates the patriarchal language of the era, the midwestern mentality augmented these feelings of humiliation and helplessness as African Americans were blamed for their own inability to get ahead. Cincinnatian Martha Fox explained her aggravation, "All my family is educated and well-liked, but they never get the jobs they are equipped for. Don't tell me that isn't frustrating."[41] Cleveland Marshall, who worked for the post office in Omaha, told a *Sun* newspaper reporter that Blacks' biggest problem is "in industry as well as government. They don't want to recognize Negroes with dignity."[42] Added to this was the degradation of "the stream of white workers and proprietors who drove into the Negro area in the morning to staff the businesses and factories and then return to their homes in the suburbs" each evening.[43]

The mechanization and deindustrialization of major midwestern industries left Blacks underemployed or unemployed. Simultaneously, in communities where whites controlled commerce, often exploitatively, African American consumers and workers had access to few opportunities for redress. As one Milwaukee arrestee noted, "I was hitting [visiting] that Youth Opportunity thing every day. Me and my buddy, we hit that place five or six times a day.... They'd send us over on the [predominately white] south side for a job, and the guy would say, 'We're all filled up' and here this white comes in and the next thing you know he's working."[44] Maurice McCracken, a Cincinnati grassroots political activist, argued that the uprisings had "only been possible because of the seedbed of overcrowding, poverty and disillusionment which have been sown through the years ... usually sparked by what appears to be a very trivial grievance, but they flare up out of a background of dehumanization, degradation and cruelty."[45] Race, class, and region worked together to trap working-class African Americans in industries with discriminatory practices and in redlined neighborhoods where shops could operate with relative impunity while maintaining a collective expectation that Blacks should pick themselves up by their bootstraps.

The midwestern myth convinced both white and Black residents that hard work could open doors of opportunity. Blacks, however, had yet to receive the fruits of their labor. Previous avenues for change, like pickets, federal job programming, and union apprenticeships, had not led to substantial economic betterment, so working-class Blacks sought new tactics to achieve their objectives. Historian Ted Gurr argued that "the potential [for collective

NAACP picketers protest discrimination in Cincinnati's building trades in front of city hall, August 4, 1965.
Courtesy of Ohio History Connection, Columbus (p267401coll32-28910).

violence] would be greatest in a nation whose citizens felt sharply deprived with respect to their most deeply valued goals, had individually and collectively exhausted the constructive means open to them to attain those goals, and lacked any nonviolent opportunity to act on their anger."[46] These feelings of subjugation and indignity offer a glimpse into how urban rebellions not only mobilized political power but also became a means to upend typical patterns of power, prestige, and honor within the Black community.

Blacks organized in their own interests because even when government entities acknowledged their grievances, these officials tended to be unresponsive, framing African Americans' complaints as unjustified. In a summary report to the Kerner Commission, the Cincinnati mayor's office wrote that unrest was influenced by many beliefs "held by a substantive number of Negroes," but "the administration does not believe that many of these have a basis in fact." After dismissing outright the complaints of Black Cincinnatians, the authors outlined fourteen assertions that influenced "the emotions of the Negro Community." These included "#1 Civil rights legislation did not provide expected tangible improvement for the mass of Negroes; . . . #6 There is a white power structure which is not responsive to Negro problems; . . . #7 Traditional Negro leadership is not representative of the Negro community; . . . #10 Business in Negro areas provided inferior products and services;" and, finally and most importantly, "#14 A strong feeling that the entire social, economic, and political structure is geared to keeping Negroes second class citizens."[47] Municipal officials had a very precise understanding of Black community frustration yet felt no obligation to respond to these grievances or even interpret them as legitimate. Analysts made similar observations in other cities.

The Governor's Commission on Human Rights in Nebraska stated in a 1966 open letter that they found it "distressing" that local and state leadership had long "ignored or denied to responsible Negro and civil rights organizations the request for action that is now being provided after the irresponsible acts of a number of desperate people."[48] In summary, Pete Lakers, the chair of the commission, stated, "We can only conclude that Omaha and Nebraska are following the patterns that have been established in other cities and states: those persons in responsible positions will only listen to irresponsible leadership and that social reform is only possible through the use of violence. We deplore that such a conclusion must be reached and request all elected officials to bring about necessary reform so that irresponsibility and violence are not the proper tools for needed change."[49] But perhaps Omaha community activist Bertha Calloway best captured this sentiment: "It is too bad the ridiculous had to happen before the obvious was made known."[50]

Black midwesterners drew their collective interest across color and class lines. Historian Gustave Le Bon, in his account of the French Revolution, noted, "When the crowd changes into a mob, its individual members lose their identity . . . as a part of a mob, however, he becomes conscious of the power he shares with others."[51] Omahan Frank Peak reflected upon the uprisings, "It was a time where Blacks as a community got an opportunity to vent their anger, but also proclaimed their place over the broader community, not just as blacks, [but] menial blacks."[52] Similarly, in Milwaukee, Earnest D., a twenty-two-year-old foundry worker remarked, "We was trying to show that the poor man wants just as much as the rich man if not more. That's why we did that last night. . . . It's going to take some years and some people are going to have to die. I'm not afraid to die, not for my equal rights."[53] Rebellion participants recognized that violent protest represented an effective way to articulate their class-based interests and combat vulnerability in multiple social hierarchies denoting a changing consciousness of young working-class African Americans.54 As Talitha Saunders recounted in her book *The Negro in Avondale*,

> Just after the riots I talked with an intelligent young man and was astounded at his way of thinking. He said that Negroes would never be given their Civil Rights if they did not fight for them; that Negroes had been patient for over a hundred years, and that to a certain extent we are still in bondage; and our only salvation would come from bloodshed—or we would live the rest of our days in a hell on earth. I asked the young man if he realized that violence might impede our progress rather than help it. He gave an emphatic "no." He tried to convince me that he was right, and that as a result of the riots, doors previously closed to Negroes were opened.55

African Americans' cognitive liberation impelled activists to agitate at the intersection of their identities, civility be damned.

BLACK AWAKENING

The confluence of the midwestern myth, economic decline, and social marginalization led working-class African Americans to partake in violent upheaval in response to both racial and economic marginalization. The slow pace of integration embraced by many civil rights leaders sent countless desperate Blacks searching for new tactics—tactics where African Americans no longer relied on gradualism, token leadership, and the adoption of white norms as dominant features. Sociologist David Boesel wrote that "tactically, black coercive protest [uprisings] may be seen as a logical extension of some of the principles of the civil rights demonstrations—creating a crisis and using it as a means of negotiating with authorities; and its goal—full participation in American society—may be seen as an extension of the more narrowly conceived integrationist tendency."56 Ironically, "the alienation that was manifested in black riots and in the ideology of black power" grew from the regional indifference and the glacial pace of change.57

In July 1963 Lerone Bennett reported on a "new 'Negro' mood," marked by a "go-for-broke" attitude in the southern movement as well as a growing "mood for blackness." The *Ebony* writer offered that the "Here-Now-All mood" was driven by "impatience with the slow pace of desegregation, frustration over continued deprivation and a healthy disdain for tokenism."58

Stokely Carmichael rallied a Cincinnati audience of 800 in April 1967, echoing, "If we do not enjoy the benefits of this country, we will burn it down to the ground."[59] This growing Black pride emerged from a new generation who came of age in the North, was familiar with discourses of Black nationalism, and became frustrated with the stagnation of the civil rights movement. These elements aligned to create a mindset where working-class African Americans began to think differently about themselves, their allies, and their enemies.

Although not inevitable, growing Black consciousness, increased grievances, and feelings of inefficacy fueled working-class African Americans who viewed rebellion as an alternative protest strategy. Kerner Commission director of investigations, and former Central Intelligence Agency officer, M. C. Miskovsky noted that national organizations such as the Student Nonviolent Coordinating Committee (SNCC), Revolutionary Action Movement, and CORE "by their extensive proselytizing . . . made talk of violence or rebellion everyday fare in inner city communities."[60] The critical shift leading up to the urban rebellions is reflected in the increased discourse legitimating violence as necessary to achieve Black objectives.

At the local level, violence felt not only plausible but imminent. The Cincinnati Human Relations Committee described "the emergence of spokesmen in the Negro community who reject the normal discourse of petition for change." While noting that these groups did not openly advocate for violence, the committee reported that there were "attempts to neutralize or eliminate leaders in the Negro community with less militant views."[61] Local activist Ernie Chambers commented in a March 1966 article in the *Dundee and West Omaha Sun* that "a bomb is the only answer. Someone will have to blow up downtown Omaha to convince the white power structure that we mean business, that we are damn sick of imprisonment in this stinking ghetto." When asked if a nonviolent protest would be effective in Omaha, he replied, "No, there is not enough non-violen[ce] left in Omaha Negroes to support such an effort."[62] After a teenage boy died in police custody, Chambers wrote a letter to the Department of Justice asking them to investigate the matter. "Otherwise people like me who have tried to be 'responsible' will be totally repudiated by the dissatisfied elements in the Ghetto, and there may very well be the Devil to pay. I hope it will not take a miniature Watts in Omaha to convince the Federal authorities that Omaha is a tinder box which is so volatile that a chance ray from the sun on a hot day could ignite it."[63] Many perceived traditional methods of protest as pointless, pushing them in the direction of a new political tactic. As Tejumola Ologboni sarcastically emphasized, "You don't get nothing from being peaceful but a butt-whooping."[64] By the mid-1960s, civil unrest became a reasonable weapon in the arsenal of reform.

Contemporary social scientists offered tremendous insight to uprising participants' psyches in the aftermath of revolt. Polling urban residents in the months immediately before and after, these scholars charted the relationship between individual's perceptions of social position and political efficacy. In a study of Newark, New Jersey, sociologist Jeffrey Paige found that those with high feelings of efficacy and low levels of trust provided the critical mass for uprising participation.[65] Gathering information from the relatively middle-class and integrated Los Angeles neighborhood of Crenshaw as well as the predominately working-class Los Angeles communities of South Central and Watts, researchers found that the entwined ideological orientations of powerlessness and peripherality influenced which tactics African American Angelenos used to agitate for equal rights.[66] Conservative civil rights activists had low feelings of powerlessness and tended to be more peripheral or aligned with dominant group values. Conversely, uprising participants felt strongly alienated from controlling their destiny and were less peripheral.[67] Studies conducted in Detroit and Newark documented that uprising participants held strong feelings of racial pride and even racial superiority, while counter-rioters, often those in established rights organizations, ranked lowest on several measures of racial pride. Overwhelmingly, uprising participants internalized a positive Black identity.[68] In the urban Midwest, African American disillusionment with racial inequity, denial of structural impediments, Black middle-class co-optation, and criticism of their own perceived inaction caused them to be more peripheral, positioning themselves apart from the midwestern myth. But for a younger generation, the myth was a dream deferred, intensifying their feelings of powerlessness.

Young Blacks came to this more militant ideology not only through their disillusionment with the midwestern myth but also through a resurgent Black nationalist discourse percolating throughout the region. Robert Washington sent his fifteen-year-old son out of Cincinnati for the summer because of a general climate of racial unrest. He reflected, "The young ones can't take as much as the older ones. . . . They're sick of being pushed around by police who break up street corner gatherings, who follow them and 'act antagonistic.' . . . It's like you're not a human being."[69] Victor, a Black Milwaukee teenager, dismissed his southern, day-laboring father, scoffing that he knew nothing about Black Power and that when the man moved to Wisconsin, he thought he "had given heaven to his family," concluding "people like my daddy are not going to throw rocks."[70] Rebels were "socialized in the North and were responding specifically to Northern grievances, using Northern-engendered responses."[71] Following the melee at the Omaha Civic Auditorium, JoAnn Donaldson, a junior at Central High School, screamed at Governor Wallace, "You're going to get it, baby. Just you wait. You're going to get it this summer. . . . Nebraska's going to be a ball of fire this summer. It's going to be the hottest state there is."[72] An employee at the Community Action Commission in Cincinnati observed, "Everywhere you go you hear [young people] say, 'Man, somebody's going to be killed.'" To which the teenagers replied, "Man, we're ready."[73] As another Cincinnatian confirmed, "I might as well die at [the corner of] Reading and Rockdale as in Vietnam."[74] For young midwestern Blacks, the feelings of powerlessness occurred not in the deprivation they felt relative to a distant southern experience but rather to the standard of living and opportunity that whites were afforded in their own midwestern cities.

Black midwesterners sought solutions to their oppression, but traditional forms of direct action were insufficient to bring about significant change. The young men and women who came of age in midwestern urban ghettos were much freer than the generation that came before them. Rev. Harold Hunt noted that many wanted "a greater share in the American way of life. The Negro is not afraid of the white man's guns, he is saying give us our rights or exterminate us."[75] James Mimms, a young man at the time, recollects his response to popular movement slogans. "We wasn't fighting for freedom and that's what I remember about the riots. They kept talking about fighting for freedom. . . . It wasn't about freedom, it was about discrimination. We could work, worship, live, and learn in freedom, we just wasn't equal, that's what we was angry about."[76] Midwestern Blacks had been socialized to believe they were entitled to the same opportunities as whites. They perceived Blackness as a positive attribute and exhibited racial pride. As Bloom notes, "this new generation of urban blacks was politically sophisticated and well informed. It felt capable of affecting policy."[77] In the aftermath of the first Cincinnati rebellion, the Victory Neighborhood Service organization noted, "Black power activists want freedom and manhood for the Negro, opportunities to set policy and run things in the ghetto. They distrust the present institutions and establishments to even provide equal opportunity and justice. There is a distrust of persons over 30 and of the Negro middle class."[78] These feelings of pride and efficacy encouraged them to establish new agendas and protest methods. African Americans in midwestern cities set forth new strategies to agitate for equality within their own local communities.

Despite the national widespread belief among Blacks that violence was an acceptable protest tactic, all uprisings were not equal. A Kerner Commission researcher wrote that although Milwaukee possessed a heightened racial climate, "I had the impression that relations among the races there resemble those in other large cities five years ago.... This impression may be present because of Father [James] Groppi. He is a white man leading a non-violent Negro protest. By comparison with other cities, this seems to be an anachronism." When Bernard Dobranski and John Boswell interviewed Assistant US Attorney Frank Gimble, he noted, "One problem that appears to be unique in Milwaukee is the political immaturity of the Negroes."[79] Gimble did not mean this as a slight on African Americans; rather, citing an example of the previous year's school board election, he demonstrated that African American protest in the city looked very different than it did in other urban locales.

In that election, the lowest voter turnout in the city occurred in the African American ward, resulting in the defeat of all the liberal candidates and the lone Black candidate. Worse yet, Gimble felt that "there is no sign of a growing political maturity on the part of the Negro community.... The largest part of the Negro community are sympathetic to Father Groppi, but not willing to go out in the street and march with him."[80] While Black militants held fundraisers in Cincinnati and Omaha for Black Power activists to build Black nationalist institutions, Milwaukee Blacks remained committed to a white clergyman but were unwilling to march with him. By parsing out Milwaukee's unique political development, not only does this challenge the dominant historiography about Black Power ideology and development in the city, it also supports the need for more granular stories of regional histories in their locales.

On the ground in Milwaukee, Black Power rhetoric, not consciousness, could be found. The Commandos, the NAACP Youth Council's offshoot militant group, epitomized this mischaracterization of Black Power. Founded in 1947, the group garnered local and national notoriety for a number of reasons. Members structured their group paramilitarily, providing ranks and titles based on an individual's commitment to the cause. The group also attracted attention because of their militancy, particularly in their sustained daily marches in support of open housing. As Kerner Commission researcher Charles King observed, "The unique aspect about the Commandos is that whereas they emphasize Black Power, they also emphasize integrated Black Power. Black Power to them means black or white people joining together to highlight the black man's problem."[81] The Milwaukee NAACP Youth Council functioned very differently from other self-identified Black Power groups in the United States, who maintained a deeply nationalist, often separatist, and radical perspective.[82]

Like other northern cities at this time, commission observers noted that "there is some good Negro leadership, but the community suffers from organizational competition, and consequently it has not been able to develop a strong coalition for the pursuit of common goals." One researcher noted that the terms "apathetic," "complacent," "disorganized," and "fragmented" were the words most frequently used to describe the protest climate in Milwaukee prior to the uprising. He reported, "except for a Negro boycott of the schools to protest against intact busing, there had been little to disturb the city's self-regarding slumber. New York, Chicago, Detroit, and other large cities had become accustomed to demonstrations and angry Negro demands." Moreover, when Stokely Carmichael came to Milwaukee in 1966, Black youths did not respond to him with "the enthusiasm that he had experienced in other cities; they did not seem to know what to make of him."[83]

The allies that Black activists chose to align themselves with also reflected this resistance to a muscular form of Black nationalism. White Milwaukeean Dr. Jay Larkey and his wife, Hinda, who wore a Black Power button to her meeting with Kerner investigators, asserted that "in Milwaukee there's still room [for white people in the movement]—that if any kind of success can come of the efforts which they have been making, the room will still be there." Ultimately, interviewer Tom Popp commented that the Larkeys were "'good' people, thinking, iconoclastic, straightforward types. But their involvement stems perhaps chiefly more from the satisfaction they get from 'being involved.'"[84]

The interviewers offered an even less-than-glowing assessment of Father Groppi, the white priest who served as the adviser for the Young Commandos. An investigator reminded the priest that "many of his statements were more militant than black people utter" and questioned whether this caused conflict. Groppi retorted that he "did not consciously recognize this [that he acted and talked Black], and he had no knowledge of when this transition took place, when he began improvising so strongly black that he began feeling black." The interviewer continued, "Incidentally he stated that he felt the greatest compliment ever paid to him was when one of the white protesters against the march called him a 'white N———.'" He concluded that the only hope for white people is to understand Black people's plight so deeply that he becomes in "essence a black man with a white skin."[85] The lack of cohesiveness of Milwaukee's movement, and its somewhat reluctant embrace of Black nationalist ideology, prevented it from creating and articulating political demands in the aftermath of the 1967 rebellion from a position of power.

As Malcolm McLaughlin noted, "uprisings by black communities against the social order in America, their defiance of authority and assaults against property, inevitably meant conflict with white authority and white property."[86] Thus, it is essential not to discuss uprisings as a homogeneous mass of events. Each must be rooted in their own context, movement development, and political economy. While clearly these events reflect the nationwide dissatisfaction with efforts to bring about meaningful change, not all uprisings deliver the same impact. The fluidity with which they occurred and the mechanisms to which they are afforded political meanings are complex processes in and of themselves. Yes, all uprisings are actions of resistance and politics at their very core, but, as Milwaukee demonstrates, the intent can vary widely.

The rebellions were specific reactions to the changing tactics and goals in the Black Freedom Movement. The movement comprised several approaches, each responsive to particular social and political conditions. The early nonviolent direct actions, many of which began in the Midwest during the Great Depression, by the mid-1960s had given way to a more militant, proto-nationalist type of protest. With time, however, these marches, boycotts, and sit-ins were no longer viable protest options. The failure was not because activists no longer attempted to ameliorate their conditions; rather, local government no longer responded to protest, necessitating more aggressive tactics. Militant, proto-nationalist leaders first brought about this intensification, willing to go to extreme actions to bring about change in their communities. Like the traditional nonviolent direct-action protest activities, these too lost their strength. Additionally, working-class Blacks began to organize in their own interests more aggressively. The uprisings became a reaction against the "system," both racial and economic. Young African Americans, who constituted most uprising participants, expressed their grievances through revolt against oppression and any symbols therein.

Black working-class people had already concluded that they had been systematically shut out due not only to their racial position but also to their class position. Many factors created the psychological vantage point from where individuals understood their position in the midwestern hierarchy prior to the uprisings. As Robert Vernon penned in his book *Black Ghetto* about early sites of unrest, "Watts, Harlem, Philadelphia, Rochester show that throwing a few scraps and bone of civil rites [sic] to the Negro middle class does not solve the problems of class oppression."[87] The uprisings demonstrate the ways in which participants fomented protest against not only an oppressive racial structure but also class structure. In the context of the urban Midwest, economic and racial bias acted as co-conspirators. The discrimination that Blacks felt in the North often manifested itself in more economic factors than overt de facto segregation. Black middle-class leadership still oriented local struggles to mirror the southern movement, lacking the vision of authentic protest for their own communities. The grievances demanded in the aftermath of the rebellions showed that Blacks were unwilling to completely jettison the American system. They demanded that the institutions that shaped their lives be controlled by people who looked and thought like them. Here lies a significant difference between the Black working and middle classes. The middle class typically wanted a world where they were included in a classed hierarchy, whereas working-class Blacks had already begun to articulate a nationalist, proto–Black Power ideology that would create either parallel institutions run by working-class Black people or altogether new organizations. The civil rights movement and Black Power movement mark these two distinct strategic periods within the Black freedom struggle. The urban rebellions served as the bridge between these separate, strategic eras.

Working-class African Americans, previously abandoned by the Black middle class, had the opportunity to use violence to force the municipal government to be responsive to their needs. In the years immediately preceding the urban rebellions, three factors—growing class fissures, increased militancy, and the failure of nonviolent direct action—contributed to this inadequacy, making the Midwest particularly explosive. The aftermath of the rebellions marks an important transitional period in which African Americans, unified in some ways by the uprisings, began to come together to codify what Black Power looked like in their communities. It is this ideology that began to solidify in the rebels' minds, forever changing the strategic vision of the Black Freedom Movement. The congealing of these factors in creating a new ideology was not enough to bring about actual change. Only in the fires of the urban rebellions could a new political order be forged.

THREE

A Creative War

In a television interview on Milwaukee's *Crosstalk* program, civil rights activist, attorney, and state assemblyman Lloyd Barbee shocked host J. G. Sykes with his provocative comments. When questioned what he believed to be the next step in the civil rights movement, Barbee responded, "You talked about the creative war in Viet Nam, I suppose we're going to have a creative war here in Milwaukee. . . . I feel the thing we witnessed this summer in the Inner Core, the thing the people call a riot—I don't think [it] has been read and interpreted to the degree that meaningful efforts are being made to solve the problems. Therefore, the demonstrations will become less non-violent."[1]

Barbee, a person with formal political power and class privilege, acknowledged that the protest that African Americans sought to manifest through the urban uprisings was unsuccessful. This failure stemmed from municipal government co-opting the rebellion for political gain and neglecting to view the uprising as authentic Black protest. Barbee asserted that Black Milwaukeeans would have to be more aggressive, creative, and ultimately violent, to have their grievances addressed. Where Milwaukee's unrest failed to bring meaningful change to the Black population, Cincinnati's and Omaha's first uprisings were moderately effective. The key difference to how these three cities fared centered on how rebels and others mobilized the urban revolts as political tools.

The 1960s urban rebellions represent a continuation of previous political jockeying and protest. In these moments of unrest, participants and governmental officials conveyed, interpreted, and reimagined political ideologies. Through the employment of extra-institutional tactics, activists temporarily held parallel footing with the state as nontraditional political actors, operating outside established spheres of power. The Black working class, effectively powerless in local electoral politics, abandoned ineffective, nonviolent direct-action tactics to coerce the government to address their grievances. Violent uprisings prevented cities from functioning normally, disrupting ruling-class interests. The rebels' actions forced elites to end the uprisings by either cooperation or suppression.[2]

Urban rebellions constitute political protests not only through participants' intent but also in local governments' response.[3] Even the most conservative views of the rebellions, such as the notorious McCone Commission, acknowledged the underlying political rationales of these events. While then–California governor Ronald Reagan considered the participants to be "lawbreakers and mad dogs," the commission conceded that Los Angeles's political, social, and economic environment "underlay the gathering anger which impelled the rioter."[4] Rebellions are often read as political, but the formal and informal political consequences are overlooked.

Through the uprisings the Black community temporarily shifted patterns of control, creating an untenable environment for key stakeholders and exposing the fallacy of the midwestern myth. Rebels used this tactical innovation to force those in power to address their demands to restore order. There are limits to this innovation, however. Subsequent uprisings did not bring about the dramatic response that the first occasions did, as governments also adjusted. This tactical adaptation neutralized the power of the uprisings.[5] The numerous revolts that took place in the mid- and late 1960s not only unseated nonviolence as the dominant strategy for achieving racial equality but also provided rhetorical power for Black nationalist movements and the coming backlash of the New Right.[6] In reading the political actions of rebels and the state, the function of urban revolts shifts from wanton violence to strategic negotiation.

OMAHA'S REBELLION (JULY 2–5, 1966)

Omaha's first uprising occurred over the Fourth of July weekend in 1966. Late Saturday evening, July 2, a group of about 150 Black youths loitered in a parking lot owned by Safeway grocery and Skaggs Drugstore. At 12:49 a.m. on July 3 a neighborhood woman, who witnessed a teenager lighting fireworks in the parking lot, called the police. Two officers arrived in patrol cruiser #33 to investigate. The teenagers hurled cherry bombs and rocks at the patrol car, breaking the rear window. Feeling threatened, the officers left the scene and returned with reinforcements. Property damage began around 1:00 a.m., and reports of police brutality began to circulate among the gathering crowd.[7]

The group dispersed from the parking lot and poured onto the main business strip of the Near North Side. Their pent-up anger, frustration, and helplessness manifested in the fires they set and the glass they shattered along North Twenty-Fourth Street. Police gathered at a makeshift response post housed at the fire station located on Twenty-Second and Lake Streets. Over 100 law enforcement officers reported to the Safeway parking lot, where youths again threw rocks, bottles, and stones in the direction of the officers. For the next two nights, participants broke windows and looted several stores along the central business corridor.[8]

At 12:30 a.m. on July 5, law enforcement personnel moved to Twenty-Fourth and Lake Streets to disperse yet another crowd that had gathered. Recognizing they were outnumbered, the police immediately requested National Guard assistance. Under the command of Brig. Gen. William Bachman, the First Battalion, the 134th Infantry, and the 867th Engineer Company assembled. These Nebraskan men, many the same age as the uprising participants, marched to the Near North Side armed with rifles, clubs, and gas masks.[9] The crowd attempted to provoke the guard, with taunting comments like "whitey," but no physical confrontation occurred as most of the youths had dispersed. Bringing in the National Guard seemed to help diffuse the violence, but Mayor A. V. Sorensen disappointed the Urban League and NAACP by not consulting with the organizations prior to calling in the troops. An afternoon rain shower on Tuesday, July 5, quite literally dampened the rebels' desire to take to the streets, effectively bringing the uprising to an end. The rain, however, could not wash away the deeper meaning of what had happened.[10]

One hundred young Black men aired their grievances about police brutality, joblessness, and the lack of recreational activities at a meeting coordinated by YMCA director Sam Cornelius and attended by Omaha's mayor, public safety director, and community relations coordinator. The NAACP accused Mayor Sorensen and Governor Frank Morrison of listening too much to the rebels and not enough to the established leadership in the Black community. Moreover, Sorensen angered moderate leadership after keeping them waiting for a scheduled meeting, while the mayor "hammer[ed] out recreation and job providing plans with a committee of the youngsters at a secret meeting in the Sheraton-Fontenelle Hotel."[11] The mayor deemed the meeting a success and indicated he would eagerly meet the youths again, day or night. Sorensen stressed there were two ways to deal with a rebellion. The first was doing "as some cities have done with tear gas and machine guns," creating "an atmosphere of antagonism and hatred."[12] The second was listening to the people involved, believing that Omaha's civil rights problems could be solved "if every citizen, Negro and white, will accept his personal responsibility," which is what Sorensen said he intended to do.[13] By the next day, the young leaders presented a list of demands. They requested more educational training facilities, more recreational outlets, an immediate end to police brutality and abuses, more jobs, and the release of youths jailed in the disturbance.[14] Sorensen and the municipal government responded favorably to the demands, instituting several recreational and job programs within the week.[15]

CINCINNATI'S REBELLION (JUNE 12–18, 1967)

Racial tension embroiled Cincinnati in the summer of 1967. In addition to long-standing African Americans grievances, several recent incidents amplified Black Cincinnatians' feeling of marginalization. On April 29 local law enforcement, without provocation, arrived at a Stokely Carmichael event in riot gear. In early June, just a few weeks later, the promised and much-lauded jobs fair was canceled due to lack of industry participation.[16] These incidents, among others, reiterated to Black Cincinnatians their unequal status. The arrest of Peter Frakes, however, became the specific event that catapulted Cincinnati into racial unrest. Throughout 1966 a series of rape-murders of elderly white women put Cincinnati on edge. As Betsy Neel recalled, the city's female residents "broke. . . . They just gave up any social life at all because of this one man."[17] Months later, in the spring of 1967, an assailant murdered a thirty-year-old white secretary in the Price Hill suburb. African American jazz musician Posteal Laskey was arrested, charged, and subsequently convicted of first-degree murder in the case. The jury recommended the death penalty even though Laskey had not been charged with any of the other murders. Black Cincinnatians were enraged by the sentence as that same month a jury had convicted a white newspaperman of murdering his mistress and recommended parole.[18]

Peter Frakes, Laskey's cousin, most vocally objected to the conviction, situating himself at the corner of Reading Road and Rockdale Avenue wearing a sandwich board that read "Laskey Innocent, Cincinnati Guilty."[19] "Without benefit of advice" from a supervisor, a Cincinnati police officer arrested Frakes. Both local and federal authorities, aware of the tension in the Black community, feared that any small incident would provoke a full-on uprising, creating "another martyr for the Negro community."[20] Moderate Black leadership, sensing rising community tensions, asked for increased patrolling. Their decision once again magnified the distance between African American leaders and the masses.

Black Cincinnatians' anger flared on Monday, June 12, when a jury convicted Frakes of loitering and disturbing the peace. That evening militant community leaders Leonard Ball and Clyde Vinegar convened a meeting to discuss police harassment and develop protest strategies.[21] Before the meeting, small groups of African American teenagers prevented truck drivers from entering Avondale. The young men informed the rebuffed drivers that no deliveries would be made until Black drivers operated the trucks. By 8:00 p.m. the audience at Vinegar and Ball's meeting in the Rockdale School lot had grown to more than 300 people. Cincinnati Police Department informers stated that the speeches were "highly emotional and incendiary" and that Vinegar delivered an "inspiring radical speech."[22] Civil rights activist Floyd Spencer tried to counteract the militancy of Vinegar's speech with a more "go-slow" approach, which the crowd shouted down and threatened his life.[23] In the aftermath of the meeting, the situation escalated rapidly with the city recalling all Cincinnati police officers by 11:00 p.m.[24] By Tuesday evening police sealed off a five-square-mile area, effectively placing Avondale under martial law. As a result, the violence that began in Avondale soon spread to other neighborhoods. With the situation remaining uncontrolled, City Manager William Wichman requested the National Guard at 10:30 p.m.[25] Patrols roved through the neighborhood with armed guardsmen and a police officer perched atop quarter-ton trucks. When fire trucks responded to calls, eight guardsmen on a three-quarter-ton truck accompanied them. The arrival of the National Guard and this supersaturation of law enforcement nearly eliminated violence in the disturbance area.[26]

On June 14 at 3:00 p.m. Mayor Walton Bachrach called an open council meeting that the *Cincinnati Enquirer* reported "sounded more like a head-on collision as speaker after speaker heaped abuse and criticism on the city and its history of relations with Negroes."[27] As Floyd Spencer approached the podium, teenager John Poole (so identified by police lieutenant Thomas

Dixon) seized the microphone and asked for all those arrested to be released. When Rev. Fred Shuttlesworth addressed the assembly, Clyde Vinegar burst into the room criticizing the police and National Guard presence outside the council meeting, "seeing this as evidence of mistrust and another show of force."[28] Vinegar stormed out and other African Americans departed, seemingly at a prearranged time: 5:00 p.m. That two young activists interrupted established civil rights figures demonstrated the waning respect for traditional leadership. Despite the indications of a power shift within the Black community, the city council remained uninterested in hearing the opinions of young people. That evening several black-T-shirt-clad African Americans attended Vinegar's meeting. No councilmembers were present.[29] By Saturday evening, June 17, the full force of the uprising had passed, and the guard fully demobilized on June 19.[30]

MILWAUKEE'S REBELLION (JULY 30–AUGUST 4, 1967)

On Saturday night, July 29, 1967, the Milwaukee chapter of CORE sponsored a teen dance in Garfield Park. CORE director Cecil Brown asked two police officers who appeared at the dance to leave because their presence disturbed the 1,000 mostly Black partygoers. Around 11:00 p.m., as the event ended, a fight started between two girls. When the police arrived, they ordered the remaining 300 attendees to disperse. As the groups left, they moved along North Third Street breaking a small number of shop windows.[31]

In the late evening hours of July 30, Sgt. Hubert Pschachler of the Milwaukee Police Department noted that crowds of several hundred Blacks "had commenced a disturbance" in the Black enclave. Participant Tejumola Ologboni articulated more preplanned motives: "We had been waiting for an inciting incident, so we [could] go out and do what we knew needed to be done. See because all this marching and stuff we knew was a dead end. That ain't really disruption."[32] Small groups of rebels traveled down Third Street, breaking windows and setting the multifloor Gimbels-Schuster's department store ablaze.

The uprising escalated rapidly. Mayor Maier responded by imposing a citywide curfew and calling in the National Guard at 2:35 a.m. By Monday afternoon July 31, 750 local police, 250 state police, and 950 National Guard sealed off an 840-square-block area in the predominately Black North End. For the next twenty-six hours law enforcement prevented anyone from entering or leaving the city except for medical professionals, the press, and emergency service providers.[33] On Tuesday, August 1, civil authorities committed the entire police force and placed 4,084 National Guard on reserve. This massive show of force effectively stifled the unrest. Anger once again flared on Wednesday August 2, when police shot and killed Black teenager Clifford McKissick for attempting to firebomb a paint store, although this account remains highly contested.[34]

As the violence dwindled, local authorities began to draw back their response. On Thursday, August 3, Mayor Maier again adjusted the curfew, from midnight to 5:30 a.m. Unlike in Omaha and Cincinnati, Milwaukee's elected officials did not invite an organic presentation of grievances by grassroots leadership; instead, Mayor Maier mandated top-down solutions to solve ghetto problems in consultation with handpicked advisers from the Interdenominational Ministerial Alliance, a Black, conservative, middle-class organization. Most disconcertingly, although working-class African Americans constituted the main participants in the uprising, Maier insisted that his thirty-nine-point plan was "not intended to help just one group, but to help all by making this a better city."[35] The mayor effectively used African Americans' protest to advance his own objectives, ignoring the specificity of their grievances.

TACTICAL INNOVATION AS POLITICS

African Americans expressed their dissatisfaction by vandalizing symbolic and nearby targets, including post offices, police cars, and fire trucks. As James Mimms recounted, "Our thing was, when the fire truck passed, hit the fire truck! Hit the firemen! That's all we could do."[36] In Cincinnati, rebels also targeted the Metropolitan Housing Authority administrative building.[37] Robert Fogelson astutely noted why rebels frequently selected stores in their neighborhoods during uprisings: "Most whites and white institutions act at their worst in the ghetto, and thus it is at their worst that most blacks perceive them."[38] Former police officer Marvin McClarty lamented that "Hinky Dinky [grocery store] did not buy grade A chicken, [but] they sold it at grade A prices."[39] In Milwaukee, Tejumola Ologboni recalled the rationale behind striking exploitative stores: "If you ever bought anything there, you overpaid. . . . They took all your money all these years, they sent all their kids to college. Take all their stuff!"[40] Inner-city business owners deployed a different philosophy of doing business in Black communities than in other retail locations, buying bargain goods to sell at a profit, following Black shoppers around the store, and living far away from the communities they worked in.[41] *Omaha World-Herald* photojournalist Rudy Smith elaborated on this general

After Cincinnati police disrespected youths at this location, youths targeted the Lomark drugstore in retaliation during the 1967 and 1968 unrest.
Cincinnati Enquirer/Gannett.

perspective, saying that these stores "represented the national mood, they represented the anti-Black feeling, and they represented what was bad in America."[42] Many residents with a growing Black nationalist consciousness saw these merchants as outsiders, demonstrating feelings of economic and racial marginalization.

The deep feelings of resentment toward these business owners influenced decisions to target certain retail outlets. Dr. Robert Reid recounted to Kerner Commission investigators that he witnessed police reference Black teenagers participating in the truck blockade at the Lomark drugstore using a racial epithet. Although he was able to convince the youngsters to leave, a squad car immediately began following them. The youths nodded at Reid, stating, "Don't worry about it Doc, we'll take care of it." That evening the shop had all of its windows broken.[43] Tejumola Ologboni of Milwaukee explained, "If it was Black we didn't touch it. But we did try our best to eliminate all the 'leeches,' white stores that were drawing the money, the lifeblood of the community." He summarized, "We burned out all the white business because they ain't doing us no good."[44] Beyond the vandalizing of openly racist stores, many people looted to obtain goods that they did not have.

William Haynes remembered "televisions being pushed in shopping carts. . . . I remember the man coming out of Jack's [grocery store] with all this meat. . . . They looted day and night."[45] Rebels frequently robbed stores that sold a wide range of consumer goods because those stores included necessities like diapers and groceries that people needed but could not afford as well as items they lusted after. Grocery stores, furniture retailers, jewelers, and liquor stores thus became popular targets during the uprisings.[46] Participants' actions spoke loudly of their race- and class-based dissatisfaction. Their explicit grievances provide additional insight into how they imagined these discrepancies could be remedied.

Individuals desired to "alert America, not overturn it, to denounce its practices, not renounce its principles. . . . They wanted a change in norms, not in values."[47] For many participants, this change in norms meant that all Americans would have access to quality educational, labor, and recreational resources. The disorders should not be interpreted as attempts at municipal takeover, however, but as a disruption of "the world in which the people taking part lived out their lives, day to day."[48] President of the Omaha NAACP Lawrence McVoy, when speaking to the Youth and College Chapter, stated, "This revolt is not agitation, active or non-violent, toward an overthrow of present values. It is not an effort to overthrow social, economic or political values, but rather it's a seeking of full participation, full partnership and full responsibility toward total freedom—to join the majority in getting to good things."[49] In the aftermath of the unrest, uprising participants put forth specific demands framed as righting the system, not a coup. The efficacy of these negotiations reflects each city's political climate at the time.

In Omaha, A. V. Sorensen worked with youth participants, reflecting his long-term commitment to the African American community and young people in general.[50] His willingness to meet with teenage rebels in lieu of the established Black leadership reveals that the legitimate leaders, those who could "speak" authentically for the Black community, had changed. Ernie Chambers remarked, "When they [municipal government] become aware that these guys [conservative Black leadership] are not in the loop at all and if [Sorensen] wants to have any chance of keeping his city from exploding . . . he needs to talk with the people [who] have the bombs and the Molotov cocktails."[51] Alternatively, Cincinnati municipal leadership consistently played both sides, hearing the demands of grassroots organizers but favoring traditional advocacy groups because of their go-slow approach. Finally, Milwaukee mayor Henry Maier met with only established conservative leadership, even though more militant grassroots organizations continually petitioned him.

The articulated grievances and demands provide an important lens for understanding the community nature of the uprisings as well as the commonalities of Black midwestern life. By comparing demands made by grassroots organizations in Cincinnati and Omaha to the mandated fixes in Milwaukee, the fissure between traditional Black middle-class leadership and the concerns of the Black working-class community is glaring. The specific complaints brought forth by rebels reflect a growing Black Power or Black nationalist ideology largely absent in previous rights struggles. Malcolm McLaughlin rightly argues, "The riots and rebellions were spontaneous, fleeting, and lacking in the sort of organization that would have been necessary to nurture a sustained social movement. What seems rather clearer, with hindsight, is that the experience of urban rebellion, and the idea of a nationwide uprising, encouraged the development of a Black Power politics that created new ways to confront the injustices of ghetto life."[52] The uprisings bridged discreet formal civil rights struggles and Black Power strains of organizing. African Americans fused the goals of the civil rights movement with burgeoning ideas of self-determination and community control. The rebellions represented a community in transition.

Omaha

The Omaha municipal government's response to the demands of the young rebels could be divided into three categories: police relations, recreational activities, and job training. Although the programs created did ameliorate immediate conditions, they were ineffective at altering long-term discrimination patterns. The city-backed Operation Summertime sponsored five new programs, including sports clinics taught by professional athletes, an outdoor basketball league, dances, and a young-adult hire-out service. In addition to these programs, the city opened a teen center at the Blackburn building, averaging over 524 patrons a night.[53] A "blue-ribbon" committee appointed by the mayor recommended that the city purchase additional playground equipment and consider converting the Safeway parking lot where the uprising began for community use.[54] Created by the newly founded People's Recreational Council, a play lot was funded by an "unnamed industry" solicited by newspaper reporter Charles Washington and

Human Relations Board chair Norman Hahn. A substantial increase in parks and recreation funding subsidized an additional summer camp at Fontenelle Forest.[55] A. V. Sorensen also created the Mayor's Patrol, composed of young Black men between the ages of nineteen and twenty-nine who had maintained order in the Safeway parking lot. The group's name is somewhat misleading since North Omaha businessmen, not the mayor's office, paid their salaries.[56]

Although innovative, the Omaha initiatives had limited reach as they represented temporary fixes to more systemic problems. A downtown job-training center opened at the Paxton Hotel with mixed success. Hundreds of young African Americans showed up to obtain the skills that had partially shut them out of the job market. The presence of so many young Black people, however, frightened area shoppers and led to complaints from the business community. Within the year, pressure from major retailers caused the site to be shut down. The state's Labor Department also established a North Omaha satellite office open seven days a week but, due to a reluctant business community, could not find enough jobs for the applicants.[57] Despite the shortcomings of such initiatives, young Omahans forced the local government to create meaningful changes that impacted their lives.

Cincinnati

Beyond youths advocating on their own behalf, the creation and presentation of grievances became a collective community effort. In the Kerner Commission staff paper on Cincinnati, the authors summarized the uprising by stating, "The general picture which emerges out of the events of the week in the Negro community is of a process of rebellion—in which violence used by youth, tacitly supported by many adults—became a substitute for, as well as complementing, the more traditional forms of protest. While the use of violence was not controlled in a formal sense, the coherence and reciprocity involved in actions taken by different Negro leadership segments, and the hinging of actions on white response, gives the picture of a community in movement for collective goals."[58] The urban rebellions do not constitute a significant break in civil rights activism. Violent protest amplified grievances presented by previous rights organizations. In so doing, this encouraged rebels and traditional leadership to collaborate in negotiating with the state. This approach brought widespread change to the city, allowing Black Cincinnatians to develop a coherent set of objectives in how they envisioned equality for African Americans.

On the morning of June 13 twenty-five clergymen and civil rights leaders, including grassroots organizers Clyde Vinegar, Bailey Turner, Donald Spencer, and Peter Frakes, attended a meeting at the Cincinnati Human Relation Committee. Rev. Harold Hunt, the group's spokesperson, presented a list of eleven grievances. Business owner Robert Weaver warned the council that "the time for empty promises is gone."[59] Reverend Hunt reminded the group, "Those who are called leaders and who are negotiating with City Hall are not in the community with the man on the street and have lost contact with him."[60] In many ways Dr. Bruce Green became the example for Black middle-class collaboration with the state. Green received numerous threatening phone calls stating that if he spoke at the city council meeting, he should fear for the safety of his wife and children. This tension between grassroots and formal leadership occurred in shifts. During the day, civil rights leaders would try to negotiate with authorities, and city government issued threats against would-be participants. At night, however, the "16-year-old soldiers" exercised their own political capital in the streets, with the older men "staying in the background."[61] In the end it was the young men's grievances that the city addressed.

Cincinnati exemplifies how rebellions are political actions deployed by multiple entities. Black community representatives made three sets of demands, the longest of which was put forth by H. Rap Brown when he visited the city. The first set of demands articulated specific grievances that members of the Black community endured, along with ameliorative steps. Of the eleven points for discussion, five dealt with police and community relations. Of the remaining grievances, four addressed economic concerns, including that the city should provide employment for Black youth and permanent employment for those unemployed, that financial institutions should lend money to Blacks to buy white-owned businesses, and that Black truck drivers should deliver goods in the community.[62] By proposing specific solutions, rebels assertively named the source of their woes rather than allowing city government to disregard the violence as aberrant.

Drafters of the second document issued a series of demands titled "short term goals." These consisted of items that local government could change immediately, representing a negotiation of the terms of peace. This included the release of all prisoners and that those who participated would have their juvenile record expunged for their involvement. Of particular interest in the second set of demands is that the creators of the document referred to themselves as a "negotiating team." By self-defining as legitimate agents, the rebels asserted their authentic claim to make demands of the government and wield real political power. The initiatives met the needs of working-class Black Cincinnatians, including the "placing of a Negro in the City Manager's Office, who is acceptable to the Negro community, including the grassroots people."[63] Additional demands included the passing of a local ordinance that would require a minimum of thirty days' notice before any person could be evicted from a rented dwelling. The document creators framed themselves as Black working-class representatives in securing economic rights that the broader civil rights struggles overlooked. By tying Black control to mainstream structures, the negotiating team fused integration objectives of the civil rights movement with Black self-determination and control found in Black Power movements.

As in Milwaukee and Omaha, the Cincinnati negotiating team requested that Black city employees receive promotions, and that the city should withdraw from all contracts with discriminatory unions. The team specifically demanded that all "delivery trucks in Negro communities [should have by] tomorrow . . . black drivers or *no drivers* at all." This specific request demonstrates that the initial youth who blockaded deliverymen from entering Avondale helped shape the demands. The final demand and perhaps the biggest testament to Black Cincinnatians' feelings of alienation asked that "the City Manager make periodic tours in the Negro community, visit homes, and be exposed to the concrete elements present in the ghetto communities."[64] This demand asserts not only that the city manager was out of touch with the lives and experiences of Black people but also that Black municipal representatives did not adequately convey the struggle of the community.

Finally, it is important to discuss H. Rap Brown's demands on behalf of Black Cincinnati. Whereas the first and second rounds of grievances presented to the city council reflect local concerns by local people, Brown's contributions are clearly written by an outsider. In it he echoes broad themes relevant not only to Cincinnati but also to the nation. Brown's grievances reflected his growing Black nationalist framework desiring to "stock all libraries in black communities with histor[ies] of black people" and that "any white proposal or white representative objected to by black representatives must be rejected automatically." Although rhetorically important, Brown's demands did not reflect the specific needs of Cincinnati's Black community. Brown swooped down from a Dayton speaking engagement to advance his assertion that "SNCC had declared war" on America.[65] His submitted grievances reflected some of Cincinnati's issues, but overwhelmingly Brown used the rebellion as a political tool to push forth his own agenda and in the process provided conservatives with a villain, minimizing opportunities for reform.⁶⁶ Brown is but one example of an individual who, although not an uprising participant, mobilized the rebellion as a symbolic weapon. No person, however, was more successful in turning a disturbance into his own political tool than Milwaukee's mayor, Henry Maier.

Milwaukee

A unified grassroots group called Common View met at the office of the Organization of Organizations and issued a five-point statement calling the uprising a "reaction to the indifference projected by the white power structure." On August 7, 1967, they submitted a list of recommendations to the mayor. These aims targeted several spheres of Black Milwaukee life including housing, employment, education, police–community relations, the court system, and recreation. The Common View group, in the release of their document, spoke of their disappointment in the government, stating, "The white power structure continues to ignore the need for meaningful communication with the black community. The structure also refuses to recognize the long time, deep-rooted circumstances and inherent consequences of not establishing plans and programs to resolve the situation."⁶⁷ In their statement, Common View contextualized the urban rebellion as a continuation of protest that the city had long neglected, framing it as legitimate strategy and not merely criminal opportunism.

Common View's demands represented the African American community's decades-long struggle against the state. Under housing, they demanded the inclusion of Black citizen involvement in city development and for unconditional support of fair housing legislation. More tellingly of the grassroots initiatives that Common View advocated for, they asked that one-third of the representation to the Milwaukee Housing Authority (MHA) and tenant selection committee be made up of actual MHA tenants not just business leaders. Furthermore, the demands promoted better enforcement of sanitation codes and the ability for tenants to hold their rent in escrow until conditions were improved in public housing. Their objectives for better employment also reflected a more working-class focus. Common View sought greater enforcement of nondiscrimination clauses in city contracts and better job-training programs. Similarly, their educational demands reflected the desire for greater community control, including more African Americans in administrative positions, and for the mayor to mediate the current dispute over integrated education.

In the realm of justice and law enforcement, Common View's demands reflected the concerns of a people constantly harassed by the police. This included the appointment of a Black commanding officer for the predominantly African American 5th District. Additionally, they asked that the police department reopen negotiations for law enforcement assistance grants to develop police–community relation programs. As with the housing concerns, Common View demanded representation on major boards, including a joint citizen police advisory grievance system, and an African American appointee to fill the next vacancy on the Fire and Police Commission. Their most forceful demand in this area was to "immediately suspend, without pay, all policemen involved in any questionable fatal shootings until the case is investigated and resolved." This appeal directly addressed their grievance that the city had placed the police officer who killed Clifford McKissick on administrative leave *with* pay. Common View also requested a Black judge, a bail bond system that was less "excessive and punitive," and greater public defender rights. Finally, Common View requested an expansion of recreational facilities.[68]

Although Common View directly tied their grievances to prior struggles, Maier depoliticized the uprising by refusing to meet with the rebels or Common View, ignoring their roles as political agents. Maier from the beginning doubted the authenticity of the uprising, claiming that race relations were so sound in Milwaukee that Black militants "had to hit us," to "embarrass him politically because of Milwaukee's interracial success."[69] If anyone had conspired to create a political crisis, it was the mayor himself, as Kerner investigator Bernard Dobranski wrote that Maier "had been preparing for some incident for approximately 15 months. The general feeling seems to be that [he] tried to use the disturbance as a means of projecting himself into national prominence. By calling it a riot and then squashing it immediately, he is able to claim that he is the first big city mayor to effectively deal with racial disorders."[70] Still members of the mayor's inner circle willingly met with mainstream Black activists.

Julius Modlinski, a social worker at Marquette University, invited Paul Moynihan, the chair, and Calvin Beckett, the executive secretary of the Milwaukee Committee for Human Relations, to meet with a civil rights coalition that included Father Groppi, Organization of Organizations representatives, and 150 local people. A Mr. Jesse questioned the mayor's absence, asserting, "If the Mayor isn't coming, I'm going." When Moynihan informed the group that the mayor would not be attending, the chair adjourned the meeting.

Twenty participants left the venue chanting, "We ain't gonna march no more—we're gonna burn this town down."[71] By adjourning their meeting and rearticulating their belief in the efficacy of violent protest, the attendees regained some of their political agency.

READING POLITICS THROUGH THE STATE'S ACTIONS

Mayor Maier did not attend Modlinski's assembly as Maier had already created his own committee of alleged leaders. After consulting with prominent African American clergyman Rev. Earl Parchia, Maier felt that a biracial committee comprising individuals appointed by the middle-class Interdenominational Ministerial Alliance constituted the best approach. Parchia exposed his commitment to the old way by stating that "[a biracial commission] was a worthwhile idea, since the current problem seemed to be emanating from leaderless persons who could not be reached by anyone, but who are enjoying the publicity and attention they were receiving." Despite the previous existence of an independent group of concerned citizens in Common View, Maier called a two-and-a-half-hour meeting with the so-called grassroots Inner Core residents.[72]

Maier exerted his authority over the attendees at this meeting by forcing the invited guests to show identification to two police detectives stationed at the entrance of the city hall meeting room. Although the Mayor's Office refused to provide a list of the attendees, the group was made up of middle-class Black representatives, including real estate operators, business owners, and union officials. Since the assembly was closed to the press, what transpired can only be ascertained by the invitees' comments afterward. A mayoral staff member disclosed that an informal show of hands to endorse the formation of a biracial committee appointed by the Greater Milwaukee Conference on Religion and Race resulted in forty-four yeas and three nays.

John Jackson, a barber, left before the conclusion of the meeting. Frustrated with Maier's circular talking, Jackson told the press, "He calls a group of core businessmen and he talks about the tax structure of the city and the city is burning down around his ears.... [Maier addressed] nothing germane to the riot, nothing germane to civil rights even. I think he's got pretty many of the people snowed because most of the people don't know the mayor as he really is—a con artist." When Maier saw Jackson talking with reporters, the mayor pointed at him and boasted, "there's one of my dissenters. I only had three dissenters." Jackson, a member of the Community Relations–Social Development commission, criticized the mayor for only appointing "middle class Negroes to boards and commissions." Although he was the only person to be called out individually by the mayor, Jackson was not the only dissenter. Ray Alexander, community relations director for the Northtown Planning and Development Council, did not even attend because "it is the usual approach of the Mayor to pick the people he will condescend to talk to . . . this does not appear to be a sincere effort on the part of the Mayor to meet with people of the community." Marshall Jarreau best summed up the experience by stating that the meeting was a "vague nothing" and that he did not consider the individuals attending to be grassroots representatives, "I don't really come in contact with people who really have the problems—the kids tossing the gas bombs."[73]

Maier's apparent cluelessness in choosing his advisory board was not unintentional. The mayor had long been advocating for greater county, state, and federal support of the urban city. The uprising provided the rhetorical and political justification he needed to make further entreaties to those who could grant his wishes. Maier's co-optation of the uprising as a political tactic was reflected in the solutions the committee submitted, known as the thirty-nine-point plan or "Milwaukee's Marshall Plan." The points constituted broad sweeping hopes that lacked focus, concrete plans, or the specificity of locally created demands. Of the nearly forty points, the mayor could only directly influence six. Even these proposals were nebulous, including "The Mayor initiates ways and means to increase Negro employment opportunities." Additionally, four of the six mayoral initiatives involved Maier asking the federal government for assistance. To solve Milwaukee's specific urban problems, the responsibility needed to be borne by a host of co-collaborators, from the local to the national. These suggested measures were toothless at best, and intentionally vague at worst. Point nineteen demanded that "the nation step up federal programs to develop and improve open space and beautification projects in urban areas."[74] Specific solutions would have to be mandated from on high and could be vetoed any number of times along the way. There would be no immediate amelioration of ghetto problems. Milwaukee's mayor seized the uprisings—specific Black working-class political protests—to advocate for his own pet projects.

On Thursday, August 3, Mayor Maier took out an ad in the *New York Times* titled "A Statement of Concern about the Crisis in Our Cities." Amid Milwaukee's largest emergency, which resulted in the mobilization of the Wisconsin National Guard, Maier felt it was vital to address a national audience. In the advertisement he restated his position that the "fight for [federal] resources must be won" to help central cities prevent the "formation of urban wastelands." The *Times* ad cost $2,218 ($19,035 in 2022).[75] Although paid for by concerned civic groups, the national press spot showcased Maier's commitment to becoming a first-class mayor in the vein of Richard J. Daley of Chicago or John Lindsey of New York City—and not in addressing the legitimate concerns of Black Milwaukeeans.

Maier's co-optation of the rebellions is evident in Black Milwaukeeans' opinions of these initiatives. In a series of television interviews, attendees outside of a mayoral meeting noted that the biracial council did not speak for the Black community at large. An unidentified man in his late twenties wearing a hat and sunglasses opined, "they don't really know the common man, his grievances, that is out in the street." An older Black gentleman with a slight southern accent stated that he felt that the mayor's commission would fall short because "to better the condition of the young folk ... it seems like they wanted their own representative, a better representative."[76] One can especially see this indifference to young African Americans' quality of life by not taking up the grievances most meaningful to them. When compared to the demands local leaders made in Omaha and Cincinnati, Milwaukee's thirty-nine points did not mention the issues most salient to Black youths, including the release of prisoners involved in the uprising, the end to police brutality, and Black representation on the committees and boards that had the most influence in the Black community.

TACTICAL ADAPTATION AS POLITICS

The state's operational tactics during the uprisings reflected a conscious decision to shut down not only the physical uprising but also potential ideological uprisings. Incarceration represented the first strategic political tool in a city's arsenal. The state employed curfews and the creation of riot zones as a second strategic political tool. Finally, local governments responded to the tactical innovation of the rebellions by using the most potent response it had, the mobilization of the National Guard. The actions that the state took were not an overreaction but strategic and pragmatic decision-making. Locally and nationally, rumors percolated throughout the community. In Cincinnati, "reliable sources" informed FBI agents and the National Guard commanders that out-of-town protesters would be arriving with a truckload of dynamite to destroy power stations and that Chicagoans wearing gold T-shirts came to agitate.[77] Local activist Marian Spencer recalled that a man working at the Black newspaper told her husband that outsiders targeted the couple "because you all are leaders in the black community and they want to control the black community."[78] Although apocryphal, rumors of nonresident agitators engaging in all-out race warfare remained potent. The state's adaptations had to be effective not only to stop the uprising but also to psychologically deter participants from protesting in this manner again.

The use of incarceration, although often temporary, served the state in two ways. First, it cleared the street of potential rebels. Second, incarceration discouraged others from participating. By labeling those picked up as criminals and not protesters, the city relayed important information to the Black community on the responsible way to participate in the polity. Although the local government saw the grievances made by negotiating teams as valid, they carefully noted that uprising participation was aberrant and not an appropriate way to address local problems. Omaha's A. V. Sorensen, one of the more progressive mayors in dealing with the uprisings, applauded the "literally hundreds of residents" who did not participate and "continue[d] this fine expression of responsibility."[79] By congratulating responsible leadership and nonrebels, Sorensen reinforced fissures within the Black community. In manufacturing a binary between good and bad activists, Sorensen and other contemporary commentators ignored the reciprocal relationship between violent and nonviolent protest. Rooted in their own feelings of political efficacy and seeking to gain official approval, much of traditional leadership disregarded violent protest as irresponsible although it proved to be an effective political tool. By deeming participants of the uprisings as criminal or reckless, these parties actively discouraged Black community members from participating and reified their positions as being the authentic spokespeople for the community.

Judges meted out punitive punishments for uprising participation, so African Americans sought to avoid arrest, fines, and jail time by limiting their participation. During the Cincinnati uprising, Municipal Judge William H. Mathews warned that anyone convicted of a riot-connected offense would get the maximum sentence. He made this announcement after handing down $50 fines plus costs and thirty-day workhouse terms to each of twenty-three individuals convicted on charges of loitering in the disturbance area. Mathews defended these harsh sentences, arguing, "Cincinnati is practically in a state of siege," and framing uprising participants, or even those unlucky enough to be at the wrong place at the wrong time, as enemy combatants.[80] On June 15 he gave twelve rebels, several between the ages of fifteen and seventeen, yearlong sentences and $500 fines for violating the State Riot Act.[81] Enforcement of the loitering law and rioting act reflects the capriciousness in the application of these ordinances. Police and prosecutors used these laws as a catch-all to arrest suspects for whom little evidence was available, creating a major deterrent for not only actively participating in the uprising but even observing the event and supporting those engaged.

The state tactically adapted not only through the rigorous enforcement of riot and loitering acts but also by criminalizing all members of the Black community through the establishment of riot zones and curfews. Residents, although not illegally engaging in the uprisings, could be arrested and arraigned on riot-connected charges for simply being outdoors in their own neighborhood. Although the municipal government explicitly applauded the hundreds of responsible citizens, such punitive arrests tacitly sent a message of Black criminality to the broader white community. As municipal governments touted their large arrest numbers, they demonstrated that they, and not the rebels, were in charge. The aggregate arrest numbers, however, often included large numbers of individuals who were not participating criminally. Mayor Maier imposed one of the most sweeping riot curfews, remaining in effect for forty-eight hours. He only relented and lifted the curfew after the business community complained about the inability of workers to get to their jobs, cutting down on productivity and profit. Maier valued the curfew for two reasons. First, police could contain the disturbances more easily by focusing their attention on the uprising area. Milwaukee police, in lieu of deciphering who was criminally participating and who was coming home from work or the store, could round up everyone. The court then decided to arraign the individual on loitering or more serious charges.

Second, Maier expressed that the curfew had important psychological implications. When the suburbs, all white because of discriminating practices, voluntarily implemented their own curfews, Maier pronounced, "There was a common identity in the metropolitan area. . . . I hope the experience could bolster efforts to achieve a greater metropolitan sharing of the poverty burden in Milwaukee."[82] Maier again used this rebellion suppression tactic to push forward his political aims. Despite his belief that the curfew united the suburbs and city, the police and National Guard only mobilized in the Black Inner Core neighborhood. Breaking curfew in the suburbs did not carry the same consequences that it did for Black residents. Despite its small population, police arrested 1,700 people in Milwaukee during the uprising, compared to approximately 125 and 450 in Omaha and Cincinnati, respectively.[83] Of the 1,700 people taken into custody during the uprising, police arrested only 193 for non-loitering offenses.[84]

Milwaukee's citywide curfew enabled police to arrest such a disproportionally large number of people by making it a crime to be outside of your house for any reason. The curfew, in addition to criminalizing African Americans who tried to get food or other emergency necessities, also prevented people from discussing the political meaning of these events. As one woman lamented, "If we could have had some role in the community now, even after curfew hours, to mix and see what the man on the street feels and be able to relay it back to the city and the power structure."[85] Mayor Maier effectively depoliticized the events for African Americans while simultaneously framing the uprising for his own purposes.

A discussion of the urban rebellions and potential tools of the state is incomplete without discussing force or state-sponsored violence. In Milwaukee, Kerner Commission officials noted that several Inner Core residents remarked that "the only people in Milwaukee who rioted were the police."[86] In Cincinnati, Police Chief Jacob Schott highlighted the omnipresence of unpunished violence against the Black community. In response to the community's fourth grievance of police brutality and panic during the uprising, he flippantly offered that "for the police not to have used force could be likened to giving a carpenter a hammer and instructing him to build a house but not to use the hammer."[87] Schott acknowledged that one of the most effective tools the state had to suppress uprisings was the threat of physical harm with relative impunity.

Max Felker-Kantor wrote of Los Angeles, "The uprising was ultimately a demand for an end to police practices that maintained white authority, control, and order in black spaces."[88] In the anger stemming from the urban uprisings, police violence temporarily lost its threat. Many inner-city residents faced this type of force daily, and in a moment of rage and impulse, police violence lost its efficacy. In the case of Omaha, youth participants taunted the police.[89] In Cincinnati, a policeman allegedly used the butt of his riot gun to hit a young man who was trying to encourage a crowd to go home. Some jeered the officer for thinking himself tough for having a "big gun," stating that they had faced bigger guns in Vietnam.[90] In the face of very real danger perpetrated by the police, many Black Americans knew that this was a uniquely powerful moment to assert their humanity.[91]

Municipal leaders tactically adapted by deploying the National Guard as the ultimate culmination of their power. When the police no longer physically intimidated participants, the state called out the National Guard, converting Black neighborhoods into militarized zones. White Cincinnatian Betsy Neel recalled that, during the uprisings, there were only four routes to travel through the uprising area to her place of work at University Hospital: "We would follow a Jeep with four soldiers and a bazooka and it was like being in

The Wisconsin National Guard marches near Teutonia Avenue and Center Street on August 1, 1967, during Milwaukee's unrest.
© *Milwaukee Journal Sentinel*—USA TODAY NETWORK.

Okinawa," where her husband had previously deployed.[92] Mutope Johnson recalled sitting on his porch as a young child and counting more than 100 National Guard jeeps, trucks, and armored vehicles.[93] Rosalind Baker understood that the mobilization of the guard posed an imminent threat to her. While experiencing a gall bladder attack during the uprising, she decided to wait for the National Guard to pass before venturing out to find help "because I didn't want to have no confrontation with them about why I was out on the street . . . at that time of night." Baker crawled back to a major throughfare where a nightshift worker saw her, guided her to his home, and called the ambulance.[94] As Malcolm McLaughlin noted, "The indiscriminate use of force implied an acceptance that the innocent would be terrorized, maimed, and killed alongside the guilty. It amounted to a collective punishment."[95] The mobilization of the National Guard into Black communities converted these areas into an occupied territory, shifting power back to the state, in a "deliberate strategy of incapacitation."[96] While the uprisings represented an opportunity where Blacks temporarily controlled Black communities, the calling out of the National Guard reinstated the status quo.

The uprisings have traditionally been interpreted as wanton violence without order or intention. These events signified a tactical innovation for Black working-class urban dwellers whose previous forms of protest had been disregarded by municipal authorities. These uprisings were not one-sided affairs. The state reacted to tactical adaptations by innovating their own approaches not only to stop the violence but also to respond in a politically savvy manner. The nature of the uprisings is read through the participants' actions as well as the state's. Rebels demonstrated their political concerns by targeting certain entities and presenting specific grievances. The state exhibited its political influence by employing the judicial system, co-opting Black middle-class leadership, and mobilizing the National Guard. Although the events represented politically overt protest within the municipal community, the uprisings also highlighted individuals' own deeply held political rationales. Moving from the macro level of the city to the micro level of the individual, the following two chapters determine the way uprising participation directly correlated to one's understanding of their personal place within racial, class, and gender hierarchies.

FOUR

It's Time to Stop Asking and Start Taking

Amid Cincinnati's urban uprising, a curious thing occurred just a few blocks north of the action. In lieu of joining the fray, African Americans in North Avondale chatted outside watering their lawns and sipping iced tea on their porches. *New York Times* reporter Gene Roberts noted that "through it all, Negro homeowners in the area were as aloof to the violence as were the whites in Indian Hill, one of the city's wealthier suburbs."[1] These residents were Cincinnati's Black elite; they earned their livings as schoolteachers, entrepreneurs, and health care professionals. In contrast, Blacks living in Avondale proper were generally poor, vulnerable to long periods of unemployment, and actively participating in the rebellion.[2] Four decades later one interview subject described this tension between the residents: "They thought they were much [pauses for several seconds], well, they were mostly professional people [let's put it] that way."[3] Race alone provided insufficient cause to participate in the uprising and identify with its participants. Class represented an equally salient determinant to why local African Americans chose to violently protest to express their grievances, inexorably linked to the midwestern myth of opportunity.

This myth amplified the already extant fissures within the Black community. Many working-class African Americans felt that the middle-class-dominated civil rights movement had left them behind. Working-class Blacks acted in their own interests to achieve social, economic, and political equality. Although these individuals dominated what would be considered rebellious participation, the Black middle class and white working class also engaged in the revolts. Ultimately the intersection of race and class, proxies for perceived efficacy within the formal political system, informed each of these groups' actions during the uprisings. The multitude of ways, both sanctioned and illicit, that individuals participated highlights the centrality of intersectional identity in the revolts.

WORKING-CLASS POLITICS

Working-class insurrection dominates American history, and when participants are white, these are frequently lauded as historical events. From the 1863 Draft Riot, a protest against a "rich man's war, a poor man's fight" following the National Conscription Act, to the prolonged gun battle when Amalgamated Association members and their wives opposed 300 armed Pinkerton agents sent to protect replacement workers, violence has been employed as a tool by marginalized people.[4] Class violence has been ever present and necessary in the struggle for equality in American history. The urban uprisings are an inseparable and indisputable part of that legacy.

Although scholars of the 1960s revolts draw connections between social position and violence as protest, none have placed these disturbances in the broader context of working-class protest behavior.[5] The extensive literature on crowd violence as politics largely concerns itself with Europe in the eighteenth and nineteenth centuries and the United States in the postbellum era. Historians included bread riots, peasant revolts, and coups d'état as the objects of their analysis, but modern-day comparisons end with the labor protests in the interwar era.[6] Not coincidentally, it is at this exact time that Black working-class activists began to mobilize this tactic. Despite the prevalence and significance of working-class rebellion in US history, scholars have not used an analytical framework of labor violence to understand the urban rebellions.

The confluence of economic decline, social marginalization, and midwestern myths led working-class African Americans to frequently engage in violent upheaval as protest. Demographic studies of the rebels support this. In Cincinnati, the average uprising participant was a young, working-class,

Black male resident of Avondale. After omitting arrestees who listed "student" as their occupation, 45 percent were employed, 20 percent were currently unemployed, and 11 percent did not disclose their employment status. Indicative of racial discrimination within Cincinnati's industries, 39 percent of the Black arrestees were unemployed.[7] Additionally, police apprehended seventeen Youth Corps workers in Cincinnati, which accounts for one-quarter of all Youth Corps arrestees nationally. While the *Cincinnati Enquirer* speculated that the high percentage of poverty workers arrested could be due to a community rumor that "outsiders were imported by neighborhood poverty program workers who fear they will lose out in cutbacks made by the last Congress," enrollees of these programs often remained unemployed.[8] For many working-class African Americans, the combination of being young, Black, and working class limited their options for finding employment in cities with deeply entrenched racist labor practices. Those actively participating in employment opportunity programs directly felt this economic marginalization.

Recognizing that most revolt participants held jobs, occasionally in federally sponsored programs, combats the misconceptions that participants came largely from the lumpenproletariat. Such "riffraff" pseudo-theories lurked in mainstream conceptions of the urban rebellions to discredit political intent. Municipal leaders frequently asserted that only a small percentage of African Americans participated in the rebellions. Milwaukee's mayor Henry Maier expressed that over the course of the uprisings, "we learned that 99.8 percent of the non-white population of our city did not desire to be participants in the disturbances. . . . This significant fact indicated that the vast majority of our Negro population wants to join hands with the white citizens to work for constructive programs that will improve our city."[9] By quantifying uprising participation—and, by extension, community support—through arrest statistics, the state viewed these events through a carceral logic. In so doing, they obscured the ways that the Black community tacitly condoned the uprisings through noncriminal support roles or simply by not divulging rebels' identities. By characterizing Blacks who participated criminally as the lowest rungs of society, plagued by substance abuse and lawlessness, those in power could disregard the political intent behind these actions.[10] In so doing, municipal authorities continued championing a slow, steady, and interracial approach to addressing inequities in Black life.

In the postwar economy, African Americans believed that equal status and dignity could come through labor opportunities. But the mechanization and deindustrialization of major industries in the Midwest left Blacks underemployed or unemployed. Working-class African Americans partook in the revolt in response to both racial and economic marginalization. In 1967 Dr. Karl L. Flaming, in his Urban League–sponsored report *Who "Riots" and Why? Black and White Perspectives in Milwaukee*, conducted 119 interviews with individuals arrested in the disorder, excluding those arrested for curfew violations. African American arrestees lamented not receiving equal pay for equal work and were more critical of social, political, and economic inequities than the Black control group of nonarrestees.[11] As concluded in the Cincinnati West End survey, "high rate[s] of unemployment among the Male, coupled with low-income jobs, makes it difficult for him to maintain the family in adequate American standards."[12] In Milwaukee, 88 percent of arrested participants felt that job growth opportunities for Black Milwaukeeans moved too slowly, compared to 61 percent of the control group.[13] As a community activist wrote in his summary report, "One major grievance voiced by the spokesman for the Negro community has to do with jobs. A cry for jobs is a request for responsibility and for full participation in the mainstream of American society."[14] The midwestern myth convinced both white and Black residents that hard work could open doors of opportunity. Blacks, however, had yet to receive the benefits. When Black working-class individuals chose to violently protest these conditions, the offending parties became prime targets.

Rebels did not vandalize at random in the revolts. Both the properties targeted for destruction and the people threatened with violence signaled racialized working-class disillusionment. Although collateral damage occurred, overwhelmingly participants strategically targeted their sites. Participants rarely selected Black-owned businesses or schools, but exploitative merchants frequently sustained damage. The Kerner Commission, in its analysis of the 1967 uprisings, found that the majority of arson targets were white-owned businesses known for price gouging in the Black community. Consequently, during the unrest rebels targeted white passersby, residents, and media personnel as proxy symbols of white supremacy. Critically, and contrary to popular misremembering, most participants committed misdemeanor violations such as disorderly conduct or loitering, not violent crimes.[15] Property, not people, were the main targets of the uprisings. For those who chose to participate in the rebellions beyond minor infractions, their deeds illustrate strategic intention as a means for Black working-class individuals to agitate in their own interest.

Highly visible in Black neighborhoods, white storeowners became symbolic proxies for African Americans' political impotency, diminished class status, and lack of control in their own neighborhoods. Floyd McKissick codified this strained relationship at the 1967 Black Power conference in Washington, DC: "White landlords, white storekeepers, white corporate managers and a white, Anglo-Saxon Wall Street, conspire to keep the Black Man in his place."[16] For African Americans, especially those who identified as working class, financial and consumer institutions served as powerful daily reminders of their diminished status in American society. An Office of Economic Opportunity representative stated before the Consumer Subcommittee of the House Government Operations Committee on October 12, 1967, "There is increasing evidence that suggests that discontent and disorders in cities across the country are in no small part a consumer revolt against a system that has for years permitted the unscrupulous to take advantage of those least able to pay. A system that has, at the same time, deprived the poor of any real choice in the quality of goods they can buy, the prices they pay or the method of financing or source of credit available to them."[17] In addition to the aforementioned forms of the exploitation, the relationship many white entrepreneurs had with the Black community also made them unpopular.

In his dissertation, "The Role of Ghetto Retail Merchants in Civil Disorders," sociologist Richard Alan Berk surveyed the attitudes of both Black and white store owners in fifteen cities including Cincinnati and Milwaukee. The merchants, although perceived as outsiders by uprising participants, saw themselves as part of the community, with nearly seven out of ten donating to local charities and nearly a third offering advice on personal problems. Yet only a quarter of merchants lived in the neighborhoods where they worked, with a ten-mile average commute to their shops.[18] African American merchants both lived in the neighborhood and considered their customers personal friends. But despite this affinity toward their clients, a significant majority of Black ghetto dwellers, nearly 70 percent, felt that there was "not much difference" in the treatment they received from white and Black merchants in terms of dignity and fair pricing.[19] These attitudes toward retailers demonstrate the fluidity with which uprising participants negotiated the intersection between their racial and class identities. Although most African Americans felt that Black and white merchants treated them about the same (poorly), very few Black stores were looted or set on fire.

The clichéd admonishment—still in circulation today—that Black people are "destroying their own neighborhood" is a fallacy, as participants hardly saw the exploitative businesses they targeted as their own. One Milwaukee rebel using the alias Johnny Davis explained, "I was mad. I wanted to show them I got a right to everything they got." When asked about the damage he was inflicting upon the community, he retorted, "Baby, this is war. . . . For 300 years we have been asking the white man for what's rightfully ours. Now it's time to stop asking and start taking."[20] Marjorie Parham, fifty years later, offered a similar assessment of the property damage that occurred. Participants "lived there but they owned nothing. They did not tear up their neighborhood. They had to tear up the neighborhoods of landlords and business operations that they felt had been oppressing them."[21] Absent genuine political and economic power, a significant disconnect existed between Black residents and the predominately white entrepreneurs in the community. During the urban rebellions, power shifted—albeit temporarily—from those with the capital and resources to exploit a vulnerable community to those who had been exploited.

By looking at the buildings and objects targeted, the practical and symbolic nature of illicit participation comes to life. Rebels looted Milwaukee's Gimbels-Schuster's department store on Third Street, a neighborhood institution with a lousy track record for hiring African Americans.[22] Several Black teenagers broke into the Millvale Public Housing offices operated by the Cincinnati Metropolitan Housing Authority and removed administrative records and furniture to the courtyard, destroying it in a gigantic bonfire.[23] This is perhaps the best example of symbolic property violence. Black Cincinnatians long suffered overpriced, substandard housing, and agency officials treated those who secured public housing assistance paternalistically.[24] Easily identifiable police cruisers and fire engines also became frequent symbolic targets, with Cincinnati participants damaging seventy-seven police vehicles.[25] One Omaha fireman observed, "We know they don't have any use for us down there. We're just more white trash."[26] By targeting specific symbols of oppression, particularly those associated with law enforcement, uprising participants demonstrated their dissatisfaction with the treatment they received from these entities.

Although physical assault did not comprise most charges brought against those arrested, interpersonal violence did occasionally happen. Assailants perceived their targets as those who did not belong in the community. Milwaukee experienced a significant amount of gun violence during the uprising. Alderperson Vel Phillips recounted that police tried "to scare people off with gunshots, and there were gunshots back." On the first night of the disturbances, there were two fatalities and fifty-six injuries, including six police hit by sniper fire and three civilians injured by gunfire.[27] In Cincinnati on the first day of the uprising, participants assaulted several white journalists. Passersby moving through Black neighborhoods also met abuse.

Pauline E. recalled an older white couple who came to Avondale to "see what the N words were doing" and a group of Black youths began to attack the car. Pauline implored the assailants "please don't hurt them, please don't hurt them," to which they shouted for her to "shut her mouth" and then proceeded to hit the man in the head with a brick and rolled the car down the street.[28] Even an African American man, Charles M., was stopped and beaten on Twenty-First Street and Walnut Avenue. The man speculated that he was targeted because he had a large antenna on his car and figured the group assumed he was a police officer.[29]

Participants' targets for looting, arson, and physical violence reflected Black working-class individuals' frustrations with the pace of civil rights gains and their political and consumer impotency. White passersby stood in for a racist American society, allowing some African American participants to take out their anger and frustrations on unsuspecting, and often innocent, bystanders. By setting fire to grocery stores and other exploitative retailers, rebels upended the power dynamic between consumer and owner. Although most participants acting criminally during the urban rebellions were working-class individuals, these were total community events. Middle-class Blacks and working-class whites also participated in the uprisings, demonstrating that insurrections held significant meaning for individuals community wide. Although these other two groups' actions did not parallel the dominant patterns of Black working-class participation, the ways in which these individuals joined in the urban rebellions were also informed by their race and class identities.

Working-class residents realized they possessed great power in affecting change through collective action and the threat of violent protest. Both Cincinnati and Omaha experienced multiple uprisings, and Milwaukee sustained a four-month-long daily march for open housing where the constant threat of interracial violence proved to be a very effective course. In addition to creating sentiments of political and social potency on a grand scale, African Americans' specific actions during the revolts allowed them to upend typical relationships of power. Arsonists and looters attacked stores that charged exorbitant goods for inferior products. Cincinnatian Marjorie Parham recalls one Avondale entrepreneur's wife wondering aloud what would happen to her husband's business. Parham responded, "That's going to depend largely on how they've [the working-class Blacks] been treated in that drugstore."[30] Spectators verbally challenged police while others created roadblocks and sat vigil, preventing outsiders from gaining entrance into their communities.

In what Doug McAdam termed "cognitive liberation" in his political process model, an individual's realization that they can change his or her own conditions impelled many participants.[31] A twenty-something unidentified man told Cincinnati television cameras,

> We're not afraid of your force because it has always been there[;] the only thing that you have with the National Guard is just a little more force. . . . We're here to tell your people today that we are tired. We're sick and tired of you people taking all the goodies and leaving us none. Ever since we've been in this country we've been in a trick bag. About this procedure thing, about this law and order. We're not concerned about the law and order anymore because you make the law and you keep the order. What we're concerned about is getting someplace in this country for black people. And either we are all going to have peace or ain't nobody going to have no peace. We don't mind dying because we have been dying ever since we've been in this country. And for the first time in our lives we are alive. And we see ourselves as black people on the move.[32]

These and other specific rebellious actions demonstrate how the Black working class organized in their own interest.

MIDDLE-CLASS PARTICIPATION

Middle-class individuals shared multiple perspectives of the events, ranging from expressions of racial solidarity to the admonishments on the "appropriate way" to protest inequality, highlighting the complexity of race, class, and privilege. Kerner Commission investigators observed that "middle-class people tended to be less involved. Many apparently felt confused and ashamed, believing that the riot threatened them and their position more than it threatened whites."[33] In Omaha, fourteen ministers released the following statement: "We deplore the recent acts of vandalism and looting and we feel further that the acts are unfounded. . . . Such uprisings only lead to the total destruction of our community."[34] Others felt that change must come from already established mechanisms. Floyd McKissick publicly shamed those who made such comments, retorting that "some so-called Negro leaders even have the audacity to join The Man by calling a liberation struggle, a riot—his brothers hoodlums and criminals—and damning his brothers who seek to overthrow the yoke of oppression."[35] By registering violent protest as deviant, Black middle-class commentators legitimated extant social institutions as

Class proved to be just as salient as race in determining
participation in the 1960s urban rebellions.
Dundee and West Omaha Sun.

sufficient mechanisms to address grievances, encouraging all Blacks to be more middle class in their values.[36] In calling attention to their own distance from the working-class, middle-class Blacks often exercised racial privilege by way of class privilege, deploying an artificial binary between responsible and irresponsible engagement.

The fissure between Black middle-class and Black working-class individuals was not always insurmountable. Some activists worried about the safety of rebels and the efficacy of the protest. Joe Hall, executive director of the Cincinnati Urban League, stated, "I think the demonstrations [uprisings] had a place and served a real purpose, but in the end people had to sit down and talk through what were the issues and what can we do about this concern."[37] Mildred Brown, editor of the *Omaha Star*, also acknowledged both viewpoints and toed a moderate line on the uprisings:

> We cannot commend the methods they [rebels] used to draw attention to the fact that they were frustrated and despaired because they could not feel or see any appreciable betterment of their lot. Likewise,

we cannot commend those who have failed over the past three years to listen to the traditional methods of calling attention to the fact that in Omaha there is discrimination in housing, education, employment, and health and welfare services.... We think that less attention should be paid to the methods they used in calling attention to their plight and more to finding some solutions to the causes which brought their actions about.[38]

Middle-class commentators, using both their political and social capital, often framed the rebellions within a broader protest trajectory. In so doing they connected these events to the considerable failures of traditional rights activism and government indifference. These occasions of interclass collaboration aside, Black working-class individuals agitated in their own interest, as they believed that tangible gain would come from such action.

Police arrested very few middle-class African Americans as they did not see their actions as riotous or criminal, but they were still integral parts of the unrest. More often than not, Black middle-class leadership participated in more subtle ways, encouraging participants to leave the area out of concern for the young people's lives. Members of the Black middle class often acted as counter-rioters, encouraging rebels to return to their homes, mobilizing community resources, and acting as spokespersons during the urban rebellions. Marian Spencer recalls that her husband "was standing up to, trying to get those people to do right, he was talking to them, he was saying, you know, 'stop all of this rioting, we don't need to do this, we can do better, we can do different.'"[39] By providing a moderate voice during an especially tense time, the Black middle class tempered the rage of the rebellions. In some cities, local government thought established civil rights leadership was so critical to ending the unrest, they circulated to police a list of persons authorized to enter the disturbance area.[40] Elsewhere the distribution of identification cards actualized an important rhetorical distinction: between sanctioned and unsanctioned engagement, good and bad actors. Although Black middle-class leadership's ability to convince participants to return home was questionable, they leveraged the limited power that they had within local government, marking their participation as legitimate. Cities offered their blessing to those willing to side with municipal authority. Even with these measures, police did detain some middle-class residents, seeing their race and not their class and often unaware or indifferent to their political intentions, drawing consternation from these arrestees.

The twenty-four-hour citywide curfew in Milwaukee caught many more middle-class individuals in a carceral dragnet than those in other cities, even if not for an outright criminal infraction. The experience of Mr. and Mrs. M., a successful real estate agent and his wife, demonstrate this racial class entanglement. When Mr. M. heard that police were closing Third Street, he asked his wife to pick him up from work on Sunday afternoon, July 30. Police officers hassled Mr. M. as he departed the building, telling him to move faster. Mr. M. responded, "I didn't do anything wrong. Go get the ones that are." This remark led to his arrest. Witnessing the scene, Mrs. M. attempted to get the car keys from her husband by opening the cruiser door; police then "'snatched her up,' called her a bitch, handcuffed her, [and] threw her into the wagon." While on the way to the station the officers joked, "What shall we charge her with?" At her arraignment, as Mrs. M. told her story, the judge jumped down from the bench, wagged his finger in her face, and called her a liar, accusing her that it was "because of people like her there was so much trouble in the city."[41]

This anecdote illustrates the overlapping class and racial identities that many middle-class African Americans faced. Mr. M. clearly did not identify with those violently participating in the uprisings, telling the officers, "Go get the ones that are," distinguishing himself from the criminal participants and disavowing their activities. The police officers, however, saw Mr. and Mrs. M. as African Americans who did not respect police authority, evidenced by their talking back to the officers and resisting arrest. Finally, the judge who presided over Mrs. M.'s case blamed "people like her," categorizing her not as part of the Black elite, who had different goals and concerns, but as just another rebel. The salience of class and racial identity were fluid and situationally dependent. Whereas the Black middle class could exercise class privilege toward working-class African Americans, they still maneuvered in a deeply racist society where they faced discrimination. Complicating the interplay of race and class further was that during the urban rebellions many middle-class African Americans faced harassment not only from the police but also from uprisings participants.

Perceived as outsiders, the Black middle class often incurred the wrath of roving groups of rebels. Both Cincinnati city council member Myron Bush and Milwaukee alderperson Vel Phillips were verbally threatened by participants during the uprising. Bush recounted to the Kerner investigators that as he and his wife drove down Gilbert Avenue during the uprising, someone broke his station wagon's rear window with a rock or, he speculated, a bullet.

In their report the investigators noted that "some of the damage inflicted by rioters appeared to be unreasoning and non-discriminating as evidenced by a report of Negro Councilman." While it may seem illogical to those unfamiliar with Cincinnati, the situation makes sense in the community context. Locals felt that Bush, a successful African American lawyer, had distanced himself from the Black community, which solidified his outsider position and made him a legitimate target.[42]

The threat of violence toward elected officials demonstrates that although African Americans had some political representation, they felt disillusioned and dissatisfied with these individuals. The only Black alderperson, Vel Phillips, frequently criticized Police Chief Harold Brier for his excessive policing of the Black community, but when he telephoned her to help calm the masses, she agreed. As she rode through the city for nearly three hours, rebels stoned her car. During the uprisings she also received threatening phone calls from white supremacists.[43] Although the threat of physical violence remained a real possibility for some in middle-class leadership, for one Kerner Commission investigator, demurring to such pressure was unconscionable.

Traditional civil rights leaders' actions could be interpreted in a variety of ways. Diane Phillips, a Kerner Commission student researcher, remarked, "I don't think that it is necessary for me to say much about Dr. [Bruce] Green as a Negro leader. The fact that he went home Tuesday night and had to be convinced by a white man [Mr. Hobson of the Committee of 28] to leave his home is an indication of something." Dr. Green told Phillips during their interview that unnamed militants threatened to harm him and his family if he spoke in front of the Cincinnati City Council during the open forum. She continued, "Dr. Green has been threatened before—by whites. The question one must raise is why he bowed to the threats from Negroes, when he hadn't to the ones from whites. I think it is fair to say that Dr. Green is not 'in touch' with the 'folk' of the ghetto." Phillips felt that Dr. Green shirked his responsibilities to the Black community at the height of their need. Alternatively, instead of cowardly hiding, Dr. Green stepping aside could be read as letting those actively participating in the uprising express their grievances. Phillips further recorded that "he expressed bitterness to me about the fact the NAACP is being called an 'Uncle Tom' organization."[44] Despite racial solidarity and Dr. Green's previous activism, the more militant working-class African Americans saw him as unable or unwilling to represent their own perspectives and thus threatened him, collectively working for their own interests. Green, recognizing that a new age of African American protest was upon Cincinnati, relinquished control.

The distrust many working-class African Americans had of middle-class Blacks and traditional civil rights leadership was born in the years before the uprisings, nursed during these events, and came of age in the aftermath. The commission concluded that in Cincinnati, "while no attacks or threats against middle-class or conservatives Negroes have been reported since the riot, it is significant that two Negroes asked that they be excused from jury duty on cases involving riot arrestees." One middle-class woman feared retaliation if she reached a guilty verdict against any participant. She defended her decision: "It has taken me twenty years to pay for my home and I don't want it firebombed." The commission felt that "the possibility of violence being directed against [middle-class Blacks] by poorer Negroes, seems to be acting as a consideration for propertied Negroes in defining their allegiances on community issues."[45] In this scenario, like Mr. and Mrs. M., the female homeowner identified more readily with her class position than the common race she shared with uprising participants. Her interpretation of the events suggests that race was not the only factor that participants used to select targets for vandalism; they also used class.

As observers in Cincinnati noted, the "Negroes in the middle class have been confused and ashamed. [They] feel [the] riot threatened them and their position more than it threatened whites."[46] Due to the comparatively small distinctions within the socioeconomic structure in the Black community, a seemingly insignificant misfortune could be all that was necessary to lose the markers of middle-class status, such as home ownership. In Milwaukee, similar tensions between working-class African Americans and middle-class Blacks existed. At the time of the uprising, dentist Peter Murrell lived north of Capitol Avenue in Milwaukee with other Black middle-class residents in what he described as "an area of professionals." Although he did not believe the rumors that rebels were heading north to strike the wealthier Black enclave, throughout the night he "kept looking out the window" just to make sure.[47]

Mayor Maier invited Black and white businessmen to speak with him about the uprising but "the vast majority of them told the Mayor's Office that they wanted to meet with the Mayor but are fearful of what might happen to their homes and their families while they were gone." Skilled laborers in Milwaukee who were arrested during the uprisings lost their positions. Charlie J. lost his job of eight years after his employer found out he had violated the curfew. Clarence F., who already worked sixty hours a week, felt that his arrest "will keep him from getting a good job."[48] Thus, two of the significant markers of Black middle-class status—homeownership and stable, high-prestige labor—were directly jeopardized by the actions associated with the rebellion. Despite the reluctance of some in, or aspiring to, the middle class, the majority of middle-class African Americans, especially those with previous civil rights organizing experience, helped bridge the gap between more radical and mainline visions of progress.

Kerner Commission staff authors reported, "[In Cincinnati] the uniting of the militants (and the riot itself) has also had the consequence of making traditional organizations and leadership more demanding."[49] Traditional middle-class leadership was able to balance the violent, aggressive, and militant rhetoric of the rebellions and hammer home a more mainline, integrationist approach for African American equal rights. Cincinnati civil rights activist Rev. Tecumseh X. Graham remarked,

> We had to knock them in the head to get their attention. After we got their attention we talked about what needed to be done. I emphasize that, because a lot of us so-called middle-class intellectuals disagree with the revolution, as I like to refer to it, and the way it was brought about. As I tried to explain to them [middle-class leadership and municipal government] if the revolutionaries had not taken the time and the courage to go down and throw a few bricks, although I disagree with that approach, . . . we would have not gotten the few things we did.[50]

Although the grievances articulated by the participants reflected the concerns and aspirations of working-class African Americans, in the actual implementation and establishment of solutions, traditional leadership often brokered the peace.[51]

Black middle-class leadership also dedicated their time and money to supporting those who participated criminally in the uprisings. In a leaflet dated June 22, 1967, the Cincinnati Defense Fund solicited money to raise bail for "many of our people who are still in jail from our recent rebellion against the status quo in Cincinnati. Many of these persons have been booked on sham charges. . . . We need your support and we are sure you need ours." The Avondale Community Council (ACC) allowed the fund to use its offices as headquarters. The fund was endorsed by the chair of the ACC, Bailey Turner with several other prominent civil rights leaders signing onto the letter as well. The NAACP and Rev. Harold Hunt both collected donations for the fund. Other supporters included Dr. Robert Reid, Dr. Bruce Green, and legislators William Bowen and William Mallory.[52]

After the 1969 uprising Omaha community members established the Vivian Strong Memorial Fund, in honor of a fourteen-year-old girl murdered by police and discussed in chapter 5. Their announcement in the *Omaha*

Left to right: **Donald Spencer, Walter Tucker, and Adolphus Ward of the Avondale Task Force stand in front of the burned-out business they hope to rebuild.**
Cincinnati Enquirer/Gannett.

Star proclaimed, "Our money will not restore Vivian to life, nor will it bring the murderer to justice, but it will show our great concern and help the family."[53] People wishing to make donations could do so at Greater Omaha Community Action, the Spencer Street Barber Shop, Omaha Opportunities Industrialization Center, Urban League, the LEAP Program, and the Martin Luther King Jr. Center. Although the money gathered through the fund assisted Vivian's family and not those who participated in the uprising, it sent an important message of solidarity. In demonstrating their frustration that the officer who shot Strong was not convicted, middle-class leadership shared a moment of racial solidarity alongside the working class's feelings of political impotency.

Just as the Black working class performed in the uprising in ways that were representative of their class position and needs, so too did the Black middle class. These individuals operated within the revolts in ways that reflected both their feelings of political efficacy as well as their racial and class position. But because of the privileged positions they held in the community, they often advanced a moderate, more palatable viewpoint and acted as intermediaries between militant factions and the municipal government based on the earlier alliances they had made.

WHITE WORKING-CLASS PARTICIPATION

Although the deindustrialization and mechanization of the Midwest disproportionally affected African Americans, working-class whites also suffered in these cutbacks. Moreover, as Adam Ochonicky argues, "The availability of productive (often physical) labor, the reduction of sexual orientation solely to heterosexuality, the primacy of whiteness, and the symbolic value of the nuclear family all have strongly informed the Midwest's popular image since the early twentieth century. Consequently, midwestern narratives revolve around the strategic use of nostalgic violence to prop up superficial signs that these vanishing elements persist and remain dominant, despite the fact that they are simply components of reductive regional mythology."[54]

For white working-class males, the perceived erosion of their positions as breadwinners and family men was caused by more liberal attitudes toward racial and sexual politics. The real economic hardship coupled with false feelings of Black underserved entitlement left many working-class whites feeling threatened and willing to employ violence to secure their positions in social hierarchies. Only 17 percent of Black rebellion arrestees in Milwaukee felt that job growth opportunities for African Americans were moving too fast. Conversely, 67 percent of white arrestees agreed that "in the North, Negro groups are generally asking too much."[55] Those whites who participated in the urban rebellions were more inclined to feel slighted by the advances African Americans were agitating for but had not yet won.

Whereas popular accounts typically depict these events as expressions of Black angst, a significant minority of participants were white. These events could have devolved into the interracial conflicts that plagued the 1919 Red Summer, but "a strong police response to the potential use of weapons by whites prevented the outbreak of a true racial riot."[56] White individuals' participation was not characterized by the property destruction or loitering offenses that many Black arrestees committed but interpersonal violence and weapons charges. By looking at the demographic profiles, charges, and opinions of these white arrestees, an alternative framework emerges for understanding changing race relations in both the region and the historical era. By understanding the significance of the urban rebellions for white midwesterners and the tensions many working-class whites felt throughout the Black Freedom Movement, the subsequent rise of conservative political ideology becomes evident.

Unlike African Americans who were engaged in civil disobedience to secure greater expansion of rights, white participants engaged in interpersonal violence strategically to maintain social hierarchies. Ochonicky describes this "nostalgic violence" as a "cultural regulatory mechanism" employed to "strike down and discipline individuals who would challenge the surface-level placidity of Midwestern iconography."[57] In 1969 social scientist Robert Hill published his nationwide study of uprising participation, consisting of nearly 8,000 individuals in thirty-seven civil disorders from 1964 to 1967. Hill concluded that only 5 percent of Black males arrested were for weapons charges, compared to 15 percent of white males. Additionally, white males were disproportionally arrested for shooting firearms. Although they accounted for only 11 percent of the total males arrested, they comprised 40 percent of those arrested for shooting or sniping.[58] African Americans participating in the rebellion rejected their second-class citizenship, and many white participants felt it was their duty to remind them of their place through the threat of extralegal violence.

Undoubtedly many whites feared for their safety, just as many African Americans did, but white arrestees used their weapons for purposes other than self-defense. While only 3 percent of Black male arrestees lived outside the uprising city, 11 percent of white male arrestees lived outside the city they were detained in. Additionally, only 2 percent of Black male arrestees lived in the state of the rebellion but not in the uprising city; whereas 9 percent of the white male arrestees lived elsewhere in the state but outside of the rebellion city.[59] Finally, in the latter stages of the uprisings some "white nuts" attempted to stir up a violent reaction against Blacks in the suburb of Wauwatosa but were unsuccessful.[60] These findings demonstrate that armed white participants consciously choose to drive, often great distances, into Black neighborhoods to criminally participate in the uprisings. Put simply, white midwesterners were the outside agitators.

As with African American participants, the ways that white men (no white women are recorded as arrested in the case study cities) performed in the urban uprisings were a function of their perceived social position.[61] A significant faction of white participants came into the Black community intent on causing damage to African Americans and their neighborhoods under the false pretense of protecting their community. Omahan Fr. Jack McCaslin recalled sitting on his front porch watching the fires, ducking behind a pillar every time a car passed, fearful that white vigilantes would kill him, as he was "public enemy number one."[62] In Cincinnati, arrest records show that forty-four white males were charged, comprising nearly 15 percent of the arrested. In Milwaukee nearly 38 percent (about 500) of adults arrested were white, as were 30 percent (86) of juveniles.[63] Investigators in Milwaukee found that 42 percent of whites arrested in the July 1967 uprisings were carrying concealed weapons.[64] Clint Reynolds recounted to a Kerner investigator that while walking through a southern Appalachian migrant neighborhood with a patrolman, the officer asked if Reynolds had noticed all the men with their shirts untucked. When Reynolds replied noncommittally, the officer chided, "because you know damn well or you should know, that under those shirt tails is a .25 caliber Beretta in their belt." The area had become an "armed camp," and the acting executive director of the Cincinnati Human Relations Committee feared that, had a Black person accidentally wandered into that neighborhood, there would have been a "great deal of bloodshed."[65]

The after-arrest interviews add complexity to these statistics and accounts, providing important information on the intent behind white participation. In recounting their uprising experiences many of the Black participants used the occasion to inquire about jobs or training opportunities. White arrestees, however, used the opportunity to express their race-based anxieties. Eldred A. stated that after attending one of Father Groppi's first housing marches, "his attitude toward Negroes [was] tainted," saying specifically that "the way they behaved and the language [they] used turned him against them." Whether it was the militant posture of marchers or a general distaste for open housing, Eldred was not alone in his assessment. Another white participant echoed these sentiments, stating that he had "no use for Fr. Groppi."[66]

Many other white participants expressed concerns about protecting themselves and their families during the uprisings. William B. felt that he was illegally arrested because his gun was disassembled in a case, "and he merely wanted to protect himself in his apartment—because he could hear the yelling outside his window." The man did not explain why he was on the street with his weapon when arrested, however. Within Avondale proper, David and Elaine Davis recalled a "white redneck" that positioned himself on the second-floor landing of their apartment building. The newlywed white couple expressed that throughout the whole episode, this neighbor, not Black residents, was the man they most feared as he had a "I'll shoot the first one [Black person] who comes through the door type of attitude."[67] This general sentiment of arming oneself for an all-out race war was not limited to those arrested during the uprising.

In the aftermath of these events, the white majority used the fear of continued racial violence, African American criminality, and the decline of cities to rhetorically shift political regimes in these communities. In Omaha, B. D. Super, the manager of Hansen's Sporting Goods, stated, "I've never had such a week in the gun business." He reported handgun sales at more than three times the volume than in the same period the year before. J. C. Penney also showed a 25 percent increase in the sale of rifles and handguns. Police registration records in Omaha showed that four times as many owners registered pistols in the two weeks after the 1968 uprisings than they had in a comparable period before March 4, with daily registrations increasing to fifty a day.[68] Additionally, Milwaukee's gun sales increased after the Detroit uprising, some 400 miles away. Arrestee Eldred A. noted that he was concerned about "the possible riots this summer, [saying] many of his friends are buying guns to be ready if any rioters come in their neighborhoods."[69] White individuals who participated in the uprising, and those who did not but purchased weapons, felt uneasy about their position in society as both men and workers. These men participated in the uprisings not because they had nothing to lose but because they had something to protect—namely, their families and white privilege.

Most white Milwaukee participants held jobs but felt economically threatened, whereas 50 percent of Black arrestees were without a full-time job.[70] In Cincinnati, groups organized to protect their communities in the unlikely event that African Americans entered their neighborhoods. Additionally, some suburban whites came to Black neighborhoods and set fires to buildings. In the Over-the-Rhine neighborhood, where many white, southern Appalachian migrants lived, the Office of Economic Opportunity supported "the Hub," which provided referrals for displaced workers and was frequented by unemployed African Americans. During the uprisings anti-Black feelings grew in the neighborhood, resulting in a large group of whites throwing projectiles at the building.[71] By targeting the Hub center, which could have also provided employment opportunities for them, white Cincinnatians expressed their anger that Blacks received "undeserved advantages" because of their race, augmenting extant feelings of unearned African American entitlement.

It is important not only to interpret the actions of the many whites who actively participated in the rebellions but also to understand how the uprisings served as an important touchstone to white municipal citizens in understanding the changing urban community. In Omaha during the 1969 uprisings, emergency call transcripts provide in-the-moment insight into the powerful resentments many whites cultivated toward Black participants, the police, and local city government. One woman told the operator, "We've lived down here. They don't own nothing, never did own nothing. . . . Why do people who are not of this mess have to tolerate it?"72 After enduring this harassment and fear twice before, white business owners were enraged during the 1969 uprising. When a storeowner requested that the Fire Department send rigs to put out the fire in his store, the dispatcher replied that they could not go in.

> *Male:* So all a man can do is sit there and have his place burn down, is that it?
> *Operator:* I guess . . .
> *Male:* That's the protection I get from the City of Omaha.
> *Operator:* No, that's . . .
> *Male:* I mean, where in the hell is the Police Department to take these guns away from these people, and mow them down and drive the trucks right through, huh? You have your business burn to the ground and the people you pay to protect, they don't protect you. So what the hell is the use of paying taxes, huh?
> *Operator:* Well, I pay them, too. And I don't know what to say.73

Many white midwesterners' interpretations of the uprisings—and, for that matter, the Black experience—came from detached observations, not contextual understanding. They saw that African Americans were destroying property in the streets and looting stores but did not comprehend that Black participants sought out the same economic security that white property owners were trying to protect. In many ways these violent insurrections severed the tenuous ties between Black and white midwesterners, exacerbating long-held prejudices.74 One such frustrated white Milwaukeean wrote to Mayor Maier nearly six months after the uprising:

> We think it's high time we put our foot down and put a stop to this constant fight for more rights. So we are going to put a stop to this lawlessness on our own. The sooner the whites will riot for equal rights and for putting a stop to N.A.A.C.P. and putting the n——s back in they'er [sic] places all the whites will unite and whipe [sic] out the n——s before this gos [sic] any farther. We are tired of the negroes getting what they want "FOR NOTHING" and the white men working they'er [sic] fingers to the bone for what we need.
>
> *Signed The Whites.*75

In the aftermath of the urban rebellions many white midwesterners jettisoned previous attempts at a "slow and steady" allocation of rights to African Americans. These insurrections caused whites to turn their focus inward and to begin to agitate for a more aggressive retrenchment of white privilege.

Nationally, the urban rebellions sparked the growth of several white vigilante groups. In 1967 the Minutemen, a Philadelphia white vigilante organization, distributed flyers that read "The N———s cry 'Black Power' and 'Get Whitey' and threaten to burn America to the ground. We tell you these N———s are not kidding, they intend to do just that. The American people must be prepared to physically oppose them anytime we can." Additionally, several Minutemen drove cars pasted with bumper stickers that read "N———S BEWARE. IF YOU DON'T STOP THIS YEAR YOU WILL DIE."[76] Kerner investigators noted that within the Midwest there had been "a proliferation of local 'white patriot' organizations."[77] Staff investigators in Cincinnati succinctly observed that after the rebellion, the "situation in Cincinnati [is] worse, not better. Fear and bitterness in Negro community . . . could possibly be a true race riot with poor Southern Appalachian whites fighting with young Negroes in the same area." The researchers also noted that "even white elites are buying guns."[78] The fear that Black protest was synonymous with antiwhite violence caused many white Americans to begin to arm themselves in continued service of maintaining regional hierarchies and sustaining the midwestern myth.

On September 14, 1967, 4,000 whites gathered to counterprotest the open housing marches in Milwaukee, attacking African Americans who drove past in their cars. White racist groups, such as the National Association for the Advancement of White People founded by Bryant Bowles in 1953, the Ku Klux Klan, and the White Rangers, all increased their membership and actively threatened advocates of open housing with violence.[79] A Congressional Research Service representative requested that the assistant US attorney contact local public officials regarding the inability, or unwillingness, of local law enforcement to contain the mobs that had been gathering in South Milwaukee.[80] Although Mayor Maier was eager to call out an equal number of National Guard during the July disturbance, he took a decidedly hands-off approach when white Milwaukeeans physically threatened Black marchers, clearly demonstrating who he considered a violent threat.[81]

Individuals participated in the urban rebellions at the intersection of their race and class position. Black working-class people sought to end the disenfranchisement, marginalization, and lack of equal access they faced from both the Black middle class and the white establishment. The Black middle class straddled the privileges that being economically secure afforded them and the commitment to racial solidarity. Although most in the Black bourgeoisie did not participate criminally, they helped in many ways during the course of the rebellions, including acting as a counter-rioter, securing bail money, and serving as intermediary between the masses and city government. Finally, African Americans were not the only people affected by and participating in these events. Many white working-class men took part in the rebellions, attempting to protect their white privilege. As white property owners suffered damages in these events, the delicate midwestern liberal détente that existed prior to the unrest began to break apart. The one commonality in the aftermath of the uprisings was that no person, Black or white, middle- or working-class, was left unaffected.

FIVE

Black Men (and Women), Are You Ready?

On Tuesday night, June 24, 1969, Omaha police officer James Loder and his Black partner, James W. Smith, responded to a break-in at 1701 North Twenty-First Street in the city's Black enclave. A group of youngsters, attending a record party nearby, scattered when they saw the officers arrive. As the children ran from the police, Loder raised his service revolver, leveled the weapon, and fired a single shot, hitting fourteen-year-old Vivian Strong in the back of her head as she ran away. Doctors pronounced the child, dressed in green shorts and a white blouse, dead on arrival. Eyewitness and Vivian's friend Lenford Vaughan described the incident, "He raised his arm, aimed and shot. He just fired one shot and Vivian fell. The cop didn't yell 'halt' or nothing. He just stood there and shot." Loder later testified, "If I had known it was a female, I would never have shot."[1]

As news of the girl's death circulated throughout the community, 200 people gathered in solidarity outside the Logan Fontenelle Housing Project, where the Strongs resided. Gradually the crowd moved from the public housing development to the E-Zee Liquor Store, where protesters committed the first acts of vandalism. One thousand people gathered the next night on a baseball field adjacent to the homes. Community activists wove in and out of the crowd passing out leaflets that inquired, "How many black children have to be murdered by cops before something is done?" On the street, uprising participants taunted police officers to "come and get us, you white bitches." By the end of the week, forty businesses had been damaged, destroyed, or vandalized. Frank Peak recollected witnessing "one lady in particular, an older lady. She was just smilin'. She'd got some new clothes out of there, and it was a real neat thing to see her so happy." Peak, a former member of Omaha's Black Panther Party, did not join the organization until he reached his "breaking point," the murder of Vivian Strong.[2]

These snapshots of Omaha's 1969 rebellion urge more complex questions regarding the uprisings, beyond racial and socioeconomic considerations. Loder's guilt in shooting a female, but not a Black child; participants' use of emasculating epithets; and Peak's happiness at seeing a woman gathering new clothes gesture toward connections between gender and the urban rebellions. Investigators, scholars, and rebels have all employed highly gendered ideas in their uprising interpretations and actions. The urban revolts must be placed in dialogue with class, gender, and racial analysis to understand the full impact these events had for not only the Black populace but also America as a whole, providing a critical lens for understanding the Black Freedom Movement. By examining such prevalent notions, lasting assumptions about race, class, masculinity, and femininity in social movements become evident. In interpreting criminal and noncriminal participation through the lens of gender, this chapter demonstrates that the uprisings represent a collective community action, extending beyond illicit acts.

THE CRISIS OF BLACK MASCULINITY

Gender roles and relations are not created in a vacuum. They correspond to racial, classed, and regional considerations that factor into the valuation or devaluation of an individual's status.[3] Throughout the 1960s, public policy analysts, African American leaders, and everyday citizens heatedly debated gender roles, pondering whether Black masculinity had reached a point of crisis. These conversations influenced popular and federal perceptions of the uprisings. The US government published two significant reports contemporaneously with the first wave of uprisings, social scientist Daniel Patrick Moynihan's infamous *The Negro Family: The Case for National Action* in 1965 and activist Dorothy Height's addendum to the 1964 *Report on Four*

Consultations by the President's Commission on the Status of Women. Both reports focused on the seemingly atypical structure of Black families in which the authors argued that the "reversed roles of husband and wife" led to the emasculation of Black males in the home and ghetto community.[4] Lingering assumptions about the interplay between race and class contaminated this contemporary gender analysis, ignoring the systemic problems that contributed to the perceived emasculation of the Black male.

In a chapter titled the "Tangle of Pathology," Moynihan charged that the Black American family was not only cause for "national action" but also partially to blame for the rebellion that took place in the Watts area of Los Angeles. He suggested that the rebellion represented Black males' response to the matriarchal structure of the Black family "so out of line with the rest of the American society, [which] seriously retards the progress of the group as a whole, and imposes a crushing burden on the Negro male."[5] In his assessment, the blame for problems within the Black community lay neither with discrimination nor disenfranchisement, lack of jobs nor redlining, but with the assumed nontraditional role of Black women.

Similarly, in her addendum Height partially blamed Black women for men's feelings of inadequacy: "When she [a college-educated Black woman] earns more than her husband, his resulting insecurity and jealousy may dissolve the family and thus continue the matriarchal family pattern," adding that "the children of many Negro mothers who must work are not cared for properly during their mothers' working hours." Commentators echoed this sentiment during the rebellions. One Black Cincinnati woman remarked, "The mother here can't control their kids. They just sit and watch. It's stupid. This may not sound like a Christian [thing to say]. But if one or two would get sniped—I mean shooting to kill—this would stop."[6] Many Americans held Black working mothers responsible not only for the dissolution of two-parent homes but also for "wild" children running the streets.

More disconcertingly, given her own impressive political activism, Height completely depoliticized Black women by ignoring their own issues and grievances. She summarized, "If the Negro woman has a major underlying concern, it is the status of the Negro man and his position in the community and his need for feeling himself an important person, free and able to make his contribution in the whole society in order that he may strengthen his home." She continued, "Thus, the progress of the Negro woman—her personal advancement and that of the whole family—is inextricably bound to the improvement of opportunities for the Negro male."[7] In Height's opinion,

Black women's objective during the apex of the civil rights movement was not to overcome their own triple oppression as working Black women but to ensure that "their" men felt manly enough.

In the context of the Midwest, economic and racial bias acted as co-conspirators, preventing working-class Black men from fully benefiting from the wages of manhood, defined as asserting masculinity through physical prowess, the subordination of women, providing for one's family, and exercising control over their own and others' lives.[8] The constraints of structural racism and classism thwarted African American men in their attempts to assert their masculinity. Whitney Young argued that "both as a husband and as a father the Negro male is made to feel inadequate . . . in a society that measures a man by the size of his paycheck, [the Black man] doesn't stand very tall in a comparison with his white counterpart. To this situation he may react with withdrawal, bitterness toward society, aggression both within the family and racial group, self-hatred, or crime."[9] Beverly Hills psychoanalyst Dr. Frederick Hacker noted that the Watts rebellion had a positive effect in the community because before "Negro children saw their fathers as helpless and frightened objects of the arbitrariness of white men in uniform," but afterward the children saw their fathers as heroes.[10] While this is a simplification of the totality of Black men's day-to-day experiences, without a doubt Black citizens in their interactions in the workplace and with police had limited control over their lives. For Marvin McClarty, these spheres overlapped.

In 1967 Ernie Chambers wrote a letter to Omaha's safety director, L. K. Smith, describing an incident that took place on January 18. That evening African American police officer Marvin McClarty stopped by the Spencer Street barbershop after his shift to chat with the proprietor, Dan Goodwin, and their mutual friend, Chambers, about a race-related issue. The men were vocal, if unofficial leaders in the Near North Side, and the Spencer Street barbershop served as a meeting point for Black men to discuss a wide range of issues. Cruiser car #86 stopped in front of the shop and Sergeant Brock—despite being of a lower rank than McClarty—alighted his car and verbally reprimanded the officer for "being out of his district." Chambers wrote that the "whole spectacle was insulting to Officer McClarty and insulting, in the extreme, to us."[11]

Chambers was concerned that McClarty had little respect within the police force—respect that he deserved both as an officer and a man. Chambers argued that not only was this an affront to McClarty but also offensive to Black men throughout the community, writing, "We [the Black community] see a man—who is one of the few links the Omaha Police Division has with the Ghetto—one of the few Officers we can respect—treated in this uncivilized manner."[12] In Chambers's opinion, McClarty lacked control of his own life and the respect he deserved because he was reprimanded by an officer whom he out ranked. Chambers was concerned with the symbolism that it held for the Black community. If one of the police department's own could be disrespected with impunity, what chance did civilian Black men have?

Black men faced the arbitrariness of stop-and-frisk procedures, as they did in many other communities, but they also lacked control over their own medical records and privacy. In 1966, the police department, desperately searching for the suspect in the rape-murder (which Posteal Laskey would later be convicted of), violated Black men's medical privacy in order to "narrow" their list of suspects. The department obtained the hospital records of 10,000 African American males within the area with type O blood. They then cross-referenced this illegally obtained information against public records of committed sex crimes. Any Black man who previously had blood drawn at the hospital could now be investigated as a potential sexual assault suspect. African Americans were so disgusted by this treatment and the violation of their constitutional rights that the assistant US attorney feared that this investigation could produce an "explosive situation."[13]

Police also subjected Milwaukee Black male teenagers to excessive search measures like stop and frisk. The Memorial Community Center sponsored a summer dance, and when the event concluded organizers provided girls with rides home and instructed the boys to walk. On the boys' way back, state agents forced the male teens to line up against the wall for investigation. The Milwaukee police, however, were not responsible for this search but rather a random fire truck patrolling the area.[14] Clearly this was outside of their assigned duties, but the firefighters self-deputized to control Black lives and movement. Therefore, because of their gender, the Black teenage boys were expected to see themselves home while the girls received escorts. For the young men, their working-class status ensured that they did not have their own vehicles to drive, so they walked. Finally, their race made them susceptible to unnecessary searches even by those without the authority to do so. These constant indignities accumulated over time and boiled over during summers of unrest.

As activists and politicians read the uprisings through the lens of masculinity, Black women became disadvantaged. In lieu of looking at the institutions that prevented Black men from obtaining equal status in the workplace and politics, commentators focused on how Black women, employed out of necessity, emasculated Black men. Middle-class advisers writing on Black working women reiterated that Black women in the workforce not only made Black men weaker but also raised a cohort of hellions. Women possessed no authentic claim to protest, except to support Black men. It is in this deeply troubling context that the urban rebellions occurred.

BLACK MASCULINITY IN THE REBELLIONS

Racial discrimination, deindustrialization, and mechanization ensured under- or unemployment for African American men, resulting in their continual struggle to provide materially for their families. This same intersectional prejudice prevented Black men from engaging with other men, including employers, politicians, and authority figures, as equals. Political powerlessness and frustration with token Black middle-class leaders contributed to Black working-class men's disillusionment. Additionally, due to the mainstream devaluation of Black womanhood, African American men struggled to protect Black women from verbal, physical, and sexual assault. When CORE president Floyd McKissick proclaimed to his delegation, "The year 1966 shall be remembered as the year we left our imposed status as Negroes and became Black men," he did not do so casually.[15]

As a growing Black nationalist rhetoric radiated throughout the community, African American men asserted that their inferior race and class status also constituted an affront to their manhood.[16] Black men struggled to meet many of the traditional markers of being manly: mobilizing political power; providing for one's family through gainful employment; protecting Black women from abuse; and controlling their own communities.[17] The impediments to achieving full Black masculinity were complex and deeply rooted in the discriminatory structures of the urban Midwest. Ghetto life, not Black women, emasculated its residents. The same concerns grieved during the rebellions—namely, excessive policing, political inefficacy, and lack of full employment—demonstrated the challenges Black men faced in fully expressing their masculinity. To escape these limitations, Black men employed a masculinist discourse. Race privilege would come via gender privilege.

Black women were also often targeted by police. In May 1962, Cincinnati patrol officer John A. Virgin, handler of police dog Ted, was driving in his cruiser when he saw two women fighting. According to Virgin, Gwendolyn Barnes ran at the officer with a half-opened pocketknife. While trying to defend himself, his hand was severely cut and he backed himself up against a wall drawing his weapon for protection.[18] African American witnesses told a different account. The NAACP took eighteen statements where it became obvious that women were often the victims of police brutality and that the men who came to their defense were subject to attacks and arrests. One witness stated, "I saw an officer pounding and beating a girl ... cursing and kicking her with his gun drawn." Another uninvolved witness stated, "I am the mother of nine children. I was bitten on the abdomen by the dog before I knew what had happened." When backup arrived, instead of speaking with the crowd to calm them, the officers released more police dogs to control the group.[19] Thus, in this situation Black men were unable to prevent these women from being attacked by police dogs, undercutting their masculine imperative to protect "powerless" Black women. In the aftermath of Martin Luther King Jr.'s assassination, an already tense Black Cincinnati community exploded into violent rebellion when rumors began to circulate that a police officer had killed a Black woman. Although an African American woman had been shot and killed, it was a tragic accident, not police brutality. Her husband, a caretaker for a jewelry store, fought for control of his shotgun against young men attempting to loot the store and the gun fired, killing his wife. The extant feelings of police disrespect and rumors of yet another incident when an African American man failed to protect Black women from these dangers became too much to bear for a community already in mourning.[20]

The rebellions afforded Black men the opportunity to regain control over their lives, if only temporarily. Prior to the uprisings, African American men possessed limited opportunities to fully exercise their masculinity, particularly in exerting control over their lives. An investigation of "manly" behaviors within the rebellions highlights masculinity in the revolts. These actions can be classified into three types of behaviors. First, Black men shifted the normative power structure by taking back control of their neighborhoods. Second, both white and Black participants sought to protect "their" women and institutions. Finally, participants in the uprisings emasculated their opponents and employed masculinist rhetoric to encourage others and augment solidarity through "brotherhood."

For a brief period, in many places just a matter of hours, Black inner-city residents took control of their own neighborhoods. This takeover consisted of residents preventing outsiders' entrance, protecting vital community institutions, preventing firefighters and police officers from performing their duties, and targeting stores that exploited the Black community. In Cincinnati Black youths refusing white deliverymen entry into their neighborhoods became the opening salvo to the 1967 uprising. In the aftermath of Dr. Martin Luther King Jr.'s assassination, the city's Black leaders followed young people's lead by instructing all whites, including police officers, mail carriers, and milkmen, to stay out of the Black community, providing Avondale residents the space to grieve. Black Panther Party members guarded the buildings for the *Omaha Star* newspaper, Greater Omaha Community Action center, and Mothers for Adequate Welfare. Activists took up these strategic positions to protect against potential damage as suffered when the NAACP Youth Council Freedom House in Milwaukee burned down.[21]

Police–community relations in Black neighborhoods had always been tenuous, but relations became particularly strained during uprisings. Rudy Smith recalls that he nearly lost his life while covering the 1966 uprising as an *Omaha World-Herald* photojournalist. "I see these National Guardsmen everywhere and I saw this one church in the back, and I took a picture of it, click, click, click, and a policeman and a National Guard looked at me and said, 'There's one there!'" Smith attempted to explain to the officer that he was on assignment for the newspaper: "Here's my credentials, and here's my camera, I'm just taking pictures." The officer responded by putting a gun to his head. At that moment Smith saw Mayor Sorensen touring the area and shouted desperately, "Mr. Mayor! Mr. Mayor! This is Rudy, from the *World-Herald*. . . . These guys are gonna shoot me!" After recognizing the then nineteen-year-old Smith, the mayor told the Guard to stand down. Nearly fifty years later, sitting in his comfortable living room with journalistic accolades surrounding him, Smith reflected on the haunting experience: "It was terrifying, but to me, I had learned previously that danger would always follow you as a Black person, you'd always be involved in danger and would never be far from extinction. It brought back memories of being put out of the house at five and missing meals, being homeless, hungry, and so I said, you know, so be it, because even back then I didn't expect to live long anyway."[22]

Incidents of unrest provided African American men the opportunity to temporarily suspend normal power dynamics and the ever-present fear of extinction. Instead of police terrorizing Black individuals, first responders found themselves as targets. African Americans physically and verbally challenged police officers, unafraid of deadly force. The Cincinnati Police Department notably documented this trend in arrest records. Of the over 450 records, nearly forty African Americans received charges for using obscenities and challenging police authority. Police arrested only one white man on similar charges. Officers frequently complained in their arrest reports that African Americans laughed at them, claiming, "You're only stopping me because I'm colored," or used derogatory language such as "you simple motherfucker," eschewing typical patterns of deference.[23] Such actions highlight a shift in normative police–Black citizen relations, demonstrating that the disorder of the rebellions opened space for defiance and the embodiment of certain tenets of masculinity.

African American men also upended typical Black–white relations. Despite the lack of Jim Crow laws in the Midwest, prior to the uprisings Blacks did not enter certain neighborhoods or establishments without being scrutinized. During the uprisings African Americans inverted this practice by targeting white passersby, using physical violence to intimidate and prevent them from returning. As one participant bragged to emergency room admitting nurse Carol Brown, "I kicked a honkey in the ass," subsequently spraining his foot.[24] Ronald Hudson, a white Omaha resident, recalled driving with his girlfriend in his cherry red '63 Super Sport nicknamed "the Red Baron" when, after attending a concert at the Omaha Civic Auditorium, "we see flames going straight up in the air . . . so we drive down there and I get out of the car, next thing I know I'm in the hospital." Due to the injuries sustained from being dragged from his car and beaten, Hudson remembers little from the incident but is left with a dent in his head as a reminder. Sipping coffee at an area McDonald's, Hudson offered that he held no hard feelings toward African Americans after the incident, primarily because many of his friends and coworkers were Black. He described North Omaha as a "no-zone for white people" following Vivian Strong's death because of fear of retaliatory violence.[25] These incidents of physical violence, although undoubtedly harrowing for the victim, occurred infrequently. By physically intimidating outsiders who ventured into the neighborhood, Black residents shifted norms of who could enter their neighborhood safely.

Black men also took control of their lives through looting stores, particularly for the goods they desired but could not afford due to economic deprivation or exorbitant prices. In Cincinnati, these stores included Green's Department Store, McDevitt's Men's Shop, Woolworth's, Schiff's Shoe Store, Guenther's department store, and a watch repair store. In Omaha this included Crosstown Pawn Shop and Loan as well as the E-Zee Liquor Store. The goods that men looted served as implements that embodied traditional gender roles. Deborah DuBose, a girl at the time, recalled that neighborhood boys "brought some meat to our house. . . . They had just a big cart of meat, I mean we had so much meat!" These young men, although not members of DuBose's family, took on traditional gender roles in literally bringing home the bacon to a poor family.[26] Arrest records note that Black males' contraband often included liquor, electronics, cigarettes, suits, watches, and condoms. Rebels took items linked to manliness via perceived wealth, good looks, and sexuality.

In burning certain buildings, Black residents also punished those who had previously mistreated them. Kerner Commission investigators noted that participants frequently hit racist industries and that stores identifying themselves as Black-owned businesses were left alone.[27] In Omaha rebels burned the Reed's Ice Company and Skaggs Drugstore, both of which engaged in discriminatory hiring practices. Participant James Mimms said, "I wanted to get downtown, Schlito's, Penny's . . . F. W. Woolworth, had this counter where you could go eat, they wasn't allowing us to eat there, we wanted them stores but we couldn't get to them."[28] The targets of physical abuse, looting, and arson reflected Black men's desire to reassert their manhood against those who had politically or economically marginalized them as well as take the goods they felt would also serve as appropriate trophies of their manhood.

Direct negotiations served as one of the most important ways working-class men took control over their lives during the rebellions. Prior to the rebellions, Black middle-class leadership served as an ineffective intermediary between the masses and city hall. Through the uprisings, working-class African Americans directly communicated with those who had previously held power in their lives. The grievances these men presented, including employment and investment opportunities for Black workers, reflected their class and racial identities.[29] By negotiating the terms of the peace, rebels demonstrated that they wielded real political power. Incensed negotiators punctuated this actualization by walking out of a city council forum when Mayor Bachrach mobilized the National Guard in the building. By leaving the meeting in protest, Black men took control over their lives, no longer groveling at the feet of a racist government.

In addition to inverting the typical patterns of power in their communities, working-class men, not just African Americans, acted in gender normative ways through the protection of "their" women. Nationally, nearly every city had examples of Black men protecting Black women from bodily harm or harassment. Most notably are the cases reported in Harlem, 1943; Dixmoor, Illinois, 1964; Chicago, 1965; Los Angeles (Watts), 1965; and Omaha, 1969.[30] In each of these examples, a police attack, either actual or rumored, on Black women catalyzed the response of Black men.

Black women also faced the danger of sexual harassment and rape in their own neighborhoods. In some cities white men would cruise main thoroughfares in Black communities, believing that all African American women were sex workers or, at the very least, sexually available.[31] After an extensive interview with one woman, she confided a few days later that she had omitted two incidents that she had personally experienced from her initial account. The first occurred when she was fifteen when "an older white man [approached] teenage African American girls who were on their way to Lincoln Junior and Senior High. [He would] ask them to sit down on the sidewalk, spread their legs and show him their panties." She was one of the young Black girls he approached. Years later, when she was nineteen or twenty years old, two white men tried to kidnap her and sexually assault her. The woman made a point to reach out and share this additional information after her interview because "in America, black people are not seen as human but as things to be used by white society at their whim."[32] Dan Goodwin recounted in an interview how white men would stalk through North Omaha harassing Black women and girls at bus stops and that he and other men would run them off: "These are our women, our children, our mothers you know, these white guys were making everybody a prostitute. . . . That kind of stuff was just hard to take. . . . These are our ladies, these are our women."[33]

This trend became amplified during the rebellions. Cincinnatian Pauline E. recalled, "Black men were Black men then, and they were protective of their family and their community." Her statement captures this correlation between Black masculinity and an imperative to protect people and institutions of importance. Pauline's husband had made the decision during the uprising that "I will go down protecting my family." At the conclusion of the uprisings, he casually remarked, "I guess I can take my guns out of my truck." Incredulous, Pauline exclaimed, "You had guns in the truck?" To which her husband asserted, "Hell yes, they were there! If I had to, I was gonna use them."[34] The Black community, acutely aware of this reality, attempted as best as they could to protect Black women. But Black women were clearly capable of defending themselves. Betsy Neel recalls that, while working at General Hospital, "we had people, I know they had guns in their handbags, one lady's bag turned over and the gun fell out. I mean people, they must have felt the need to have guns too."[35]

As a testament to the particularly tense race relations in Milwaukee and Cincinnati, and reminiscent of struggles over open housing in Detroit, armed white men entered Black communities to engage in open combat with Black males with the misguided idea that they were protecting white women.[36] White interviewees described their involvement in the uprisings as their masculine prerogative to protect their families. Roger L., of Milwaukee, described as a "young, white, husband and father," was "concerned that possible riots next summer would mean bloodshed all over the city and he intend[ed] to get a gun when he's twenty-one to protect himself and family."[37]

White males did not limit their armed involvement to self-defense but also came to the community's defense. In so doing, they positioned themselves along Frederick Jackson Turner's frontier line as the last defense between so-called civilization and wilderness.

As early as 1966, the Truth About Civil Turmoil organization maintained that the uprisings were dress rehearsals for a Communist revolution. In an article titled "The Plan to Burn Los Angeles," Gary Allen claimed participants were stockpiling stolen items from the uprising to build an arsenal. Los Angeles police captain Harold E. Yarnell Jr. responded to these rumors: "The only arsenals we've found have been those of paramilitary right-wing groups." Yet the article's uncovered "plan" demonstrates the intersection of the economic, gendered, and racial fears animating these conspiracies. According to the document, Black agitators planned to lure officers to Watts with emergency calls to murder them, then destroy the two main sources of police communications with rocket launchers, kill off-duty officers in their homes, and burn Los Angeles to the ground, shooting all the white men. Children and the surviving women would be "rewards for the insurrectionists."[38]

This gendered and racial fever dream picked up steam across the nation. A single-sheet flyer titled "Has the Riot Opened Your Eyes?" circulated throughout Detroit following the uprising, announcing an August 22, 1967, meeting to discuss the growing violent threat that African Americans posed.[39] Sponsored by the American Legion, United War Veterans for Defense of the US Constitution, Citizens Committee for the Civil Defense, Detroit Police and Firemen Association for Public Safety, and Breakthrough, the organizations played to white citizens' greatest fears.[40] This last organization, like the Truth About Civil Turmoil, was a John Birch Society offshoot founded by city employee Donald Lobsinger. Breakthrough held rallies across Detroit to audiences as large as 1,000 people. The organization's slogan, SASO, "Study, Arm, Store Provisions and Organize," helped to drum up hysteria, calling for the arming of white citizens if the city became Black, as there would be "guerrilla warfare in the suburbs."[41] Breakthrough also encouraged their members to arrange for safe locations to send their children as "bands of armed terrorists invading from the inner city to 'murder the men and rape the women'" were imminent.[42] This gendered anxiety mirrored with visual imagery in a MUST (Men United for Sane Thought) poster, which featured a white housewife carrying a rifle, curlers in her hair, alongside the caption, "Your wife will probably kill you if you come home too late this summer."[43] As new vigilante groups cropped up throughout the Midwest, they drew from the long histories and hysteria at the intersection of race and gender that animated the region.

White Cincinnatian Betsy Neel remembered "my parents saying how proud they were of the people of Norwood who positioned their men, with shotguns at every large entrance." An independent municipality surrounded on three sides by African American neighborhoods, the suburb's residents feared that Blacks would attempt to cross into its borders. Neel noted, "My mom and dad really thought that was wonderful, they looked at them as you or I would look at Minutemen who were protecting their homes from the British or something. They thought that was honorable."[44] Other interviewees corroborated Neel's recollections. When asked about the Norwood community, Brenda Middlebrook commented after a considerable pause, "You didn't shop in Norwood, especially after the riots" as it was a "hostile environment." Her reluctance to discuss the neighborhood stemmed from an incident where she and her husband took a wrong turn during the uprising onto a dead-end street in the community. Before they could turn their car around, ten men came out from their homes "every last one had a shotgun, 'come on n——, you better get out of here n——' it was just like they we're waiting for someone to come into their neighborhood."[45] Betsy Neel recounted a story about the township, "You just knew you didn't go in there. In fact, I heard that a nice young Black girl was down there with some white friends, was pulled out of a car on Montgomery Road and was hurt. So, you know, it was all she was doing was riding through with friends."[46]

During the June 1967 Cincinnati disturbance, police arrested thirty-two individuals on weapons charges, half of whom were white males. Records indicate that many of those individuals were on the offensive against African Americans. Confiscated weapons ranged from tire irons, knives, and handguns to a bazooka. Police arrested John F., a US Army soldier, in the Avondale disturbance area with a .22 caliber rifle. Willie R., an employed twenty-year-old mechanic, fired his weapon into a loitering crowd of Black people. Three young men—Finley H., Jessie W., and Jon A.—threw bottles from their automobiles at Black passersby. These men had left their neighborhoods, pushed through police barricades, and positioned themselves to engage in open combat with Black urbanites. James Mimms noted that it was more difficult for Blacks to leave their neighborhoods to engage in similar armed combat: "The police and the National Guard, they had a line between neighborhoods, like Avondale couldn't get to Mt. Auburn . . . because the police had boundaries: cars, fire trucks, in between these communities so we stayed in our neighborhoods and burnt up and [rose] up where we live. That why it was contained and that's why we burned our own neighborhood." Mimms noted that "no whites came up to that line to shoot at blacks, the police turned them away because they said 'you're committing suicide.' . . . They were stopped at the deportation line where the National Guard were. So they pull up, 'We wanna get them n——s!'"[47] By using their physical prowess to intimidate, exert control over others, and protect their families, both Black and white males asserted their masculinity during the uprisings.

Apart from these violent displays, the masculine imperative to protect women often took more subtle forms. James Mimms stated that he joined the "battle of the riots" because he was furious that "Dr. King followers in suits and ties, dresses and hats were marching non-violent[ly] . . . while the police ran over them with horses, ran over them with dogs, ran over them with bats." Although his initial rationale for engaging in the uprising centered on police terrorizing nonviolent demonstrators, his notion of "protection" quickly shifted. Mimms indicated that men in Cincinnati's West End first began organizing around the idea of "raising hell" and protecting their neighborhood. "Our mothers, our little sisters and our brothers, they were home afraid. We're going [to] protect our families. So that's what brought us out on the street. That made me come out on the street, to protect my family, from my own self and the guys that were out there."[48] In the end, police arrested Mimms, a member of the West End Community Council safety committee, for disorderly conduct and looting.

Numerous men, both Black and white, sought to protect their spouses while attempting a return to normalcy during the daylight hours. Betsy Neel's husband, escorted by a National Guard vehicle with a mounted bazooka, drove her to work every morning. In recalling those events, she twice likened the experiences to the film *Black Hawk Down*. Brenda Middlebrook's husband escorted her to the hospital for a different reason; she believed she was in labor with their first child. She recounted, "Avondale was just burning, burning. It was pandemonium. . . . [We drove] one tank ahead of us, one tank behind us." Carol Brown, who worked at General Hospital, remembered her police officer husband informing her that "[Black militants] got a list of all the policemen's wives, and they're supposed to be coming around doing harm to them and their family." Her husband, one of the few Black officers on the force, gave her a gun to protect herself and had officers patrol their home.[49] While evidence to corroborate this final recollection has not been found, it demonstrates the intersection of political and gendered anxieties in the fear that the most coveted target of uprising participants would be not exploitative stores but police officers' wives.

Beyond using physical strength and their presence in the uprisings, men often encouraged other males to participate in the uprisings on the imperative of acting manly. In Cincinnati, Errol E. was arrested for encouraging participants of uprisings by shouting "go, boys, go!" Others rallied individuals on their shared racial and gender identities using the term "soul brother." In each city, Black business owners expressed their racial and gender solidarity with active participants in the streets by posting signs that read "Black Business" or "Soul Brother." On June 13 in the 1967 Cincinnati revolt, several African American car owners paraded through Avondale with signs reading "Black Power Will Win—Soul Brother No. 1."[50] In their makeshift caravan, individuals identified as Black men, unabashed in their communities and proudly encouraging others that it was OK to be a proud, Black male. Multiple interviewees mentioned that African American men hung women's black stockings from their car antennae. David Davis speculated that "it was just camaraderie, I think just an instantaneous [thing], Hey I don't live here, but I work here, and I am going to be driving through and I am a Black man. I've got to let them know some way."[51] Pauline E. noted, "Black wasn't going to harm Black. You put a black piece of cloth or whatever was black, you put it on your radio antenna, and they did not bother it."[52] This acknowledgment and collective assertion of Black masculinity occurred via solidarity through community protection and taking control of their lives by upending typical patterns of power within the ghetto community.

Black males did not limit their racial and gendered pride to verbal demonstrations but also communicated through the written word. A flyer distributed in an unspecified city read, "I'M TOO PROUD TO BEG FOR MY FREEDOM! I'M NOT AFRAID TO FIGHT FOR IT! BLACK MEN ARE YOU READY?" The creators of this handbill highlighted the gendered imperative of the urban rebellion. By writing "proud," "freedom," "fight for it!," and "Black men are you ready?" in capital letters, they expressed that Black men needed to prepare themselves for armed rebellion. This document demonstrated that rebels perceived earlier civil rights efforts as "begging"—for Black men to receive full rights, they must be proud and willing to fight physically. Accompanying the rallying message was an illustration instructing potential participants on how to make a Molotov cocktail, culminating in step 4: "Light rag—throw bottle at WHITEY!" The final exhortation reads, "White 'Citizens' Are Arming Themselves BLACK MEN Prepare to Defend Yourselves!"[53] The rhetoric used in the flyer demonstrated the intersection of race, class, gender, and tactical adaptation for many Black men. Participants couched the objectives of the urban rebellions in language that demanded respect and full rights for Black men, directed against racial and class enemies.

It is this rhetorical usage of words that helped reflect the transformative power the rebellions held. Many white Americans remembered the urban uprisings as overt attacks on white people, not property violence. This provided legitimatization for white men to use violence against African Americans because they felt that both white privilege and white people were under attack. Yet there is a critical limitation to the employment of masculine rhetoric and pride in being a "soul brother" to explain the urban rebellions. Dick Gregory, in his tongue-in-cheek "Gregory Report on Civil Disorders," opined on why African Americans participated in the rebellions: "White folks are not going to burn this country to the ground. The average white man cannot possibly be as bitter as the average black man. The white man has a better job and cannot afford to go to jail. He has much more to lose by participating in civil disobedience or open rebellion in the streets."[54] While Gregory acknowledged the racial and economic dimensions of the uprisings, he ignored that Black women held many of the same grievances as Black men. To truly understand the fullness of the urban rebellions, women's gendered participation in uprisings must also be unpacked.

BLACK FEMININITY IN THE URBAN REBELLIONS

Male rebels undeniably acted in the revolts informed by traditional gender roles. The rebellions, however, should not be interpreted solely as exercises in masculinity. Although the centrality of their contributions has been downplayed, women engaged fully in the rebellions. As one Cincinnati observer noted, "All ages were active in scenes of violence. In a number of locations where windows were being broken and looting was taking place, women carrying babies could be seen watching the activity."[55] Beyond the confines of spectator, women actively engaged in the rebellion. Social scientist Karl Flaming calculated that 43 percent of the Black female residents in Milwaukee's North End and 33 percent of the Black male North End residents interviewed believed that "Negroes [had] more to gain by resorting to violence than in the Civil Rights movement."[56] Black Milwaukee women felt it more necessary to engage in violent conflict than the men did, demonstrating their feelings of impotency due to their positions within a racial, gendered, and classed hierarchy.

Published documents and arrest records indicate that men dominated the ranks of uprising arrestees. Despite the potential for detailed demographic information, such documents are limited. Publicly available records do not capture those who illicitly participated but were not apprehended or those who contributed in noncriminal ways. This undercounting significantly obscures women's revolt participation. Black women as a discrete entity are hardly mentioned in the Kerner report, save for maligning their parenting skills.[57] The Kerner Commission's survey of Detroit found that 38.6 percent of self-reported rebellion participants identified as female although they comprised only 10.7 percent of those arrested. The *New York Times* estimated that police only apprehended 20 percent of the total uprising participants in Cincinnati, where a high number of women evaded arrest. Although neither the commission nor the *New York Times* explained this discrepancy, the problem lay in how each of these entities defined participation. The Kerner Commission considered a "rioter" anyone who actively participated in looting, arson, or other criminal activities. By discounting the participation of those who specifically went into the uprising area to observe and encourage criminally engaged participants, contemporary researchers effectively interpreted the rebellions through a masculine lens and defined participation as the state does.[58]

By broadening the definition of uprising participation beyond illicit activities, a fuller spectrum of uprisings activities—particularly ones that women participated in—emerges. Often erased from official accounts and local histories, working-class Black women were central to the uprisings. Black women played important roles as defenders, supporters, beneficiaries, and often catalysts; all the product of their intersectional identities. The ways that Black women participated in the urban uprisings reflect their personal experiences with overlapping discriminations. Race, class, and gender reflected a triple axis of oppression shaping the activism of Black women in the revolts and reflecting the entanglement of working-class women's politics and activism.[59]

Women's participation often adhered to traditional gender roles: victims, family protectors, helpmates, and household consumers. As addressed above, police violence against "defenseless" females often served as the immediate catalyst for revolts. But women not only defended themselves during these events, they protected their families and communities as well. Women's noncriminal support roles ranged from distracting police so men could evade arrest to providing food and shelter. In Milwaukee, two out of three women arrested were shielding their husbands from civil authorities.

On their way to work, Ruth Wallace and Barbara Buck had their car searched at a National Guard roadblock on Twenty-Seventh Street and North Avenue in Milwaukee.
© *Milwaukee Journal Sentinel*—USA TODAY NETWORK.

Women charged with looting often did so in the company of their spouses. One woman created a diversion for young male looters by lifting her skirt and calling out to the police to "come and get this," allowing the men to escape. In Cincinnati the number of African Americans visiting hospitals after the first day of the uprising dropped significantly, with both government documents and residents hypothesizing that Black nurses in Avondale operated an underground triage. These individual contributions demonstrate that the success of uprisings hinged on the mobilization of entire communities.[60]

By analyzing arrest records from the June 1967 Cincinnati uprising, a distinct pattern of women's participation emerges, providing insight into females' criminal activities during the rebellion. Women tended to be present in the uprising area when the risk for bodily violence or arrest was unlikely, typically after the main burst of activity. In Cincinnati, during the first two days of the uprising and the height of violent action, no women were arrested. At 2:30 a.m. on Wednesday, June 14, the Ohio National Guard moved in and restored some order to the area. Correspondingly, police arrested nineteen women that day. Arrest records indicate that men's criminal uprising participation tended to be between 9 p.m. and 2 a.m., whereas women tended to be arrested between 2 a.m. and 7 a.m., when there was a diminished police presence and thus a smaller chance of arrest.[61]

Although rare, women did engage in physical violence during the uprisings. A group of young Black males snatched white University of Cincinnati graduate student Noel Wright from his car as he drove through the Avondale neighborhood. They proceeded to beat the man when one of the youths took out a knife and stabbed him. Simultaneously their female companions physically assaulted the dying man's wife. In Omaha during the 1968 uprising, Black public school girls showed up and challenged students at Sacred Heart Elementary School, which had a largely Black middle-class student body, to a fight.[62] Despite the seemingly atypical nature of Black women's violent participation, by physically assaulting female victims they remained somewhat within gender norms.

Most uprising arrests involved property crimes, and women's criminal participation was no exception. Female uprising participants looted stores that used predatory pricing, taking household items they had been unable to afford. Sandra Dickerson did not participate in the riots because she "was married with very small babies, and I wasn't about to get out there. . . . I had no reason to riot. I was working, married at the time. And I just had no reason to get out there. I just didn't feel that disenfranchised that I would get out and break windows. I was more afraid of being arrested, or shot, or hurt."[63] But for many other women with a similar demographic profile, they were still compelled to go out into the streets; 30 percent of the Cincinnati women arrested were housewives. Police arrested each of these women for looting stores including grocers, clothiers, and furniture outlets. These women's spouses' salaries provided enough income to prevent them from needing outside employment, yet it did not afford them the opportunity to purchase high-end consumer goods, such as televisions and vacuum cleaners.

Deborah DuBose recalled her own mother's uprising participation in the 1967 Cincinnati unrest. Her parents and other neighborhood adults regularly gathered at the "living room," a cement slab behind a store where they would socialize "when they get back from work and drink their wine, it was like a little club for them." DuBose noticed that the streets were busy and inquired "Momma, what's going on?" to which her mother responded, "It's alright, it's going down, you know we gonna handle this." Confused, the young DuBose asked for clarification, to which her mother responded, "It's time for you to go home, find your brothers and you guys go home." Three hours later when DuBose's mother and stepfather returned, they had a "grocery cart, it was full of goodies. I'll never forget and I didn't think about looting or anything like that, that it was wrong. All I know is that I saw things that I never had." Her parents had brought home barrettes, paper dolls, jacks, balls, and water guns, "just a whole variety of stuff and it was like Christmas for us."[64]

For DuBose there was nothing strange about her mother's and the other living room women's participation in the uprisings. Years later she recalled, "My mother never had a record or anything you know, she wasn't the type, she worked all the time [in the shirt laundry]. . . . She worked there for eighteen, nineteen years, but they really didn't make anything."[65] For DuBose's mother and other working-class women like her, the uprisings provided an opportunity to acquire goods that they would not normally have, an updated form of pan-toting, where enslaved women and underpaid domestic workers would recoup their wages by taking food from their employers.[66] "Years later we used to tease her about it," DuBose reminisced at the senior center, bingo game in full swing. "Momma you was in the riot! You was looting everything!" Her mother defended herself, imploring, "I didn't burn nothing up though!" By justifying her actions as providing for her family and not destroying property, DuBose's mother interpreted her uprising participation as in line with societal expectations with her roles as mother and wife. For DuBose, then an impoverished little girl, the uprisings gave her a reprieve from a childhood without, which she lived every day: "I was excited to have all that stuff. I can still smell the little barrettes and the little paper dolls as I sit here talking about it. . . . I can still smell the newness, you know, of everything, and I played with those paper dolls forever."[67]

Many women also contributed to the uprisings through noncriminal means in accordance with traditional gender norms. During the 1967 Cincinnati uprising, Pauline E. was in her early thirties, married, with three children. Although somewhat reticent to share her story, Pauline began to unfurl her own contributions to the uprisings. In the early evening hours, as she stood on her stairs watching the carnival-like atmosphere, a group of young men parked in a lot by her house and walked up the street. To her surprise, the men came up to her and stated, "We've been driving hard to get here." Pauline recalled, "I did not ask them where they came from, they did not tell me where they came from, they just talked about how really, they were hungry." The woman had fed her family roast beef that night for dinner, so "I went back in the house and fixed these sandwiches, these roast beef sandwiches, I recall that very vividly." Along with a half pitcher of Kool-Aid, the young men sat on her steps and enjoyed their meal. Intrigued by exactly who those young men were, Pauline asked "'Are you H. Rap Brown?' and he started laughing and said, 'yes,' whether he was or not I really don't know."

After the men finished their sandwich dinners they proceeded to their cars, and "they unloaded these guns, I won't say where these guns went, but these guns remained in the Cincinnati area for almost a year before they come [sic] back to get them." She continued, "After they ate they got out on the street and you know, they were telling the young men what to do, how to do, and in fact, I stood there and listened to them." One overheard piece of information included the young travelers teaching the area men how to stack bricks to carry the projectiles more efficiently through the neighborhood.[68]

In addition to performing the traditional nurturing roles like providing food, Pauline also used the uprising as an opportunity to teach her children. Pauline's husband wanted their children to take shelter in the basement, but Pauline insisted, "No, you will come out, I don't want you on the sidewalk, but stand in this yard, I want you to see what happens in America when Black people are discriminated against." The morning of Pauline's interview nearly fifty years later, Pauline's daughter told her, "Mother, I'm so glad that I was out there and able [to see], I'm sorry it happened, but I was so glad that I could witness that, you know later in life, it opened my eyes to a lot of things." As her children witnessed the chaos from home, Pauline walked the streets, likening the scene to a "war zone."[69]

Pauline also protected members in her community by not revealing participants' identities to the police. Each night she and her dog would take a walk. One evening the police waited for her on the stoop to verbally harass her: "We know you walk your dog, we know you saw it [participants throwing Molotov cocktails at a store]." Although Pauline did not deny she saw the event, she refused to name the participants. When asked why this was important to keep this information to herself, "Well, you know, I'm not the only one. All the old timers around here had that information. . . . I don't have more than the average old person that still lives around here." In between condoning and condemning the uprising, Pauline and women like her saw the events as a teaching moment, an opportunity to provide material support to those actively engaged in the rebellion and to stand in solidarity with young Black men and women by not cooperating with law enforcement.[70] None of these activities would be considered riotous or even illegal, but such unseen actions contributed greatly to the efficacy of the rebellions while also challenging assertions that Black women did not support Black men.

White women also participated noncriminally in the uprisings in gender normative ways. Elaine Davis and her husband, David, lived in an integrated apartment building. She recalled that "we were stuck . . . in our houses and a couple of the gals got together and we made brownies and chocolate chip cookies. I think it was probably the first time some of us had ever baked, we were like, you know, twenty-two years old and didn't have a clue, but you know, we had a box and it had directions on it so we thought, 'sure we can do this.'" After their baked goods had cooled, five or six of the young women walked them over to the fire station "just as proud as could be, you know, look what we're doing for you," as the firefighters could not leave the station due to the emergency. When the ladies walked to the door they encountered a surprise, a Cincinnati policeman standing with his pistol drawn. Stuttering in her naivety, Davis responded, "But we, we have food." After her husband chided her for her bright-eyed innocence, Davis recalled, "We just thought it would be a nice thing to do, it was a nice gesture you know. . . . They were talking on the TV about how they were working double shifts, they had been there for forty-eight hours, some of them haven't been home, and we thought, 'Oh, gee, they need a cookie!'" The Davises, one of the few white couples in the area, understood the stress of the rebellions. Like Pauline, Elaine wished to support the individuals engaged in the chaos in a gender normative way, providing nourishment.[71]

When women participated in the urban rebellions outside of traditional gender roles, police often singled them out for more extensive punishment, using their own frameworks of gender propriety to interpret Black women's actions. When an officer asked a group of teenagers including two young women to disperse, the girls instead "paraded down Main Street in a loud and boisterous manner, using foul and lewd language." Police charged the young women with juvenile delinquency while their male companions walked free. In another example, police arrested a woman outside of a vandalized store and charged her with public drunkenness and prostitution; the officer charged her three male companions with looting. This woman's transgression of traditional gender norms by being publicly intoxicated caused her to be arrested on harsher charges than her associates. The intersection of women's race, class, and gender conspired to disadvantage Black women. In Milwaukee, Mary W. was arrested when she went outside to observe what was going on, she recounted to the Urban League investigators. "In court the policeman told the judge me and two college boys were in it together. I told the judge, 'I didn't know those boys, that I had never seen them before' but the judge didn't believe me. Then, because the boys were smart and in college he let them go but, because I had a record (for school truancy), he put me in jail."[72] The extant beliefs of female propriety along with the intersection of multiple oppressions influenced the ways in which women's actions were interpreted, resulting in both immediate and long-term implications.

In the aftermath of the rebellions, scholars frequently depoliticized and reconstructed female arrestees' participation so that these women appeared to be more feminine and adherent to traditional gender norms. In an analysis of news footage, Black women appeared eight times more frequently than white women, and most of these scenes depicted them in an emotional state, either grieving, crying, or acting antagonistically.[73] Dr. Karl Flaming conducted a major opinion study of arrestees of the Milwaukee rebellion. In the interviewers' notes, they prominently mentioned the "feminine" qualities of the interviewees and the ways in which the women upheld traditional gender roles. Of the seven female interviewees, all but one was described in the study's research notes as "attractive." One research assistant went so far as to describe Willie T. as "a very attractive young negro wife and mother. She was dressed beautifully but the house she lived in was terrible,"[74] demonstrating that although the interviewee lived in an impoverished environment, she still took care to meet certain domestic standards, such as motherhood and physical attractiveness.

The research assistants neglected to include the political rationales for women's participation, in contrast to their notes for the males they interviewed. In nearly all of the seventy-seven male surveys, the men's frustration with the slow pace of civil rights and the lack of job opportunities were emphasized, legitimating their criminal participation. The research team sought to justify the women's arrests as merely accidental, in the wrong place at the wrong time. Throughout the research notes, the interviewers added that female arrestees showed remorse and excelled at their proscribed gender roles as "attractive young negro mother[s] with lots of young children."[75] Researchers portrayed the women not as conscious political actors reacting against their position in a raced, classed, and gendered hierarchy but rather as apolitical women who knew their proper place in society.

Despite the centrality of women's participation in these events, municipal officials and researchers ignored the political overtones of female rebels' actions. The only tangible gains women received from the uprisings, then, were the goods they looted for themselves. As one interviewee noted, "There is so much focus on the black male, that the treatment of the black female often gets overlooked."[76] City governments met only with young men to hear the grievances of the Black community. Concessions made by these governments frequently included recreational leagues, camping excursions, and trade schools, opportunities exclusively offered to boys and young men. In 1966 Omaha, municipal officials did successfully receive a grant from Job Corps to start a women's training facility at the Paxton Hotel downtown. White shoppers stopped visiting the commercial district, afraid of the young Black men who came to flirt with the female trainees on their breaks. With sales dropping at major outlets, the center closed after a year. The intersection of multiple oppressions left Black women's needs unaddressed even though their rationale for participating in the rebellions reflected the same desperation as the young Black men who received recreational and industrial opportunities.[77] Women significantly contributed to the efficacy of the uprisings, through the active encouragement of other participants and their own participation.

Rebels engaged in the urban revolts as a function of not only their class and racial position but also their gender. The sum of these identities influenced the ways individuals responded to the uprisings as well as how scholars and the public remember these events. In investigating the ways that women participated in the revolts as gendered beings, interpretations of the uprisings shift from being solely the purview of angry Black men to incidents that enjoyed broad community support. Additionally, comprehending the mechanisms that impeded Black men from expressing their full masculinity provides deeper insight into the social, economic, and political limitations for African Americans in the Midwest. Despite the important rhetorical and symbolic value these events mobilized in usurping typical patterns of gendered control and power in the Black neighborhoods, the long-term implication for the municipal community is a more complex story.

SIX

The Changing Same

In the aftermath of the urban rebellions, the landscapes of Cincinnati, Milwaukee, and Omaha drastically changed. While rebels believed that violent protest would bring about radical change within the political, labor, and social realms, the stalwart midwestern myth remained largely intact. Media outlets, Kerner Commission investigators, and municipal residents captured this changing same in the months following the revolts. News cameras recorded one such example at a Milwaukee City Council meeting on August 16, 1967. The only Black representative, Alderperson Vel Phillips pleaded with the remaining white city council members to acknowledge the actual causes of the uprising and not just commission yet another fact-finding committee, which she derided as "poppycock." She scolded her colleagues: "If we did our responsibility, we wouldn't have even had a riot," standing to emphasize her point. "You do not need to go through a great deal of length to figure out why, unless you do not want to face why. . . . We are in a position to do something about it, we don't need a study to do what's right." The other members remained unmoved by her entreaties. One alderman, apparently dismayed at Phillips's accusations, attempted to walk out of the meeting saying, "We try to help, we try to do what's right." Incensed, Phillips responded, "Then why don't you vote for fair housing?" and then mocked him by repeating his own words: "We're trying to help you."[1] Although the rebellions shocked many well-meaning midwesterners, in lieu of substantive changes, Black grievances received only piecemeal solutions.

Whereas formal mechanisms for redress remained ineffective and perfunctory, the racial consciousness of both Black and white midwesterners drastically began to shift. In September, Lathan Johnson led Kerner Commission investigators on a tour of Cincinnati. Researchers went to the Avondale Community Center to speak with fifteen young militants. The men, all college educated and clad in dashikis, refused to shake hands with the investigators "to deny any identification with the white man's conventions." The Kerner investigators also encountered a group of three men shooting craps on the street. The men asked the commission representatives if they could help them find jobs. Two of the men had been fired because of their participation in the uprising; the other lost his job at the conclusion of a summer employment program. Each man was married, and one remarked he had to stay away from home to avoid the welfare caseworker.[2] In the aftermath of the uprisings, many working-class African Americans continued to be disproportionally disenfranchised while those with education and some labor autonomy fared better.

As in the urban rebellions themselves, individuals' responses to the aftermath of these events were largely influenced by their racial, class, and gender positions. For some, life drastically changed after the insurrections; for others, much remained the same. African American politicians wielded limited power. Working-class Blacks' economic vulnerability endured, but many in the Black middle class had the ability to espouse a more vibrant cultural nationalism, at times detached from the practical needs of the community. The effect of the urban rebellions lingered long after the National Guard departed each city. The community consequences were most evident in the years following, particularly in the reshaping of legal, social, and economic structures. This reorganization brought some tangible Black victories but also led to shifts in municipal political tactics as well as a reinforcement of white midwestern identity. The concessions won in the urban rebellions were not panaceas. They represented a liberal remedy to treat the symptoms of racial oppression, not a cure for the disease itself. Like the proactive, pre-rebellion initiatives, the post-uprising fixes were just as misguided and ineffectual. Despite the questionable long-term value of the urban rebellions as an effective protest tactic, these events held lasting political significance for both sides.

At the national level, the uprisings shifted the "geographical and political focus of the black movement" to address the issues facing northern Black urbanites.[3] These events affected the ways white citizens and the municipal government interacted with African Americans. The revolts marked a significant departure from the status quo as Blacks won tangible gains and temporarily shifted power dynamics in the city. Local government, intent on not losing future confrontations, tactically adapted to better repress urban protest. This repression occurred through increased defense expenditures and the maintenance of a midwestern identity predicated on superior race relations with African Americans. Beyond these quantifiable changes, the region also sustained numerous intangible adjustments, including shifting consciousness and the relationship between African Americans and whites in the urban Midwest.

THE WAGES OF REBELLIONS

Although the uprisings played a central role in shaping the consciousness of African Americans, these events caused significant economic and physical damage to Black neighborhoods in midwestern cities. The cost to city governments alone for additional staff, cleanup, and insurance claims was staggering. An official of the Cincinnati Insurance Board estimated fire and vandalism claims at $2 million. Other officials tacked on an additional million dollars due to the "loss of profits, payroll, and National Guard expenses." Omaha City finance director Edwin J. Hewitt stated that $40,000 would be needed just to pay the overtime of Omaha police officers for the 1969 disturbance. Additionally, the Omaha Fire Department estimated that the cost due to fire loss was close to $925,000. The city's 1966 recreation budget was $500,000. Milwaukee had a net damage cost of $570,000, which represented the amount of money lost in the city's economy, money that would never be recovered. This figure did not include insurance claims or overtime pay for first responders. City hall advised that the actual property cost would amount to $200,000 and calculated over $1 million in police and National Guard overtime expenditures.[4] In addition to these significant financial losses, the reluctance of local merchants to re-open and many insurance companies suspension of coverage drastically altered the physical landscape and economic solvency of these Black communities.

The urban rebellions intensified the instability and economic vulnerability of Black enclaves. Omaha provides the starkest example. In 1964, along North Twenty-Fourth Street from the 1500 block to the 2400 block, there were sixteen vacant storefronts. By 1970 along this same business corridor, there were seventy-two buildings that were either vacant or no longer listed. Following the June 1969 uprising police patrolman David Heese observed that the Near North Side "look[ed] like a bombed-out area."[5] The city council, after processing the list of condemned buildings, estimated that the rubble would not be cleaned up before September. As late as August 9, the Fire Department estimated that eight of the twelve severely damaged buildings had not been cleaned up. One angry merchant refused to clean up, leaving the rubble as "a monument to what the rioters did to him."[6] Undoubtedly, prior to the urban rebellions, Black neighborhoods suffered from economic decline and vacancy; however, these events exacerbated the situation, discouraging business owners, banks, and insurance companies from investing in the area.

Small-business owners were not the only entrepreneurs who remained leery of operating in Omaha's African American enclave; larger merchants also took precautionary measures. Safeway Stores Inc., decided to install an eleven-foot-high chain-link fence topped with one foot of barbed wire to enclose the store's parking lot. Safeway originally tried to fence in the lot in 1966 after the first revolt, but the community protested the proposed change. Activist Reverend General Woods offered, "Negroes hate chains, whether they are around a black man's legs on a Georgia chain gang or around a white man's supermarket in Omaha."[7] By 1968 public aversion could not sideline the corporation's plan. Thus, in very real ways the urban rebellions changed the physical landscape of urban areas. When retailers shut down, they limited the already inadequate options for employment and retail. Those stores that did remain used excessive security measures, making Black enclaves look more like a maximum-security prison than a neighborhood.

CHANGING MUNICIPAL STRUCTURE

In the aftermath of the urban revolts, participants and civil rights organizations made formal demands of the municipal government, outlining their grievances. Through the positive gains that African Americans received, we witness urban revolt's utility. These rewards took many forms, including employment, recreation, and housing. Such gains brought limited positive changes to the Black community as municipal entities soon extinguished these programs.

During the urban uprisings rebels demanded improvements in employment, recreation, and police–community relations. Both Cincinnati and

Omaha sought to address multiple grievances simultaneously through youth employment. Many social activists felt that youth employment programs not only prevented uprisings but also gave "black youth actual job experience, to inculcate a sense of responsibility and accomplishment, and to give them a feeling of self-worth."[8] Despite the positive impact for those fortunate enough to receive jobs, these initiatives were inadequate to remedy the massive unemployment of urban youth. Employment projects could not place all of the applicants, and those who received jobs had their positions terminated at the conclusion of the summer. As the Kerner Commission investigators observed in Cincinnati, "When this period [of employment] has terminated, the youth will be forced to wander into other anti-social areas of endeavor. Overall, employment seems to be decreasing rather than increasing."[9] Although these programs provided decent wages and experience, teenagers were again without gainful employment when fall arrived. Cynically, summer employment programs could be viewed merely as stopgaps to neutralize the immediate threat of additional uprisings by taking potential young rebels off the streets, not a long-term solution.

Milwaukee job programs remained ineffective for different reasons. A Kerner Commission memorandum assessed Maier's Youth Opportunity Board, stating, "One major drawback of this seemed to be its tripartite leadership. The three executives do not seem to be congenial bedfellows—politically or otherwise." Additionally, although the board took out full-page newspaper advertisements as well as radio and TV spots, they were unable to mobilize sufficient community support. Initially, the Youth Opportunity Board only located 700 jobs. In late July they initiated a final push to find additional positions. Members of the board contacted 5,000 businesses to have at least 250 employers commit to hiring an extra ten individuals in August or contribute $1,000 to support community service jobs. By the beginning of the month this intensive effort netted only $2,500 and thirty-five jobs. As investigators recognized, "considering that there are some 90,000 Negroes in Milwaukee, this is not much."[10] Other existing organizations struggled to sustain teenage employment opportunities. The Neighborhood Youth Corps, which employed 1,100, cut 450 jobs in September. Despite the steadfast adherence that hard work would net opportunity and equality, businesses and private citizens remained reluctant to support endeavors for Black youths to pull themselves up by their bootstraps. Long-standing discriminatory practices became even more glaring in adult programming.

Like teenage summer employment programs, the city government relied heavily on industry support for adult programs. Unlike the teenagers' jobs, which were created anew, adult African Americans faced major hurdles in locating positions in existing markets hostile to Black workers. In Cincinnati, the Chamber of Commerce and local Black community leaders collaborated to establish an Opportunities Industrial Center program. Captains of industry followed the lead of local government by establishing Jobs for Cincinnati Inc., which expanded employment opportunities for Black workers who did not meet industry requirements. Kerner Commission investigator Niathan Allen noted that "activities of the Avondale businessmen and Jobs for Cincinnati have delayed the rebellion for the present time, but they must be willing to sacrifice more for bettering the black lot in the city or more bloodshed will be inevitable." The City of Cincinnati also hired African Americans in sixty-four new positions, but that these employment opportunities consisted primarily of white-collar positions constituted a major shortcoming in the city's initiatives.[11]

Despite their claims of support, industry and trade union leaders remained apathetic. In the Jobs for Cincinnati project, industry representatives interviewed over 1,000 applicants but employed only 93 people. Trade discrimination still existed on a large scale. Legislators passed a state law requiring contractors to employ workers outside of hiring hall agreements. The human relations committee provided a list of building contractors that recruited and hired African Americans to encourage this policy, yet widespread union acceptance of Black workers remained elusive. Of the 700 journeymen in Cincinnati's International Brotherhood of Electrical Workers, none were Black.[12]

Government and community officials in Omaha encouraged all unemployed Blacks to register with executive director of the Near North YMCA branch Sam Cornelius so, as Mayor A. V. Sorensen stated, the city can "use our energies to put the man and the job together." Phillip C. Sorensen, the lieutenant governor, headed a six-man committee to set up a state employment office to take inventory of human resources and hired more than 200 Blacks for municipal jobs. Mayor Sorensen also convinced the Office of Economic Opportunity to double the yearly Job Corps allocation in Omaha to establish job skill programs for the "average negro John Doe." Unfortunately, these job measures were not as effective as they could have been. Only one out of every three applicants was placed in a position.[13]

Throughout each city, verbal and planned commitments to create jobs did not net widespread employment for African Americans. Industry and trade unions claimed adherence to these practices but continued to discriminate. Many working-class African Americans found white-collar city government positions out of their reach. In 1967 Judge Robert L. Black wrote, "Personally, I view the situation as volatile. We are in the midst of a national struggle with deeply-rooted causes—the struggle of a deprived and oppressed minority to attain full citizenship and their proper share of the American society. A request for jobs, jobs, jobs, jobs is a request for responsibility"[14] While those in power attempted to create solutions to the problem of Black under- and unemployment, these halfhearted initiatives did not eradicate Black joblessness. In fact, it broadcast what African Americans had said for years: they are willing to work hard, but the opportunities afforded them are few and far between.

Recreational programs represented another central demand that arose out of the urban rebellions. Both public and private entities coordinated to meet these needs. In Milwaukee, Mutope Johnson attended community arts programs and museums and had access to scholarship opportunities when he was in fifth and seventh grade.[15] In Cincinnati the Avondale planning committee headed by Clyde Vinegar and Donald Spencer negotiated with the recreational department for two swimming pools, baseball diamonds, recreational centers, playgrounds, and parks to be completed by the summer of 1968. Cincinnati's Operation Up-Tight employed the Citizens Committee on Youth as "street counselors" to refer youth to recreational programs to defuse emergency, possibly riotous, situations.[16] Omaha's recreational programming also met twin objectives, addressing recreational needs and creating better youth–police relations. City and private organizations funded a camping program in Columbus, Nebraska, eighty-two miles northeast of Omaha. Beat cops and youth fished, rode horses, and watched movies together for eight weeks. This helped the youth see the police in roles other than authoritarians and gave the police eyes and ears in the community. Many participants described this experience as one of the best in their lives.[17] These excursions were not a complete success, however. Although Mayor Sorensen believed strongly in this program, the top-down initiative did not impress Police Chief Richard R. Anderson. According to McClarty, the administration as well as the rank-and-file officers perceived the initiative to be "cuddling criminals." Officers who went on the trips often came back to find that their beats had been reassigned.[18]

The final grievance that uprising participants expressed during the urban rebellions was police brutality. The Cincinnati Police Division increased efforts through its community relations section, instituting a broader training program to deploy human relations counselors in addition to violent force in the event of an uprising. Police administration also resolved to address citizens' complaints as quickly as possible, establishing a special city service center in Avondale. Twenty-eight days later the city manager closed the location citing claims of underutilization.[19]

The Milwaukee Police Department simultaneously attempted to address the problem of unemployment and the perception of police as the enemy. Police Chief Harold Brier recommended focused recruitment efforts in the Black community, stating mockingly that he had "been told over and over that unemployment is so rampant." Additionally, he opined, "I cannot think of any other action which would more directly meet the claims of bigotry and brutality. [How] could the Negro community, for example, claim that Negro officers were bigoted and, therefore, brutal?"[20] Brier's sarcastic engagement with legitimate grievances of the Black community demonstrates that many of the solutions individuals created served their own interests and did not address the true spirit of the Black community's complaints. This less-than-authentic approach to take community concerns seriously led to fatal results.

On February 4, 1969, the police department, under executive authority, signed a contract with the University of Nebraska at Omaha for "sensitivity training programs." During these workshops, fifteen officers spent five two-hour sessions and then attended an additional forty hours of in-service training.[21] Although progressive, these sensitivity training programs did not end accusations of police brutality within North Omaha. On Tuesday night, February 25, 1969, police cruiser #104 sped down the street in front of Horace Mann Junior High. Officer James Loder leaped from his squad car, pointed a pistol at a chartered bus, and without reason threatened the students returning from a skating party. Although activist and father Dan Goodwin filed a complaint with the police department, no disciplinary action was taken.[22] Four months and one day later, Loder, an attendee of the sensitivity training program, shot and killed fourteen-year old Vivian Strong, throwing Omaha into violent chaos.[23] Loder was not the only Omaha police officer who attended the post-rebellion initiatives to be involved in a fatal incident.

Perhaps the bleakest example of the failure of innovative, proactive programming occurred in March 1968. Hours after the disturbance stemming from Governor George Wallace's appearance, James Abbot, a twenty-three-year-old off-duty Omaha police officer, checked in with central dispatch to see if any help was needed, stationing himself at Crosstown Loan and Pawn Shop. As Officer Abbott sat inside armed with a riot gun, Black teenager Howard Stevenson crawled through a broken window and started to open a door granting others access to the store. The police officer shouted

Children walk past the Crosstown Loan and Pawn Shop, where Howard Stevenson was killed during the 1968 unrest. The following year the building was burned to the ground.
Omaha World-Herald.

"stop" and then shot. Abbott fired from thirty-three feet away, and the blast tore Stevenson nearly in half. Although it was illegal for Abbott to be in possession of a riot gun while off duty, authorities never arraigned him on this or on murder charges. Heartbreakingly, these young men's paths had crossed before. Both Stevenson and Abbott had participated in the city's youth–police camping experience in Columbus two years prior.[24]

These tragic incidents provide the clearest examples of how well-meaning initiatives did little to alleviate the structural woes of racism and police power within these midwestern cities. Officers attended sensitivity training, a program respondent to rebels' grievances, yet still perceived the Near North Side as an area they could terrorize. Loder threatened unarmed schoolchildren, and, while off duty, Abbott collected his police-issued riot gun before protecting a civilian location. Although the police department did not explicitly sanction these officers' actions, both were exonerated from any wrongdoing, implying the administration's tacit approval. These events foreshadow the general trend toward policing the Black community in the post-rebellion era. As cities developed programs to allay claims of police brutality, they simultaneously endorsed a more forceful, armed police presence in Black urban neighborhoods.

As money flowed to meet the rebels' demands, separate allocations armed the police in the event of another uprising. But make no mistake, the aftermath of the uprisings was not only a moment of conservative backlash, liberals also "actively defined the response to urban unrest."[25] As Max Felker-Kantor notes, in the aftermath of the 1965 Watts rebellion, the police department, facing calls for reform, made things worse by using "the crisis of legitimacy . . . to demand more authority, discretion, and resources."[26] In both Omaha and Cincinnati, city officials purchased or borrowed military-grade supplies in the weeks following the uprisings. In Milwaukee, Kerner investigator Sam Dennis described the behavior of the police in the Inner Core as "being continually provocative." He stated that officers carried riot helmets "in the rear of squad cars, very visible; and everyone knows they are carrying rifles and shot guns."[27] Mutope Johnson stayed home during Milwaukee's uprisings as he and his friends "didn't want to be mistaken for looters or rioters" because he knew the police would kill them just as they had Clifford McKissick.[28] Equipment purchases and additional training allowed police to adopt new tactics to contain revolts that were more restrained and effective and that played better in the court of public opinion. Buried under a thin veneer of professionalism and better crowd control, the equipment expenditures and conspicuous display of weapons sent an unambiguous message to the Black community, law enforcement can and will use deadly force to suppress protest.

The National Guard, police departments, and legislators collaborated to ensure that the tactics and tools available to them would ensure victory in subsequent uprisings. The Nebraska National Guard practiced their riot control reflexes, training in a sixteen-hour exercise, and they implemented changes allowing guardsmen to carry live ammunition, training 175 snipers. Cincinnati firefighters now had the authority to carry firearms while on duty. The city's police department deepened its commitment to control over preventive measures, as less than 2 percent of their 480 hours of instructional time addressed how to interact with the people police were tasked to "protect and serve."[29]

Mayors and city council members created new ordinances and protocols to create more effective responses in the event of an uprising. Cincinnati City Council passed an ordinance mandating that harming fire personnel would carry the same penalty as assaulting a police officer, increasing the fine for violating these ordinances to $1,000.[30] Such laws provided municipal governments with broad legal mechanisms to capture a greater number of participants. In Omaha, the state adjunct general, head of the State Patrol, and the police inspector visited similarly sized cities to learn their riot controls. From their research, the men encouraged the city council to pass a new ordinance that limited the number of people allowed to gather on public streets. The provision also allowed the mayor to suspend airport operations and to restrict vehicle and boat traffic, the sale of flammable liquids, and the carrying of weapons.[31]

In April 1968, following the assassination of the Reverend Martin Luther King Jr., Black Cincinnatians once again took to the streets. The After Action Report of the Ohio National Guard documents that promptly deploying the police, reading the Riot Act, issuing a curfew, and prohibiting the sale of alcohol and gas "greatly assisted in restoring law and order."[32] These adjustments made future uprising participation more punitive and potentially deadly. Cities became skilled in using increased force, indicting rebels, and placing the entire municipality on lockdown. In the initial uprisings, cities conceded to insurgents' demands as local governments were unprepared, losing the opening salvo. In the years that followed, municipal power structures took steps to ensure that they would be decidedly declared the victor in any subsequent uprisings.

POLITICAL RAMIFICATIONS

Both rebels and local governments interpreted the urban uprisings as political. In the aftermath of the revolts, municipal political mechanisms changed accordingly. In addition to local governments kitting themselves for future uprisings through equipment expenditures, training, and new ordinances, the political apparatus of the cities also changed. In the days following the revolts, local governments eagerly sought solutions to at least consider the grievances of working-class African Americans. As the days turned to months not only did local governments return to their insincere approach in dealing with protests, they also became deeply committed to conceding nothing to Black interest groups.

Kerner investigator Sam Dennis noted that "the City of Milwaukee is 'calm' at the present time. The inner core still has the same ghetto problems. . . . The meeting with Mayor Maier was only a psychological moral victory, in that the Negro community got the Mayor to come to the inner core." Black working-class residents, due to their disenfranchisement, felt they had achieved a major accomplishment just in having the mayor come to their community, although in fact conditions remained as wretched as they had always been. The commission noted that Mayor Maier was "in the spotlight at this time, nationally and locally, and not about to risk losing his voter support in negotiating with the Negro community."[33] Maier ignored Black citizens, pandering to white constituents and prolonging his national relevance by looking tough on crime. In a similar move, other city governments attempted to delegitimize rights organizations to cater to the majority-white population.

In Cincinnati, Kerner Commission investigators met with the Community Action Committee's program officer, John E. Hansen; executive director, Halloway C. Sells; and Lathan Johnson, assistant executive director of the Greater Cincinnati Federation of Settlements and Neighborhood Centers. The men acknowledge that they had to "swim upstream" from the beginning and that the uprisings made their jobs more difficult because of token support and widespread white disapproval. In an interview with the Kerner Commission, Clint Reynolds said the uprising had been a "watershed" moment in the history of the Cincinnati Human Relations Commission (CHRC), as it "exploded the myth [and] revealed exactly where the Commission stood." Reynolds acknowledged that the CHRC had been set up as a "buffer between the City Administration and the Negro . . . [and that] the city was willing to let the Human Relations Commission absorb substantial amounts of blame when anything went wrong."[34] In the uprising's wake, old enemies found new jobs. George Sprague, the "formerly dearly hated Captain of the 5th Precinct," and John Birch Society member, was appointed to the board of the antipoverty agency.[35] The proactive race relations initiatives were mere window dressing because those in formal leadership positions were unable to effect genuine change. Similarly, many working-class individuals agitating for change continued to be ignored by local government.

The Avondale Community Council (ACC) arranged a meeting, inviting city representatives to Zion Baptist Church to state their grievances. Television crews arrived at the location "in anticipation of hearing the city fathers' replies," but the scheduled meeting arrived and not a single elected or appointed official attended. Only later did meeting attendees learn that Mayor Walton Bachrach sent a taped response to television station WCPO-TV to address the community's grievances. Don Dunkle, the news director of WLWT, observed, "Those people who were waiting for the City Council's replies weren't watching television . . . white people presumably were, and perhaps the Mayor was directing his answers to them."[36] Although the violence of the rebellions brought immediate attention to grievances and the availability of municipal leadership, after the fires extinguished, and sometimes before, politicians returned to only paying lip service to Black demands.

As local government, in conjunction with state and federal entities, implemented programs to appease the rebels' demands, they simultaneously shifted public discourse to produce a more forceful rhetoric in the event of new uprisings. The revolts mark where "the nation broke with liberalism, and a new era of conservative ascendancy began."[37] In both word and deed, municipal power brokers moved from ameliorating the issues grieved in the uprisings to framing participants as criminals looking for handouts. The Kerner Commission reported that the Cincinnati City Council "indicated that they would not respond to threats or intimidation [and] directed all who have grievances to seek redress through legal means."[38] In their statements to the press, the city council aligned themselves and their interests with the white populace, depicting the rebels as criminals who did not use the appropriate avenues for change within the community, delegitimizing their protest. Apart from the ghetto business owners and white arrestees, white Americans' isolation from the Black community shielded them from the full context of the uprising, making them more receptive to revisionist interpretations of the mass demonstrations. This reframing of the urban rebellions is significant because it demonstrates the reassertion of the central tenets of the midwestern myth post-rebellion regarding how these events were understood, disseminated, and interpreted.

MIDWEST MEANINGS

In the aftermath of urban unrest, white midwesterners began to reimagine their communities. The identity and meanings of the region carried broad impact, as the creation of a heartland was essential to the false restoration of a placid nation in the aftermath of the rights revolution.[39] By excising urban places where the revolts occurred, the boundaries of the Midwest were redrawn to retain "a pastoral storehouse for national ideals and 'traditional values.'" Specifically, by rendering urban America as Black working class and "politically charged," they created a trope that homegrown protests were outliers to the "true" Midwest. The region could maintain the preferred American characteristics of white, middle class, and nonconfrontational.[40] As media studies scholar Victoria E. Johnson argued, in the upheavals of the 1960s and 1970s, "popular imaginings of the Midwest implied that its historically *mundane* identity was, by contrast to the 'rest' of the nation, now *exceptional*—the average, ordinary everyday 'square' was also stable, functional, and representative of core national ideals."[41] The media played an outsized role in this endeavor, shifting the narrative frame of the Midwest from cautious and provincial to a place that held the "'nation's more agreeable qualities' and the lone national site of 'equilibrium' 'peace,' and 'sobriety,' post-1960s."[42] In popular and news media, the heartland became "the place where the traditional American Dream still lived *untouched* by political turmoil."[43] The Midwest became proxy for an America that never was. The urban rebellions that occurred in communities, large and small, in every American region, became manipulated as episodes of wanton, asocial violence, ignoring the actions for what they really were—attempts for inclusion in the American Dream.

Municipalities fed these delusions, again commissioning "blue-ribbon investigative committees" to understand the extent of the rebellions and validity of central grievances.[44] By focusing on who participated and how the community read these events, local government created documents to exonerate themselves and shift blame to uprising participants. Ultimately, post-rebellion reports expressed the same findings as earlier studies, life for African Americans was hard, and the institutions, individuals, and mechanisms charged with helping them were ineffective. Former executive director of the Cincinnati Human Relations Commission David McPheeters conducted a study that could have provided a more authentic account of the average rebels' perspective. McPheeters asked several provocative questions that he felt assessed the uprising's root causes, including the following:

Q9: In your opinion, how likely is it that World War III will break out *in the next two years?*

Q10: Which one of the following definitions of "Black Power" comes closest to your opinion of what the term really means?

1. Black solidarity in a holy war against "whitey."
2. The Negro's recognition and united, forceful assertion of his own basic sense of dignity, integrity and worth.
3. Black controlled communities separated, both culturally and economically, from the white community.
4. The concentration of Negro social, economic, and cultural energies in every Negro community for purposes of using these energies in any manner necessary to control organizations, programs or government.

Q31: What is your closest attitude about [how] the average Cincinnati policeman thinks of you and your neighborhood?

1. He is proud to know and serve us;
2. He is conscientious about his job;
3. He's ok (neutral);
4. He's indifferent;
5. He's a discourteous smart-aleck;
6. He's an armed legal criminal;
7. Don't know.

Q34: Do you feel that most Negroes in Cincinnati who hold public office or who occupy tax supported jobs are generally "Uncle Toms?" If yes, why?[45]

Local government was less than pleased with the results. Robert Black opined, "In all honesty, I must say that the report falls far short of expectations. . . . It is more a personal, subjective statement of the writer about his view of the Cincinnati scene; its redeeming feature is that, in this sense, it is 'true.'"[46]

Whereas other academic researchers asked questions regarding the socioeconomic status of participants and general community opinions of the events, McPheeters's keen understanding of the political climate in the Black community demonstrates that a deeper consciousness shift was taking place. Although signs indicate that McPheeters's study was never completed, he attempted to arrive at authentic feelings of Black disenfranchisement, distrust, and dissatisfaction in Cincinnati.

The midwestern identity was maintained through the proliferation of media imagery during and after the uprisings. As Mutope Johnson noted in the aftermath of the rebellion, "We need some places, some institutions . . . where folks are telling our story and not having it told by somebody else."[47] In a Simulmatics Corporation study funded by the Kerner Commission, researchers ascertained the relationship between media portrayal and public opinion of the revolts. Their analysis found that most broadcast scenes showed a "dominant, positive emphasis on control of the riot and on activities" (53.8 percent of all scenes broadcast). In comparison, actual scenes of mob action comprised only 4.8 percent of the total broadcast images, and segments featuring moderate leadership aired three times more frequently than segments highlighting militant spokespeople. The researchers noted, "We think that, in many crucial respects, they [the media] have failed to provide complex and accurate coverage of racial disorder in our society."

This failure included an "exaggeration of both mood and event" and fundamentally did not "analyse [sic] and report adequately, on a day to day basis, on race relations in America."[48]

Local broadcasters framed the discussion of the rebellions in their cities by focusing on how effectively the state managed the chaos and allowed moderate Black leaders to frame the events. City governments encouraged this emphasis as they garnered political clout while keeping the midwestern myth intact. The study noted that "newspapers tended to characterize and portray last summer's riots as national rather than local phenomenon and problems, especially when rioting was taking place in the newspaper's hometown." A significant number of news articles on hometown unrest did not originate locally, with over 40 percent contributed by wire services. More devastatingly, newspaper editors during times of local unrest portrayed racial tension as a problem that occurred in other cities, not their own, by giving a large amount of headline attention to uprisings occurring elsewhere, thus delegitimizing the local events. Black grievances received the least attention instead, with journalists choosing to focus on general and impersonal Black experiences.[49] Had media focused on local Blacks' articulation of grievances, these sources could simultaneously indict the local municipal community while humanizing the rebels. Such actions would legitimate violence as protest, affirming its utility to participants.

In Omaha and Milwaukee, local officials and media collaborated to frame these events in the best strategic light. Following the disturbances in 1966, the Omaha Police Department and the local broadcast community created a series of guidelines for covering racial disturbances. They agreed that the public safety director would hold periodic briefings for broadcast news directors during an uprising. These briefings would be "off the record," alerting the media to a possible disturbance and feeding them background information that would show local government in a favorable light. In return for this insider's knowledge, broadcasters refrained from disrupting regularly scheduled programming with news bulletins, confining their coverage to scheduled newscasts. In collaboration, the media and Omaha police established the "news code 30" protocol, which ensured a thirty-minute broadcast moratorium after a violent uprising began. During this time newscasters could only collect news stories, not broadcast them, preventing the recruitment of others into the action. Additionally, during broadcast presentations, the term "riot will be avoided unless the facts are indisputable," and charges of police brutality by the rebels "should not be aired indiscriminately." Here we see that not only the definition of "riot" but its use was deployed strategically by the state. Such measures allowed local government and law enforcement officials to control rumors, contain the violence, and frame the events in an advantageous manner.[50]

In Milwaukee, the Mayor's Office compiled a list of public relations representatives working for them. In the event of an uprising, the office would assign each official to an out-of-town news reporter to collaborate one-on-one. Additionally, one public relations employee would also feed "lines instantly as they become available to the two Negro radio stations." The Mayor's Office created several documents for immediate distribution in the event of an urban revolt. One included a public relations brief detailing the city's riot-prevention measures since the last unrest, instructing that "it should be readily in print for our PR people to distribute to out-of-town press." The media staff also coached Maier: "If you ever have to leave your own office for a press conference, open that conference with: 'I want to thank you ladies and gentlemen of the press for this press conference. It is the first time I have been out of my office in ___ hours, days,' etc."[51] The initiatives that media staff undertook enabled them to immediately frame the uprisings and highlight the proactive (but obviously ineffective) race relations solutions they had created. This strategy allowed the Milwaukee government to assert their superior race relations, as most of these documents catered to out-of-town reporters, not the local community, maintaining the midwestern myth of a region absent deeply entrenched racial conflict.

Mainstream media overwhelmingly formed the understanding and memory of the 1960s revolts. These interpretations were severely flawed, leading to skewed perceptions of the uprisings.[52] One headline read, "Arsenal Uncovered on North Side," a dog whistle that Milwaukee police had found a weapons cache in the predominately Black neighborhood—neglecting to mention the seventy-seven-year-old white gun collector who owned the weapons.[53] The most compelling testimony of these divisions came from the statements of nearly 700 interviewees with the Kerner Commission. Black citizens believed that mainstream news media distributed negative opinions about them and "were not telling the true story of life in poor black neighborhoods."[54] African Americans argued that many of the events they witnessed during the uprising were ignored and that media obscured stories of Blacks giving aid to the wounded, instances of police brutality and false arrest, and the presence of white vigilante groups who were inciting violence in uprising areas.[55]

Media coverage provided whites with a biased—and likely their only—perspective of the events. Yet resentment and apprehension grew among white citizens. Many felt that, due to victories won by civil rights activists, whites had made significant sacrifices only to be met with insufficient Black gratitude.[56] Although the commission found that the revolts "were less destructive, less widespread, and less violent than we originally thought they were," the Simulmatics study demonstrated that the average American received a very different interpretation. They remarked that television coverage gave "the impression that the riots were confrontations between Negroes and whites rather than responses by Negroes to underlying slum problems."[57] This view provided whites with a legitimate reason, they believed, to increase violence against African Americans. The media portrayal of African Americans, along with the fear that Black protest constituted antiwhite violence, caused many white Americans to arm themselves. Ultimately, if the uprisings caused white midwesterners to consider more violent protest tactics, these events caused African American midwesterners to become more organized.

CHANGING CONSCIOUSNESS OF BLACKS

Just as the urban rebellions had a major effect on how whites perceived Blacks, so too did these events influence how African Americans saw themselves. Kerner investigator M. C. Miskovsky wrote in his final assessment of the urban rebellions that "since the riots, the intercity contact between locally based militant organizations have increased with a consequent sharing of programs and an increasing homogeneity of militant rhetoric." He continued, "Within some cities previously competing organizations have drawn together, at least in the immediate response to the riot. In some cases, this cooperation has been formalized by the establishment of umbrella-type organizations; however, there seems to be diversity and disunity."[58] Prior to the urban rebellions, local civil rights groups competed for influence within the community. After the revolts there was more cooperation locally, and at the regional level many Black interest groups began working together. More importantly, at the national level the "new Negro mood" that helped shift African American's opinions on militancy crystallized. ACC president Bailey W. Turner asserted in his 1967 annual report, "There has developed within the community a strong sense of 'Selfhood.'" Turner defined this sentiment as "a strong feeling that each person is really 'Somebody.' . . . [There] is also a feeling that a community is a 'Somebody' . . . that it can and must master its ship and determine its destiny."[59] In the immediate aftermath of the urban rebellions these two assessments codified the change in Black consciousness: a sense of importance and increased unity.

This sense of importance caused a "domino-like" effect, influencing how other disenfranchised people approached protest. James Mimms likened the uprising to the agitator in a washing machine, with

> energy, up and down, up and down. Nothing came out. We didn't move out, we didn't get to the people we wanted to get to, the rich neighborhood. . . . It gave us solace, comfort. We know that America knows that we can and will burn and if we ain't got nothing else to burn, your neighborhood is next, cause we done burnt ours down. So you better watch out, keep messing with us, cause the next time we rise up, we gonna get to you cause we got nothing else to burn in our neighborhood. That's what I learned, that's what a lot of blacks learned, that the white man knows that there's a sleeping giant and we'll wake up and burn this damn place all the way to the ground.[60]

An uprising led by incarcerated men in Cincinnati demonstrates how other powerless people also used unrest as a protest tool. The workhouse, located in the city, had been built in the 1860s and closed at the turn of the twentieth century. The facility was reopened during the Prohibition era, without any renovations, and had been operating throughout the 1960s. Fifty long-term prisoners began a revolt around 3:00 p.m. on June 15, 1967, approximately twenty minutes before twelve convicted uprising participants entered the facility. As with the large-scale uprising that was taking place outside of the workhouse walls, negotiations took place between the men and representatives in power. The inmates demanded cold beverages with their meals, improved bedding, additional showers (the workhouse only had one for the incarcerated men), recreation programs, and better meals. Police Chief Jacob Schott and workhouse superintendent George Studt responded favorably, and the men were granted their demands.[61]

The successful mobilization of power in earlier uprisings gave African Americans political clout and a position of strength from which to bargain. "There is much more evidence available regarding organizations promoting violence, their plans of action and the general level of acceptability of violence in the ghetto communities. The reports received from various ghetto communities indicated that last summer's riot served as a catalyst leading to the creation of new groups advocating violence and an increase in the membership of old groups."[62] After the assassination of Dr. Martin Luther

King Jr., the ACC announced that a "Black Monday" would be declared out of respect to his memory. They demanded that all white personnel, even if conducting official businesses, keep out of the Avondale–Walnut Hills area. They also requested that all African Americans call in sick to work and wear black clothing or armbands in deference to the slain leader. Many business and public departments, including the police, complied. Finally, the organization also established a temporary Black police force to protect and maintain order in the community.[63]

Post-rebellion, many African Americans had a renewed sense of racial solidarity. Kerner investigators noted that in Cincinnati, "Leadership and organization have become more militant, more unified, and in many instances more revolutionary. The old patterns of jealousy have seemingly been attenuated by the new pattern of solidarity and cooperation against the common enemy."[64] Reverend Hunt of Cincinnati even indicated that some of the previously extant intraracial class conflict had diminished. The commission investigators noted that middle-class African Americans had become more involved; from Hunt's perspective, "even the middle-class Negro, no matter how educated he . . . [knows] that the system operated against him just as it operates against the low man on the totem pole."[65] This renewed emphasis on race solidarity brought about new protest groups, umbrella organizations, and tactical adaptations.

The urban rebellions became public symbols codifying Black nationalist consciousness. Inspired, the Black community began to lay a cohesive infrastructure for Black Power organizing, not only locally but also regionally. As an act of public protest, uprisings fomented racial solidarity and awoke the latent organizational potential in many communities, particularly militant leadership interested in Black Power. One author noted that after Cincinnati's uprisings a young man told her "that as a result of the riots doors previously closed to Negroes were opened to them."[66] An audience erupted in applause when Charles Collins of the NAACP said, "Too frequently you people on the way to your lily-white communities look but don't see." Rev. Otis Moss Jr., pastor of Mt. Zion Baptist in Lockland, said, "We are today a community in agony. And some white people are experiencing the tyranny and terror we have lived with for so many years. History is upon us and we have to do in a few hours what we have not done in generations."[67] The uprisings created conditions from which white people could not look away.

In the last weekend of September 1967, CORE sponsored a North Central Region Action Council meeting. People from all over the Midwest—Chicago, Cleveland, Kansas City, St. Louis, Milwaukee, and Des Moines—attended the event, demonstrating their continued commitment to thinking regionally about African Americans' problems. Additionally, CORE established a central communication line for the Midwest region in Chicago, which would allow activists to collectively discuss local issues. Robert Lucas of Chicago CORE led the "Strengthening the Region" session. This gathering was specifically geared to look at the ways Black activists could approach their protest regionally. Session attendees specifically referred to the uprisings as "rebellions" and said violent protests would better advance the Black cause. Furthermore, as an FBI infiltrator present at the meeting wrote, "It was believed that such rebellions, as in Detroit and Newark, served to unify black people and the feeling was predominant that without such violence on the part of the Negro, the Negro could not escape 'whitey's' trap."[68]

Violence became a fixture in Black Nationalist and Black Power rhetoric in the months following the 1967 uprisings. Lincoln O. Lynch, CORE associate director, told the audience at a SNCC rally in Chicago on August 8, 1967, "If America doesn't come around we're gonna burn it down. If there isn't a place in America for the Negro, then there won't be any America." As Director of Investigations Miskovsky noted, such commentary legitimized "the idea of violence as an acceptable tool of social expression in the minds of the ghetto population" because society and "the present channels for the redress of grievance do not work for blacks." In the aftermath of rebellion, this discourse became more sophisticated, as advocates were "no longer tossing around vague, isolated ideas [but] refined their message into a complete 'system' with the strong appeal to the disadvantaged . . . promising action programs to substantiate their philosophy."[69] The most receptive audience for this kind of provocative speech were teenagers, the foot soldiers of the urban rebellions. Kerner Commission research director Robert Shellow noted, "We are really talking about the intersection of three aggrieved groups: youth, race, and poverty."[70]

Dr. Ralph Turner said of the Cambridge, Massachusetts, uprising that the "high schools in the ghettos have become an important testing center and training ground for confrontation and racial conflict. Especially, where the youth are the shock troops of the civil disorder."[71] In the fall following the urban disturbances, the confrontation moved from ghetto streets to high school hallways. These events, although they still involved some property damage, looked different from the summer unrest as they were interracial physical conflicts. In 1968, in the wake of George Wallace's inflammatory speech and the murder of Howard Stevenson, many Black Omahans again took to the street. As night became day, the street disturbances continued at

Two Fulton Junior High students run down the street following a disturbance. The school was the site of numerous youth-led protests.
© *Milwaukee Journal Sentinel*—USA TODAY NETWORK.

Black schools in Omaha. That next morning, 1,000 students walked out of Horace Mann Junior High School. By March 8, over 3,500 of the 5,700 total student population at Central, Tech, and North High Schools were absent. White parents and moderate Black parents, fearing violence, kept their children home.72 Those who remained in school wreaked havoc there.

On April 27, Officers Duane Pavel and Richard Gillian pulled alongside a group of people playing dice. This was the second time that the officers had broken up this gathering on Twenty-Fourth and Franklin Streets.73 In the blink of an eye, the police had Carl Edward Rucker handcuffed and on the ground. They continued to spray him with mace while firing their riot guns over the heads of spectators.[74] Two witnesses, John Beasley and John Anders, stated that the police officers, after forcing Rucker to the ground, taunted the crowd to do something about it.[75] Word of police brutality spread throughout the Near North Side, and many took to the street.[76] The following night, police dispersed seventy-five teenagers outside of Technical High School who had congregated after a school function. Upset at being forced to move, the students broke numerous windows along Cuming Street from Thirty-Second to Twenty-Fourth Street.[77]

Police Chief Anderson issued an order on Sunday that two of the officers involved in the dice game breakup would no longer be assigned to the Near North Side. He declined to name the officers, but everyone assumed it was Gillian and Pavel.[78] The two officers had a long history of conflict with Near North Side residents. During the Wallace meeting, they had prominently signed the American Party petition, and just days before the April 27 incident, they had been the target of handbills calling them racists. Eighteen Black Tech students were arrested for distributing the handbills, which charged that the two officers were "armed and extremely dangerous to black people."[79] The disturbances in April ended with no lives lost, but summer was fast approaching.[80]

In Cincinnati on October 11, 1967, a large fight broke out at Hughes High School, whose population was an evenly distributed biracial population. The skirmish began as a dispute between two female students, one Black and one white, in the bathroom of the school. As the FBI reported, the students had exchanged "sarcastic comments" and then a general interracial melee commenced. The assault of several white students by a group of African American students resulted in the arrests of six Blacks. When school let out for the day, 150 students, mostly Black, peacefully remained, singing freedom songs. Other students less committed to nonviolence left the group and assaulted a white school bus driver and broke windows at nearby businesses. After the large fight at Hughes, Capt. James Klein of the Cincinnati Police Department (District 5) stated that between 40 and 50 percent of students were absent from class the next day. Police were stationed inside the school to prevent any further incidents.[81]

Student activists also petitioned the school administration, using similar tactics that rebels had employed the previous summer. At Omaha's Central High School, Black students made six demands of the administration, including the removal of racist texts, more Black student representation, inclusion of African American history, and an institutional commitment to civil rights.⁸² Black high school students heeded the lessons from the revolts, organizing collectively to advance solutions to the grievances in their community. The threat of violence following the rebellion became a powerful tool for organizing and drawing attention to the demands of local high school students.

Similarly, in Cincinnati following the Hughes disturbance in October, pupils formed a Black Student Union. The members presented their demands to the superintendent. Of primary importance to the group was to have the Black Student Union—comprising Black representatives from Withrow, Aiken, Hughes, and Courter Tech high schools—officially sanctioned by the school board. The central objective of the union was to "make known the wants and needs, academically, socially and culturally, of the Afro-American students." Their final demands reflected both cultural pride and the desire for Black autonomy including "no restrictions on the wearing of clothing that denotes cultural pride."⁸³ These demands demonstrated growing Black nationalism among high school students separate from the mainstream civil rights demands just a few years prior.

Superintendent Paul Miller was anything but accommodating to the student activists, however. In his official statement, he wrote, "Hughes High School has become a symbol of the problems which threaten the very future of our city and of our country. . . . Let me emphasize again, 95% of school personnel time will not be used to serve 5% of the children and youth. The school system shall be governed by law and order, not by the whims of harassment of people. Children and youth shall not be used as pawns in an adult game."⁸⁴ Miller's comments parallel the municipal responses, citing only a small number of participants and drawing a distinction between good and bad actors. Young African Americans had their own grievances that they wished to articulate and had learned that violent protest provided a very effective mechanism to do so.⁸⁵

The urban revolts remain pivotal events in altering the physical landscape of Black enclaves, shifting the goals of the Black Freedom Movement, and altering Black consciousness. The rebellions did not solely affect the African American population; local city governments and white citizens also underwent changes in the aftermath of the uprisings. Municipal governments frequently used the disturbances as a political tool. For white urban midwesterners, the uprisings positioned African Americans as dangerous, violent criminals. Accordingly, police personnel grew exponentially, and considerable resources were spent on riot training and equipment. The uprisings, originally construed as a tactic for increased Black political power, subsequently led to a retrenchment of white political power and social supremacy, ultimately giving rise to the New Right.

Although the grievances expressed during the uprisings brought about some immediate change, the midwestern mentality that believed in a gradual approach brought about only temporary solutions. This, coupled with a general consensus that African Americans had to take individual responsibility to better themselves, ensured that long-standing systemic inequalities remained and only became exacerbated in the subsequent decades. Still, in the wake of this considerable backlash, African Americans found new ways to unite and oppose racial discrimination. The influence and the relevance of the urban rebellions did not remain in Black enclaves but extended to the strategic plans of other marginalized people beyond the 1960s.

CONCLUSION

Revenant Revolt

*Negroes,
Sweet and docile,
Meek, humble, and kind:
Beware the day they change their mind!*

LANGSTON HUGHES

*They are lucky what Black people are looking
for is equality and not revenge.*

KIMBERLY JONES

Until recently the memory of the "long, hot summers" of the 1960s remained a vivid if distant specter. Long after the National Guard marched from the ghettos and shop owners caulked new shatter-resistant windows, the rebellions hold tremendous power in the national collective consciousness. In search of a more comfortable history, however, many Americans relegated urban revolts solely to that tumultuous decade, intentionally forgetting the numerous major uprisings that have occurred since, including those at the Attica Correctional Facility (1971) and in Miami (1980), Los Angeles (1992), Cincinnati (2001), Oakland (2009), Ferguson (2014), and Baltimore (2015). Whether we choose to admit it, civil unrest is a potent and constant fixture in American life. Violent uprisings are a fundamental cornerstone of this country's history, mobilized in word and action to pursue many agendas. But national narratives that limit Black protest to nonviolent direct action bury the frequency and legitimacy of insurrection. Our relationships with, and perceptions of, this tactic are deeply fraught, steeped in our own national mythology.

Midwest Unrest argues that the 1960s urban rebellions must be centered in not only narratives of the Black liberation struggle but also the American experience. Insurrections are tools for change. Those victories are not without cost, however, as the state responds with increased repression and violence in the wake of uprisings. Through the investigation of regional oppression and intraracial class conflict, this book registers that revolts transformed Black consciousness as well as the strategic vision of African American social movements. Beyond the historic impact of these events, the uprisings provide an important lens for interpreting and analyzing the significance of gender, class, region, and protest in Black America. Violent revolts reflect society's socioeconomic, racial, and gendered disparities in the most profound way.

The precipitating factors for the 1960s American urban rebellions were complex and interlocking. Black midwesterners arrived in the region just as deindustrialization and mechanization eroded their already tenuous opportunities for decent wages and stable employment. Despite this considerable disappointment, Black midwesterners built rich and vibrant communities affirming Black life, Black joy, and regional identities independent from white oppression. Still, African Americans resided in substandard housing, learned in outdated classrooms, played in unequipped parks, and suffered abuse at the hands of municipal police. A promise of a better life, unfulfilled upon their arrival, left many disenchanted. These deficiencies alone were despicable. Black midwesterners' lack of opportunity for genuine redress, however, made their situation untenable.

Rebels looted stores, disobeyed police orders, and committed arson in the revolt not only in opposition to racism but also due to their class, gender, and ideological marginalization within the African American community. The urban rebellions represented a critical moment in the Black Freedom Movement, amplifying long-standing concerns about class, tactics, and militancy in the community. Working-class Blacks, doubly disadvantaged in the polity, viewed violent protest as an attractive, necessary, and viable option. Their disillusionment with middle-class leadership, a growing sense of Black pride, and dissatisfaction with the pace of traditional civil rights protest led them to forgo direct action for a more aggressive protest tactic.

Although the urban rebellions played out in the public realm, these were deeply personal events. Rebels engaged in protest informed by their position in socioeconomic, racial, and gendered hierarchies. While many participants in the urban rebellions identified as working-class African American men, the participation of three outlying groups highlight the complexity of race, class, and gender in the uprisings. The Black middle class leveraged their social and actual capital by offering legal and financial support to those arrested. Contrary to lingering misconceptions, white citizens constituted the majority of those who engaged offensively, descending upon Black communities to threaten and physically attack residents. Finally, women fully engaged in the rebellions, performing important roles as defender, cheerleader, beneficiary, and catalyst. The participants' diversity challenges notions that the uprisings were only meaningful events for young Black men. These incidents reflected intersectionality and political efficacy within these hierarchies.

Despite the deeply personal factors motivating individuals to participate, these events also possessed the power of collective transformation. In the most literal sense, landscapes marred by boarded-up buildings, security gates on storefronts, and overgrown lots provided visual cues to the significant changes that had taken place. The implemented recreational, employment, and police–community programs fell short because they did not eradicate the ongoing and seemingly intractable structural violence. The rise of white vigilantism, Black nationalism, and an embrace of violence as a justified and legitimate protest tactic ended the liberal détente envisioning inclusive democracy, captured by skirmishes in high schools, armed occupation of state agencies, and prison revolts. In the fires of rebellion, America was remade.

This project began as a master's program seminar paper in 2004. At every pivotal juncture of this project, real life revolt came to the fore. I wrote my master's thesis as Parisian banlieues erupted. I organized my dissertation research notes as London neighborhoods burned. I interviewed participants in the Wisconsin Black Historical Society/Museum as images from Ferguson,

Missouri, two states away, captivated the nation. I submitted a journal article on the politics of uprisings five months before George Floyd's murder and revisions to that article a week after the US Capitol siege. What does it mean to write history while living it? I've drafted many versions of this conclusion, only to discard them, as the past is never past. History's burden gets heavier and the stakes higher with each passing year. When unrest collides with skewed historical memory, the nation clings to narratives of triumphant racial progress like a security blanket.

Widespread revolt was resurrected in the opening decades of the twenty-first century from shadowy fear to painful reality. Yet violent protest is divorced from what it actually is—an American tradition. A "myth of innocence" dominates Americans' conception of their own relationship with violence.[1] While violence maintains racial, ethnic, gendered, and classed hierarchies, our nation forgets violence's omnipresence, "its extraordinary frequency, its sheer commonplaceness in our history."[2] When those terrorized by violence employ the very tool wielded against them, shock registers across the nation. As a "color-blind" society with a deep, unwavering belief in American meritocracy, much of the public interprets violent protest as deviant, unhinged, and anti-American.[3] The contours and catalysts of millennial Black revolt entwine skewed historical memory, ongoing marginalization, and growing political consciousness reflecting and rehashing the 1960s revolts' central issues.

The Kerner Commission's 1968 prognostication that "our nation is moving toward two societies, one black, one white—separate and unequal" has also proven true in the new millennium.[4] Despite the commission's correct identification of ongoing racism as the root cause for the rebellions, the tepid liberalism advocated in the report was critiqued almost immediately. In *Harvest of American Racism*, four young social scientists employed by the commission wrote in their subversive report that "a moderate response to the summer of 1967 would only increase contempt for the white-dominated social order."[5] The commission's reliance on local action and police reform left Black communities "dependent on the good will of the very political elite and institutions that had been responsible for their predicament in the first place."[6] Fifty years later, by lauding the handful of individuals who transcend their circumstances, policymakers and the public blame those whom the system failed for their own lousy existence. The midwestern mentality, which prided itself on being progressive while ignoring the root causes of racial and economic oppression, morphed into a national ethos.

The twenty-first-century Midwest is a racial paradox. Metropolitan areas like Des Moines, Iowa; Madison, Wisconsin; and Minneapolis, Minnesota, regularly rank high on "best places to live" lists while being among the lowest on markers of economic and social parity for Black residents.[7] Six of America's eight most segregated cities are in the region, a worsening trend since 1890. Two of these cities, Milwaukee and Cincinnati, are a central focus of this book. As documented in the 2019 *Race in the Heartland* report, "of the eleven states with the largest gap in black-white unemployment, ten are in the Midwest."[8] Each of the twelve midwestern states imprison their Black citizens at a rate five times greater than white residents.[9] Black students living and learning in Wisconsin, Minnesota, Iowa, Nebraska, Illinois, and Kansas are also at five times greater risk for suspension than other students.[10]

In the aftermath of George Floyd's murder, journalists grappled with these contradictions. They touted liberal icons and gestured toward the composition of the Minneapolis City Council—twelve Democrats, one Green Party member, and two Black trans people—as evidence of the city's enlightenment.[11] But by centering the experiences of residents of color, in lieu of the self-congratulatory facade, a different narrative emerged. Robert Lilligren, the first Indigenous council member, offered a quote that could have been lifted from the 1960s: "Minneapolis has ridden this reputation of being progressive. That's the vibe: Do something superficial and feel you did something big. Create a civil rights commission, create a civilian review board for the police, but don't give the authority to change the policies and change the system." Somali immigrant Leila Ali captured this midwestern ethos with perfect brevity, "racism with a smile."[12]

The Midwest is Kerner's two nations, regionalized. Excellent schools, stable employment, and lush parks obscure the underfunded classrooms; winding lines for federal nutritional assistance; and food deserts. These disparities are not accidental or coincidental; neither is the nearly all-white character of the region. Of the nearly 1,100 counties in the Midwest, two-thirds are 95 percent white. More stunningly, apart from a handful of outliers, each remaining county has white populations over 72 percent, exceeding national demographic trends.[13] When adjusting for population density, however, 75 percent of the white and 96 percent of the Black midwestern population reside in metropolitan areas.[14] Of the ten American cities with the highest percentage of African Americans, four—Detroit, Gary, Flint, and St. Louis—are located in the Midwest.[15] Thus, the image of a midwesterner as a rural, hard-working, down-on-their-luck white man is not only a myth but a mirage.

The conflation of the Midwest with white working-class people becomes an alluring straw man for the actual conversative shift while also erasing those who are at greatest risk for poverty. As Tamara Winfrey-Harris writes, "It is a bitter irony that many of the arguments about Mr. Trump's appeal to midwesterners make sense only if you pretend black people don't exist in the middle of the country."[16] Segregation and economic disadvantage directly contribute to Black inequality in the Midwest. Colin Gordon and his research team noted, "For the region's white working class, economic loss and diminished opportunity is understood (or packaged politically) as a zero-sum contest in which others—especially African Americans and immigrants—are to blame."[17] Only in Missouri, Ohio, Indiana, and Michigan does the white poverty rate exceed the national average. The Black poverty rate, however, exceeds national statistics in every single midwestern state.[18]

This false demographic and political portrait unravels even more when we move beyond a white/Black binary. In many midwestern communities, immigrants, most of whom are people of color, are "a lifeline, bucking the pattern of population loss and revitalizing an aging workforce." Since 2000, immigrants constitute nearly 40 percent of the growth in midwestern cities, a significant contribution for a region that has experienced the slowest growth in the nation.[19] This dependence on immigrants to infuse communities with much-needed labor complicates regional identities.[20] As Britt Halvorsen and Joshua Reno write, "The Midwest's perceived connection to homogeneity, whiteness, and nostalgia is a fiction that has to be actively produced and, furthermore, is productive of conceptions of nationalism and racial projects of white supremacy."[21] This tension manifested on January 6, 2021.

The single common denominator shared by those who stormed the US Capitol is that they came from counties with significant declines in the white population. Rather than finding evidence of economic anxiety, journalists documented that participants were "awash in fears that the rights of minorities and immigrants were crowding out the rights of white people in American politics and culture."[22] While participants hailed from all corners of the United States, their presence directly links to conceptions of the Midwest and its centrality in the national imagination as the quintessential American region. In this framing, the most American (read: white) part of the nation is under threat. Within the buildup of this regional and xenophobic hysteria, high-profile cases of police brutality, political and economic marginalization, a global health crisis, and an emergent political consciousness laid the kindling for the fire this time.

George Floyd's murder sparked widespread civil unrest in 2020, but African Americans and other marginalized people learned from the 1960s unrest that violent protest could be a very effective way to express discontent and effect change. While considerable work needs to be done excavating additional understudied uprisings, when we compare incidents of urban unrest over the past sixty years, several commonalities stand out. An incident of police violence pushes people into the street as they protest the ways that economic, political, and institutional inequality have disproportionately affected them at the intersection of their race, class, and gender identities. In this sense, participation cannot be limited to just those who commit arrestable actions but also those who act as street medics, lookouts, or legal observers. Each of these roles, alongside countless others, contribute to the meaning and discourse of civil unrest. Finally, violent protest occurred alongside other efforts to negotiate with authorities, present grievances, and provide mutual aid.[23]

In this context, early twenty-first-century "flash mobs" and not Ferguson should be interpreted as predecessor events to the widespread unrest in 2020. These events provide a broader context for the attention and rhetorical power that mass disturbances create in the current historical moment. Flash mobs are groups of people who gather in a public space, organized through new media like email, texts, or social media posts.[24] While these activities originally involved harmless undertakings like dancing or pillow fights, at other times groups mobilized around more violent actions.[25] During the summer of 2011 "flash robs" occurred in Minneapolis, Chicago, Cleveland, New York, and Washington, DC.[26] Jeff Gardere, a California psychologist who studies youth motivations, tied this uptick to economic and social marginalization: "This isn't just in England or Philly or Germantown but everywhere. You've got a group that feels angry and powerless and they're trying to assume a sense of power."[27] In these occasions young Black and Latinx youth "reclaimed" spaces that previously excluded them, including a Brooklyn mall, Chicago's Magnificent Mile shopping district, and the Wisconsin State Fair in 2011 and 2012.[28] Without genuine outlets for redress, flash mob participants claimed minuscule victories with the only tool at their disposal, disrupting the daily lives of those they felt oppressed by. Unlike the 1960s uprisings, participants did not explicitly articulate demands but used social media to identify targets and create the discursive frames critical to understanding the millennial unrest. Participants comprehended both individual and collective systemic oppression and possessed a political vocabulary to articulate this knowledge. Their vocabulary constitutes the most crucial and necessary condition to foment a twenty-first-century revolt.29

The millennial uprisings diverge in several significant ways from early iterations, marking these events as a wholly new era in Black liberation struggles. The most notable differences of the 2020 street protests are their multiracial character, the brazen attacks by police on journalists and nonviolent demonstrators, and the relocation of the protests from Black neighborhoods to downtown and commercial districts. The sheer scope is also essential to understand the impact of these events. Citizens organized protests in every single state and dozens of countries. As a direct comparison, on the day of George Floyd's funeral, 60,000 people marched through the streets of Houston, the same number of individuals arrested in the urban revolts from 1965 to 1968.30 Many more people seem to accept, as one protester expressed, that "a riot is not a tactic to gain widespread sympathy. It's an expression of how inadequate other efforts have been."31 Just as significant are the strategic uses of social media and gender, particularly women's engagement in the millennial revolts.

The prevalence of the internet and social media is the most noteworthy change demarcating earlier uprisings from those in the twenty-first century, allowing individuals protesting local conditions to directly engage with national and international audiences. Social media plays an essential role in creating a political vocabulary and consciousness for concerned citizens to mobilize against police brutality. Whereas in the 1960s local governments imposed moratoriums on uprising reporting, the perpetual news cycle and social media apps allowed protesters, news agencies, and law enforcement to report civil unrest in real time. Through increased access, marginalized people shifted the dominant narrative. Outlets such as Facebook, Twitter, and alternative news sources aided in circulating protest imagery such as Trayvon Martin's hoodie, slogans such as "I Can't Breathe," and hashtags like #SayHerName, allowing these frames to become a part of the national conversation. More importantly, the increased access to information derailed the primacy of mainstream media narratives. Individuals connected through their own shared experiences, tying their personal trials to a broader system of inequity.32

With a few taps on an iPhone, an individual could boldly proclaim #IAmBreonnaTaylor, acknowledging, as one Black feminist blogger wrote, "we are all one bullet away from being a #hashtag."33 In so doing they asserted that these victims were not strangers. They could be our siblings, friends, children, partners, and, possibly, ourselves. Viral videos and tweets, verifiable proof of unwarranted abuse, publicly substantiated what Black Americans have been saying for decades. Social media's amplification enabled these testimonies and discourses to migrate into national conversations, and with them a shared political vocabulary emerged.[34] By humanizing and decriminalizing victims and connecting shared experiences of police terror, a new political context was born.

Despite the growing awareness of widespread police violence, the invisibility of certain abuse victims remains. While most Americans can recite a sad litany of the Black men and boys who are victims of police brutality, they may be hard-pressed to land on more than one or two names of Black women. But Black women and girls also have a tragically long history of being terrorized by police.[35] The tragic deaths of Aiyana Stanley-Jones, Eleanor Bumpurs, Atatiana Jefferson, Sandra Bland, and Breonna Taylor have become more frequently discussed, but the systemic and consistent ways that Black women and girls are targeted by police, especially for nonlethal violence like sexual assault, remains overlooked.[36] Brittany Cooper captures the whole sad truth: "In a world where the pains and traumas that Black women and girls experience as a consequence of both racism and sexism remain structurally invisible and impermeable to broad empathy, these killings recede from the foreground quietly."[37] In the absence of spectacle, the public struggles to cultivate sufficient outrage.

Black America finds itself amid a New Nadir.[38] To mobilize effective protest, Blacks and their allies must identify the hallmarks of this new historical moment. Racism and exploitation continue to exist, but in new forms; therefore activists must also develop new forms of protest. Milwaukee activist and folklorist Tejumola Ologboni offers, "The only way to speak to a person and have them understand it is to speak their language. And the only language America speaks is violence."[39] An intersectional framework provides a lens to understand modern uprisings, identify catalysts and regional conditions, and analyze rebels' actions to combat oppression. By understanding the texture of modern rebellions, activists, elected officials, and policymakers can begin to find meaningful, lasting solutions.

In 2004 a Chicago recording artist hauntingly rapped over a gospel choir for the single "Jesus Walks" on his debut album: "You know what the Midwest is? Young and Restless." This opening provocation taunts the audience on their knowledge of the Midwest's essence, affirming in the very next stanza that the region is animated by its youth and restlessness.[40] For those surprised, unnerved, or enraged by the past few years' protests grown from heartland soil, this declaration holds the key.

Across the country, organizing efforts of young people catalyzed global action, and in few places was their centrality on greater display than in the Midwest, where people under thirty years old comprise more than 38 percent of the population.[41] When four teens and a nine-year-old child testified for the prosecution at George Floyd's murder trial, they placed young people's power to effect change on full display.[42] Their actions demonstrate a brave continuation of young people's civic engagement as activists, witnesses, and, sadly, victims of state violence, launching a new era of Black midwestern protest. Organizing against school closures, gun violence, the presence of school resource officers, book bans, and countless other issues, this new generation of freedom fighters builds on the labor and radical dreams of those who came before.

The 2020 summer protests against police brutality captivated the world and alarmed more than a few people, convinced that they were witnessing Black discontent in a region previously unmarked by it. But Black midwestern protest is only shocking if you haven't been paying attention. Black activists of the nineteenth century organized the nation's first colored convention in Ohio to protest that state's discriminatory Black Laws and racial violence. Dred Scott's famous appeal for freedom arose from his time living in Illinois and Minnesota and was filed in Missouri. African Americans armed themselves in self-defense against racist mobs in 1917 East St. Louis, 1919 Chicago, and Omaha that same year. The 1954 *Brown v. Board of Education* case originated in Topeka, Kansas. Gary, Indiana, hosted the first National Black Political Convention in 1972. This is to say nothing of Black culture—Toni Morrison, Langston Hughes, Gordon Parks, the Ohio Players, Richard Pryor, Motown, Prince—adopted by mainstream America but birthed in the Black Midwest.

And yet the midwestern character of these prominent watersheds, integral to telling the American story, is still omitted from it. The erasure of the region's racial complexity, historically and now, is not accidental. Regional parameters are fluid by design, allowing us to lump and categorize certain behaviors in service of larger "truths." If the South, with its de jure segregation and pervasive racial terror, is scapegoated as the nation's racist uncle, the rest of the country is off the hook. In contrast, the Midwest can exist in the collective imaginary as national proxy, aligning with the triumphalist and nonracist narratives that so many wish to believe about our country. In this interpretation, the Midwest is a place without much in the way of a Black history (or a Black present) and thus without a history (or present) of anti-Blackness. When politicians in turn fondly comment on "midwestern values," as the mold for what the nation should aspire to, they are invoking a "heartland" in which white purity, meritocracy, and family values continue to reside and thrive. They imagine a region composed solely of white conservative voters, the "silent majority."

To the extent that the Midwest *is* majority white, it is because the region's very creation is predicated on settler colonialism, marginalization, exclusion, and violence. But it is not *only* white. And to consider that fact, and to consider the decades of sustained Black midwestern protest and life beyond the stories of American redemption means that folks, good midwestern folks, face an uncomfortable truth. Our challenge lies not in uncritically accepting the Midwest's conception of itself as raceless and thus a "not-racist" place but rather to use that peculiar framing as a starting point for restlessness. Over seven million people who identify as Black reside in the Midwest, more than any other region excluding the South.[43]

This is why Black midwestern erasure is central to the maintenance of American racial discourse. The experiences—the very existence—of Black people and other people of color in the Midwest challenge the fundamental nature of how white supremacy operates in this country. If we buy the myth that the Midwest is an exclusively white place without race problems, there is no issue to be managed and the protests in Minneapolis, in Ferguson, in Chicago seem anomalous. They are not. The Black Midwest not only exists but is the vanguard of a new era of protest.

In 2015 Kansas City native Janelle Monáe released "Hell You Talmbout" in response to the spate of anti-Black violence. Under a sparse drumbeat and harmonic vocals, the artists shout the names of people killed, the entire group joining in refrain, asking listeners to consider: exactly what the hell are we talking about?[44] The very question emphasizes the rupture between Black and white life in the Midwest, where Black Americans fall behind on every quality-of-life measurement. For those cloaked in a regional superiority complex, when considering these inferior life outcomes, higher poverty rates, and limited political power, they justify these differences by way of a "it's not me, it's you" tagline of personal responsibility. In fact, the opposite is true. Midwestern structural inequality, not Black midwesterners, is to blame for these significant differences.

Black midwestern restlessness, in every era and by every generation, is an attempt to right these wrongs. Without this reckoning, structural and interpersonal racial violence can be politely cordoned off below the Mason–Dixon line, ignoring that Jim Crow has found a comfy home in the amber waves of grain.

NOTES

ABBREVIATIONS

CHS   Cincinnati Historical Society, OH
Kerner Commission   National Advisory Commission on Civil Disorders, *Report of the National Advisory Commission on Civil Disorders* (Washington, DC: Government Publishing Office, 1968)
LBJ   Lyndon Baines Johnson Presidential Library, University of Texas at Austin
NACCD   National Advisory Commission on Civil Disorders
UWML   Archives Department, University of Wisconsin–Milwaukee Libraries, Milwaukee

INTRODUCTION

1. Murray Schumach, "Poitier Wins Oscar as Best Film Actor," *New York Times*, April 14, 1964.
2. Gates and West, *African American Century*, 289.
3. Karen Tumulty, "The Great Society at 50," *Washington Post*, May 17, 2014.
4. Rucker and Upton, *Encyclopedia of Race Riots*.
5. "The Black Mood: A *Newsweek* Survey," *Newsweek*, August 21, 1967.
6. "Negro Revolt: The Flames Spread," *Life*, August 4, 1967; "Newark: The Predictable Insurrection," *Time*, July 28, 1967; "Twelfth Street, Detroit," *Time*, August 4, 1967; and "Battlefield: USA," *Newsweek*, August 7, 1967.
7. Kerner Commission, 1.
8. Dougherty, *More Than One Struggle*; Ervin, *Gateway to Equality*; Ford, *Brick and a Bible*; Frazier, *Harambee City*; Johnson, *Broken Heart of America*; Jones, *Selma of the*

North; Lang, *Grassroots at the Gateway*; Michney, *Surrogate Suburbs*; Moten, *Continually Working*; Phillips, *AlabamaNorth*; and Trotter, *Black Milwaukee*. For broader discussion of this historiography, see Trotter, "Historiography of Black Workers."

9. Theoharis and Woodard, *Freedom North*; Theoharis, Woodard, and Purnell, *Strange Career of Jim Crow North*; and Sugrue, *Sweet Land of Liberty*.

10. US Census Bureau, *Characteristics of the Population*, vol. 1: part 1, sec. 2, "Employment Status by Race, Sex, and Age for Regions: 1970."

11. Kerner Commission, 323.

12. It is not my intention to advocate or encourage violence. Ultimately, I subscribe to political scientist Ted Gurr's assertion that "violence generally consumes men and goods, it seldom enhances them." Nevertheless, violent protest does not occur in a vacuum. Historically, it has been the purview of the most desperate, the most oppressed—those with very little to lose and even fewer options for recompense. Gurr, *Why Men Rebel*, 4.

13. AP Stylebook (@APStylebook), "New guidance on AP Stylebook Online: Use care in deciding which term best applies: A riot is a wild of violent disturbance of the peace involving a group of people. The term riot suggests uncontrolled chaos and pandemonium (1/5)," Twitter, September 30, 2020, 12:31 p.m., https://twitter.com/apstylebook/status/1311357910715371520; and AP Stylebook (@APStylebook), "Focusing on rioting and property destruction rather than underlying grievance has been used in the past to stigmatize broad swaths of people protesting against lynching, police brutality or for racial justice, going back to the urban uprisings of the 1960s (2/5)," Twitter, September 30, 2020, 12:31 p.m., https://twitter.com/apstylebook/status/1311357910715371520.

14. AP Stylebook (@APStylebook), "Unrest is a vaguer, milder and less emotional term for a condition of angry discontent and protest verging on revolt (3/5)," Twitter, September 30, 2020, 12:31 p.m., https://twitter.com/apstylebook/status/1311357910715371520; AP Stylebook (@APStylebook), "Revolt and uprising both suggest a broader political dimension or civil upheavals, a sustained period of protests or unrest against powerful groups or governing systems (5/5)," Twitter, September 30, 2020, 12:31 p.m., https://twitter.com/apstylebook/status/1311357910715371520; and AP Stylebook (@APStylebook), "Protest and demonstration refer to specific actions such as marches, sit-ins, rallies or other actions meant to register dissent. They can be legal or illegal, organized, or spontaneous, peaceful or violent, and involve any number of people (4/5)," Twitter, September 30, 2020, 12:31 p.m., https://twitter.com/apstylebook/status/1311357910715371520.

15. Levy, *Great Uprising*, 7.

16. Thompson, "Urban Uprisings," 111.

17. Levy, *Great Uprising*, 68.

18. Thompson, "Urban Uprisings," 111.

19. Sugrue, *Sweet Land of Liberty*, 334.

20. Jeffries and Beckham, "How Whites Shaped the Study of Urban Unrest," 112.

21. Kerner Commission, 323.

22. Kerner Commission, 65.

23. In 1967 there were eight major disorders or 5 percent of the total. The characteristics of major disorders include many fires, intensive looting, reports of sniping,

violence lasting more than two days, sizable crowds, and the use of National Guard or Federal forces. There were thirty-three serious disorders or 20 percent of the total. The characteristics of serious disorders include isolated looting, some fires, rock throwing, violence lasting between one and two days, only one sizable crowd or many small groups, and the use of state police but generally not the National Guard or federal forces. And there were 123 minor disorders or 75 percent of the total. The characteristics of minor disorders include a few fires or broken windows, violence lasting generally less than one day, participation by only small numbers of people, and the use, in most cases, of only local police or police from a neighboring community. Kerner Commission, 65.

24. Kerner Commission, 65, 323.
25. Kerner Commission, 66.
26. "The National: Running Out of Riots," *Time*, August 27, 1973.
27. Myers and Caniglia, "All the Rioting That's Fit to Print," 523.
28. Baskin et al., *Race-Related Civil Disorders*, 2.
29. Myers and Caniglia, "All the Rioting That's Fit to Print," 523.
30. On the Illini Union, see Tom Kacich, "Chaos in 1968? Depends on the Report," *News-Gazette*, February 4, 2018. In 1968 members of the New Orleans chapter of the Black Panther Party had a standoff with the New Orleans Police Department in the Desire housing projects. "Why Twenty-Four Panthers Are Political Prisoners in Louisiana," *The Black Panther: Intercommunal News Service*, June 21, 1971, www.itsabouttimebpp.com/chapter_history/pdf/new_orleans/neworleans24.pdf. University of Nebraska at Lincoln students staged a sit-in at Pershing Military and Naval Science Building protesting the war in Vietnam. Ellis Clopton, "Students Arrested," *Daily Nebraskan* (Lincoln), May 5, 1970.
31. Baskin et al., *Race-Related Civil Disorders*, 3 (emphasis in original).
32. Baskin et al., *Race-Related Civil Disorders*, 26.
33. Myers and Caniglia, "All the Rioting That's Fit to Print," 359.
34. Hofstadter and Wallace, *American Violence*, 7.
35. Howard, "American Tradition."
36. Kishi and Jones, *Demonstrations and Political Violence in America*, 5. The center defines violent demonstrations as "events in which the demonstrators themselves engage in violently disruptive and/or destructive acts targeting other individuals, property, businesses, other rioting groups, or armed actors." Armed Conflict Location and Event Data Project (ACLED) FAQ page, last updated April 25, 2024, https://acleddata.com/knowledge-base/united-states-scope-and-coverage.
37. Geoffrey Skelley, "How Americans Feel about George Floyd's Death and the Protests," *FiveThirtyEight*, June 5, 2020, https://fivethirtyeight.com/features/how-americans-feel-about-george-floyds-death-and-the-protests.
38. Deja Thomas and Juliana Menasce Horowitz, "Support for Black Lives Matter Has Decreased since June but Remains Strong among Black Americans," *Pew Research Center*, September 16, 2020, www.pewresearch.org/short-reads/2020/09/16/support-for-black-lives-matter-has-decreased-since-june-but-remains-strong-among-black-americans.
39. Newburn, "Causes and Consequences," 66.

40. 18 USC 102, §2102(a) [added by Pub. L. 90-284, title I, §104(a), April 11, 1968, 82 Stat. 76], https://uscode.house.gov/view.xhtml?path=/prelim@title18/part1/chapter102&edition=prelim.

41. Peter Levy tallies 750 urban revolts in 525 cities in his book. Levy, *Great Uprising*, 1. Seymour Spilerman, one of the most prolific catalogers of uprisings, netted 341 disorders identifying a possible 100 additional events using the following parameters: civil disorders occurring between 1961 and 1968 in cities with a 1960 population in excess of 25,000. Furthermore, he only included events if they had at least 30 participants, some violence or property damage, and took place apart from institutions such as schools or union halls. Spilerman, *Governmental Units Analysis Data*, 4–5.

42. Radical Information Project, "Racial Groups Involved in Uprisings," accessed April 20, 2022, https://radicalinformationproject.weebly.com/uprisingsdisturbancesriots.html.

43. Radical Information Project, "Urban Disturbances Code book," accessed April 20, 2022, https://radicalinformationproject.weebly.com/uploads/2/6/8/2/26824616/urban_disturbances_codebook.pdf; and Radical Information Project, "Location of Uprisings, 1968–1972," accessed April 20, 2022, https://radicalinformationproject.weebly.com/uprisingsdisturbancesriots.html.

44. Among the incidents cataloged, 17.2 percent were level 1 disturbances; 21.7 percent were level 2 disturbances; 10.8 percent were level 3 disturbances, and 9.1 percent were level 4 disturbances. The property damage code scale is as follows: 1 = very slight: will take little time or effort to fix or replace; mild consequences. 2 = minor: a few degrees stronger than no. 1; increasing consequences. 3 = extensive: will require a large monetary cost and workload to repair/replace; unfixable in some cases. 4 = enormous: total destruction of large areas. Radical Information Project, "Urban Disturbances Codebook."

45. Events categorized as "larger" or greater than 200 participants but fewer than 1,000 was the next-most-frequent gathering, at 22 percent. Medium events (< 50) comprised 20.8 percent; mobs (< 1,000), 17.0 percent; and, finally, in the thousands (+1,000) at 5.8 percent rounded out these categorizations. Radical Information Project, "Size of Uprisings, 1968–1972," accessed April 20, 2022, https://radicalinformationproject.weebly.com/uprisingsdisturbancesriots.html.

46. Biggs, "Size Matters," 373.

47. Myers and Caniglia, "All the Rioting That's Fit to Print," 540.

48. For purposes of this study, I use the Kerner Commission's definition of the North-Central region, which includes the states of Illinois, Michigan, Ohio, Indiana, Wisconsin (East-North-Central) along with Iowa, Missouri, Kansas, and Nebraska (West-North-Central) to delineate the spatial boundaries of the Midwest.

49. Eick, *Dissent in Wichita*.

50. Balto, "'Occupied Territory.'"

51. Lassiter and Crespino, *Myth of Southern Exceptionalism*, 5.

52. Lang, "Locating the Civil Rights Movement," 379 (emphasis in original); Lassiter and Crespino, *Myth of Southern Exceptionalism*, 20.

53. Hinton, *America on Fire*.

54. Eick, *Dissent in Wichita*, 208.

55. Etcheson, *Emerging Midwest*, xi.

56. According to the 1960 census, Omaha's population stood at 300,674, Cincinnati's at 487,462, and Milwaukee's at 734,788. US Census Bureau, "Preliminary Report: Population Counts."

57. "Extra Police on Duty in Wake of Near Riot," *Omaha World-Herald*, July 4, 1966; and "Violence Erupts Third Straight Night," *Omaha World-Herald*, July 5, 1966.

58. "Mob Tosses Bottles but Few Injured," *Omaha World-Herald*, July 5, 1966; and "Police Arrest 78 Adults, 44 Juveniles on North Side," *Omaha World-Herald*, July 5, 1966.

59. "New Demands after Tuesday Meeting," *Omaha World-Herald*, July 6, 1966.

60. "Mind Over Mayhem," *Time Magazine*, June 23, 1967.

61. Kerner Commission, 25, 85.

62. "Janitor Charged in Slaying of Policeman," *Chicago Defender*, August 9, 1967; and "Milwaukee Calm after Negro Riot," *New York Times*, August 1, 1967.

63. "Milwaukee Commandos," *Chicago Tribune*, October 12, 1966; and "Groppi Group Marches into Wauwatosa," *Chicago Tribune*, September 5, 1967.

64. Memo to staff from Henry B. Taliaferro, subject: "Milwaukee Trip: Monday & Tuesday, 28, 29 August 1967," September 26, 1967, 9, box E24, Series 4: Office of Investigation City Files, Jackson—General to New Brunswick—Newspaper Clippings, folder Milwaukee-General, LBJ.

65. David L. Lawrence, "Bias Felt Anywhere," *Omaha Star*, December 10, 1965.

66. Cayton and Gray, *American Midwest*, 24.

67. Abu-Lughod, *Race, Space, and Riots*, 25.

68. US Census Bureau, *US Census of Population, 1960*.

69. Draft—Staff Paper No. 7, "Analysis of Cincinnati Disturbance," November 13, 1967, 29, box E67, Series 12: Staff Papers from Office of Assistant Deputy Director, folder Staff Paper No. 7 Cincinnati: Analysis of Cincinnati Disturbance, LBJ.

70. "Black Middle Class," *Chicago Defender*, August 20, 1966.

71. Kerner Commission, 73.

72. Hobsbawm, *Social Bandits*, 110–13.

73. Upton et al., "Politics of Urban Violence," 257.

74. Miller and Schaen, "Democracy and the Black Rebellions"; McAdam, *Political Process*; and Kerner Commission, 73–74.

75. Paige, "Collective Violence and the Culture of Subordination," 43.

76. Grimshaw, "Three Views of Urban Violence," 5.

77. Kerner Commission, 73–74.

78. Stanley S. Scott, "Rebellions Not Over, Many Predict," *Chicago Defender*, September 13, 1966.

79. Skolnick, *Politics of Protest*, 145.

80. Historian Eric Hobsbawm declared that "the class mob did not merely riot as a protest, but because it expected to achieve something by its riot." Hobsbawm, *Social Bandits*, 111; see also McAdam, *Political Process*, 48.

81. Tilly, "Collective Violence in European Perspective," 10.

82. Kerner Commission, 73.

83. "Panthers Defend Black Business," *Omaha World-Herald*, June 26, 1969.

84. Johnson, "Gender, Race, and Rumors," 252.

85. Greenberg, *Or Does It Explode?*, 211; "Angry Crowd Gathers after Fatal Crash," *Chicago Tribune*, August 13, 1965; "Negro Girl Killed by a Police Bullet at Housing Project," *Omaha World-Herald*, July 25, 1969; and "Loot Stores in W. Side Unrest," *Chicago Tribune*, July 13, 1966.

86. Horne, *Fire This Time*, 54–55, 310.

87. Greenberg, *Or Does It Explode?*, 7; Cohen, *Consumer's Republic*; and Mumford, *Newark*, 161.

88. While some of the first historical works on the topic examined the structural breakdown and ultimate decline of cities, directly challenging notions of Black family breakdown and criminal deviance, there is inadequate discussion of changes in Black consciousness and intraracial class struggles within the African American community. Sugrue, *Origins of the Urban Crisis*; and Fine, *Violence in the Model City*. In their respective books, *Fire This Time* and *Or Does It Explode?*, Gerald Horne and Cheryl Greenberg argue that institutional racism and the repression of civil rights and labor organizations created a void for working-class activism. Greenberg elaborated, contending the conflagration was "essentially the raw expression of anger taught by political organizations whose collapse left a vacuum." Greenberg, *Or Does It Explode?*, 5.

89. Moynihan, *Negro Family*, 29.

90. Hinton, *From the War on Poverty*.

91. Ernest W. Chambers, "A Militant Look at Black Poverty," *Omaha Star*, December 30, 1966.

CHAPTER 1

1. "Candidate Wallace at Omaha University," *Gateway* (Omaha), March 8, 1968.

2. Lowndes, *From the New Deal to the New Right*, 88.

3. Zwiers, "Whistles of George Wallace," 17.

4. Only 750 signatures were needed to put Wallace on the ballot. In Omaha the American Party received more than 2,100. "Predicts He'll Gain Support for 3d Party," *Omaha World-Herald*, March 3, 1968; and Larry Wilson, "Wallace Party Claims Victory," *Omaha World-Herald*, March 4, 1968.

5. Father McCaslin, in his interview, implied that Omaha police officers had some knowledge that a melee would occur later in the night. Jack McCaslin (activist, Omaha, NE), interview by author, December 5, 2005.

6. McCaslin, interview.

7. Marvin McClarty (retired police officer, Omaha, NE), interview by author, November 15, 2005; Ernest W. Chambers (barber, activist, and former state senator, Omaha, NE), interview by author, February 28, 2006. The *Omaha World-Herald* describes the incident somewhat differently. Reporter Larry Wilson wrote that the "twenty-five young Negroes took a strategic position" in front of Wallace. Wallace continued to speak and told the audience, "These are the free speech folks, you know, and these are the kind of folks the people of this country are sick and tired of." Police captain Elvin Stokes then asked Palmer Anderson, age nineteen, to move aside. Anderson took a swing at the officer, and the "police quickly ran a flying wedge . . . like a Notre Dame football rush swept

the dissenters the length of the Arena floor and out the door." Larry Wilson, "Wallace Party Claims Victory," *Omaha World-Herald*, March 4, 1968.

8. Wilson, "Wallace Party Claims Victory."

9. "Reporters Find Reactions to Negro Violence Varies," *Omaha World-Herald*, June 2, 1968.

10. "Not as Simple as Black and White," *Dundee and West Omaha Sun*, March 14, 1968.

11. Benjamin E. Simpson "Take Your Choice, White America; It's Dr. King or Mr. Carmichael," *Cincinnati Enquirer*, June 26, 1967.

12. Kerner Commission, 66.

13. Barthes, *Mythologies*, quoted in Jay and Conklin, *People's History of Detroit*, 12–13.

14. While the American Dream transcends region, this myth carries particular weight in the Midwest. Such origins begin with the frontier thesis, where Frederick Jackson Turner argued that the frontier served the important function of Americanizing a community. Similarly, the Midwest's conception of itself as prototypically American manifests in the late-nineteenth and early-twentieth century where midwesterners began to conceive of the region they inhabited no longer "connoted isolation but rather centrality," particularly with the growth of manufacturing and industrial powerhouses in the region. Teaford, *Cities of the Heartland*, ix.

15. Christman, *Midwest Futures*, 83.

16. Turner, *Frontier in American History*, 155.

17. Shortridge, "The Heartland's Role in US Culture," 40–42. For examples of scholarship investigating gender and sexuality in the Midwest, see Manalansan et al., "Queering the Middle"; Kazyak, "Midwest or Lesbian?"; and Oler, *Old-Fashioned Modernism*.

18. Paul Waldman, "Opinion: Mayor Pete: What Are 'Heartland' Values, and Why Do You Need Them to Be President?," *Washington Post*, January 30, 2020; and Kim Severson, "A Classic Midwestern Dish Becomes a Talking Point in Iowa," *New York Times*, January 28, 2020.

19. Ochonicky, *American Midwest in Film and Literature*; and Johnson, *Heartland TV*.

20. Kiel, "Untaming the Mild Frontier."

21. Howard, "What to the 'Other' Is the Midwest?"

22. Hoganson, *Heartland*, xv.

23. Winfrey-Harris, "Stop Pretending Black Midwesterners Don't Exist," 169.

24. Higbie, "Heartland," 82.

25. Johnson, *Heartland TV*, 114–15.

26. Taggart, "Populism and Representative Politics," 274.

27. Watts, "Midwest as Colony," 182.

28. Sugrue, *Origins of the Urban Crisis*, 6.

29. Galster, *Reality and Research*, 19–20.

30. Markusen and Carlson, "Deindustrialization in the American Midwest," 30–31.

31. Nelson, *Farm and Factory*, 193.

32. Larsen and Cottrell, *Gate City*, 250.

33. Danton, "Omaha Experiment," 66.

34. Reconnaissance Survey Field Report—2nd Draft, undated, 7, box E44, Series 10: Field Research Reports and Field Interview Folders, folder Cincinnati—Reconnaissance

Survey Field Research Reports Draft and Second Draft, folder Cincinnati—Reconnaissance Survey—Field Research Report (2nd Draft) [1 of 2], LBJ.

35. Letter to George Beasley from James Abernathy, undated, 1, box 6, Mss 580, Urban League of Greater Cincinnati, folder Committee of 28, 1963–67, CHS.

36. O. F. Knippenburg, "U.S. Scrapping JUMP Program for Negroes," *Cincinnati Enquirer*, March 17, 1967.

37. Memo to staff from Henry B. Taliaferro, subject: "Milwaukee Trip: Monday & Tuesday, 28, 29 August 1967," September 26, 1967, 5, box E24, Series 4: Office of Investigation City Files, Jackson—General to New Brunswick—Newspaper Clippings, folder Milwaukee-General, LBJ.

38. Milwaukee, Wisconsin Team Interview Reports—Revisit, October 31, 1967, 4, box 51, Series 10: Field Research Reports and Field Interview Folders, folder Milwaukee—Arrest Data to Milwaukee Reconnaissance Survey—Field Research Report, folder Milwaukee—Team Interview Reports—Revisit, LBJ.

39. Robert D. Van Fossen, "The Coming Unemployment Problem in Hamilton County," April 1963, 1, box 6, Mss q B952, Bureau of Governmental Research, Inc., folder 11, CHS.

40. Field Community Tension Factors Report—Milwaukee, June 30, 1967, 1, box E33, Series 6: Federal Bureau of Investigation City Reports, folder NACCD—Milwaukee, Wisconsin, LBJ.

41. Robert B. Sempe Jr., "$7.5 Billion Bill, With a Rent Subsidy Proviso, Signed by Johnson," *New York Times*, August 11, 1965.

42. Taylor, *Race for Profit*, 26–54.

43. Elaine Davis (former real estate employee, Cincinnati, OH), interview by author, June 20, 2013.

44. Tejumola Ologboni (folklorist, Milwaukee, WI), interview by author, August 19, 2014.

45. "Omaha Real Estate Board Head Dedicated to Maintain Ghetto," *Omaha Star*, February 2, 1963.

46. Memorandum to Charles Nelson from John Boswell, Subj: Team Trip to Milwaukee, November 6, 1967, 18, box E51, Series 10: Field Research Reports and Field Interview Folders, folder Milwaukee Arrest Data to Milwaukee Reconnaissance Survey Field Research Report, LBJ.

47. Reconnaissance Survey Field Report—Cincinnati, undated, 28–23, box E44, Series 10: Field Research Reports and Field Interview Folders, folder Cincinnati—Reconnaissance Survey Field Research Reports Draft and Second Draft, folder Cincinnati Reconnaissance Survey—Field Research Report (Draft), LBJ.

48. Memorandum to Files, Re Milwaukee, Wisconsin, August 1, 1967, 2–3, box E33, Series 6: Federal Bureau of Investigation City Reports, folder National Commission on Civil Disorder—Milwaukee, Wisconsin, LBJ.

49. Balto, "'Occupied Territory'"; Fehn and Jefferson, "North Side Revolutionaries"; Seawell, "Black Freedom Movement"; and Wolcott, *Race Riots, and Roller Coasters*.

50. Central Themes for Cincinnati, undated, 4, box E43, Series 10: Field Research Reports and Field Interview Folders, folder Cincinnati—Central Themes for Cincinnati, LBJ.

51. Balto, *Occupied Territory*; Felker-Kantor, *Policing Los Angeles*; and Moore, *Black Rage in New Orleans*.

52. McClarty, interview.

53. Schrotel, "Supervising the Use of Police Authority."

54. Cincinnati Division of Police, "A Report of the Riot in Cincinnati, Ohio; The Week of June 11, 1967," undated, 15, box E73, Series: Investigations Cincinnati—Depositions to Elizabeth—Newspapers Clippings, folder Cincinnati: Riot, NACCD, LBJ.

55. Balto, *Occupied Territory*, 9.

56. Hinton, *America on Fire*, 15.

57. Central Themes for Cincinnati, 3.

58. "McClarty Charges Known Two Years," *Omaha World-Herald* clipping, September 14, 1967, box 5, Series 2: Exhibits to Hearings, August 1–November 10, 1965, folder Exhibit 56, NACCD, LBJ.

59. "The McClarty Charges," *Omaha World-Herald* clipping, September 9, 1967, box 5, Series 2: Exhibits to Hearings, August 1–November 10, 1965, folder Exhibit 58, NACCD, LBJ.

60. Pierce, *Polite Protest*, 6.

61. "Gov. Rhodes Issues Executive Code Proclamation," *Cincinnati Herald*, July 5, 1963.

62. Memo to staff from Henry B. Taliaferro, September 26, 1967, 10, box E24, Series 4: Office of Investigation City Files, Jackson—General to New Brunswick—Newspaper Clippings, folder Milwaukee-General, NACCD, LBJ.

63. "NAACP Calls Rhodes 'Code' Farcical," *Cincinnati Herald*, March 5, 1963.

64. Jonathan Slesinger, "A Study of Community Opinions Concerning the Summer 1967 Civil Disturbance in Milwaukee," Unpublished manuscript, April 1, 1968, 11, box 12, folder 2, Study of Community Opinions Concerning the Summer 1967 Civil Disturbances in Milwaukee, 1968, UW–Milwaukee School of Social Welfare, Office of the Dean Records, 1945–98, Archival Collection 24, UWML.

65. Slesinger, "A Study of Community Opinions," 12–13.

66. McCaslin, interview.

67. Barbara Newman and Susanne Schilling, "Political Structure and Civil Disorders," staff paper, November 9, 1967, 13, box 2, Series 7: Commission Research N-Sh, folder Political Structure and Civil Disorders, NACCD, LBJ.

68. Lang, "Locating the Civil Rights Movement," 380.

69. "Blacks Serving on Elected and Appointed Governing Boards: 1966 and 1986," *Omaha World-Herald*, September 19, 1986.

70. Memo to Charles Nelson from John Boswell, 20, 28.

71. Draft—Staff Paper No. 7, "Analysis of Cincinnati Disturbance," November 13, 1967, 30, box E67, Series 12: Staff Papers from Office of Assistant Deputy Director, folder Staff Paper No. 7 Cincinnati: Analysis of Cincinnati Disturbance, LBJ.

72. Draft—Staff Paper No. 7, November 13, 1967, 41.

73. Reconnaissance Survey Field Report—2nd Draft, 1–2.

74. Historian John Buenker argues that nonpartisan elections were adopted as an antisocialist measure. Buenker, "Cream City Electoral Politics."

75. Memo to Charles Nelson from John Boswell, 6–7.

76. Memo to Charles Nelson from John Boswell, 8.

77. Daly-Bednarek, *Changing Image of the City*, 125–26.

78. "Was 'Sing-In' Disturbance? High Court Hears Argument," *Omaha World-Herald*, May 4, 1965; and "'Pray-in' for City Hall to Follow Rights Split" *Omaha World-Herald*, July 9, 1963.

79. "Human Relations Board Target of Two Blasts," *Omaha World-Herald*, February 26, 1965.

80. Deposition of Reverend Harold Hunt, January 8, 1968, 3–4, box 2, Series 32: Depositions of Witnesses December 1967–January 1968, Subgroup: Office of General Council Cincinnati Detroit, folder Depositions Cincinnati, NACCD, LBJ.

81. "Race Strides 'Easier' Here," *Omaha World-Herald*, September 27, 1963.

82. "Housing Ace Voted Down," *Omaha World-Herald*, November 13, 1963.

83. "Omaha and Birmingham Run Neck-and-Neck in Housing Segregation," *Omaha Star*, February 5, 1965.

84. "Race Strides 'Easier' Here," *Omaha World-Herald*, September 27, 1963.

85. "Negroes Becoming Too Satisfied," *Omaha World-Herald*, June 13, 1966.

86. Marjorie Parham (newspaper publisher, Cincinnati, OH), interview by author, June 2013.

87. Interview with Clint Reynolds, in Team Interview Report, November 6, 1967, 3, box E43, Series 10: Field Research Reports and Field Interview Folders, folder Cincinnati—Team Interview Report, NACCD, LBJ.

88. Reconnaissance Survey Field Report—2nd Draft, 1–2.

89. Maier, *Mayor Who Made Milwaukee Famous*, 38.

90. Maier, *Mayor Who Made Milwaukee Famous*, 40.

91. Ologboni, interview.

92. Rosalind Baker (former Schuster's model, Milwaukee, WI), interview by author, August 20, 2014.

93. George S. Kopp Sr., "A Few Bell Sheep," *Cincinnati Enquirer*, June 26, 1967.

94. Eloise Taylor, "Puzzled," *Cincinnati Enquirer*, June 22, 1967.

95. Interview with Mrs. Francis Demet by Tom Popp and Bruce Thomas, September 28, 1967, 5 box E51, Series 10: Field Research Reports and Field Interview Folders, folder Milwaukee—Arrest Data to Milwaukee Reconnaissance Survey—Field Research Report, folder Milwaukee—Team Interview Reports, NACCD, LBJ.

96. Terry, *For Whites Only*, 41.

97. Loewen, *Sundown Towns*, 320.

98. "Reporters Find Reactions to Negro Violence Varies," *Omaha World-Herald*, June 2, 1968.

99. Mutope Johnson (visual artist, Milwaukee, WI), interview by author, August 19, 2014.

100. Ed Seitz, "The Negro in Cincinnati: Stop and Listen, Cincinnati, This Is the Voice of the Negro," *Cincinnati Enquirer*, September 15, 1963.

101. Turner, "Significance of the Frontier."

102. Helgeson, "Politics in the Promised Land," 123.

103. Harding, "History: White, Negro and Black," 52.

104. Christman, *Midwest Futures*, 91.

105. "A weather vane for democracy": Hill and Hill, *Invisible Hawkeyes*, 4, 12–13. "Conveyor of American values": Blocker writes that "between 1860 and 1928, the Lower Midwest had produced eight of the thirteen victorious presidential candidates. Because of the region's political importance, its role as conveyor of American values to new immigrants, and its fecundity in producing migrants to other regions, the pattern of race relations hammered out within its borders could well have influenced the nation's." Blocker, *Little More Freedom*, 3.

CHAPTER 2

1. "More Apps. Than Placement Orders," *Omaha Star*, July 15, 1966.
2. "Negro Cleric Hits at Some Leaders," *Cincinnati Enquirer*, June 14, 1967.
3. Marian Spencer (activist, former city council member, Cincinnati, OH), interview by author, June 18, 2013.
4. "Negro Cleric Hits at Some Leaders."
5. Draft—Staff Paper No. 7, "Analysis of Cincinnati Disturbance," November 13, 1967, 29, box E67, Series 12: Staff Papers from Office of Assistant Deputy Director, folder Staff Paper No. 7 Cincinnati: Analysis of Cincinnati Disturbance, LBJ.
6. Brown, *Fighting for US*, 78.
7. Woodard, "Message from the Grassroots," 81.
8. Cincinnati Division of Police, "A Report of the Riot in Cincinnati, Ohio; The Week of June 11, 1967," undated, 10–11, box E73 Series: Investigations Cincinnati—Depositions to Elizabeth—Newspapers Clippings, folder Cincinnati: Riot, NACCD, LBJ.
9. Foreman, Casey, and Patterson, *Colored Conventions Movement*.
10. Harbour, "'I Earn by My Own Labor,'" 347–48; Breaux, "Maintaining a Home for Girls," 236; Hendricks, *Gender, Race, and Politics in the Midwest*, xvii; Lerner, "Early Community Work of Black Club Women," 162; Shaw, "Black Club Women," 18; and Spruill, "'From the Tub to the Club,'" xv–xvi.
11. Ford, *Brick and a Bible*, 3.
12. Sulik, "Waving the Red, Black, and Green," 205; and McDuffie, *Second Battle for Africa*.
13. Hine, "Housewives' League of Detroit," 129.
14. Ervin, *Gateway to Equality*; and Moten, "'Kept Right on Fightin'.'"
15. Dawson's framework includes six designations; three dominated the Black freedom struggle: integrationist, militant, and Black nationalist. Dawson, *Black Visions*, 16–17.
16. Dawson, *Black Visions*, 17–18.
17. Dawson, *Black Visions*, 21.
18. Clarke, *Malcolm X*, 155–56.
19. Coser, "Some Social Function of Violence."
20. Carmichael and Hamilton, *Black Power*, 47, 61, 76. See also Ransford, "Isolation, Powerlessness, and Violence," 581–91; Marx, *Protest and Prejudice*, 224.
21. Bloom, *Class, Race, and the Civil Rights Movement*, 218–19.
22. McLaughlin, *Long, Hot Summer of 1967*, 180–81.

23. Boesel, *Cities Under Siege*, 333.

24. Zweig, *Working-Class Majority*, 11.

25. Zweig, *Working-Class Majority*, 13.

26. Bates, *Pullman Porters*; Cooley, *Moving Up, Moving Out*; Feagin, *Living with Racism*; Patillo, *Black Picket Fences*; Summers, *Manliness and Its Discontents*; and Trotter, *Workers on Arrival*.

27. Gaines, *Uplifting the Race*, xiv.

28. "Black Middle Class," *Chicago Defender*, August 20, 1966.

29. Interview with Dr. Bruce Green by Diane Phillips, November 1, 1967, in Team Interview Report, November 6, 1967, 3, box E43, Series 10: Field Research Reports and Field Interview Folders, folder Cincinnati—Team Interview Report, NACCD, LBJ.

30. A. Edgar Aub Jr., "Fruit of Labor," *Cincinnati Enquirer* July 2, 1967.

31. Chaney Alexander, "Kiss of Death," *Cincinnati Enquirer*, June 15, 1967; and Gene Roberts, "Cincinnati Riots Laid to Isolation," *New York Times* June 18, 1967.

32. Daniel Goodwin Sr. (barber and activist, Omaha, NE), interview by author, November 30, 2005.

33. Draft—Staff Paper No. 7, 37.

34. Pierce, *Polite Protest*, 125.

35. Bloom, *Class, Race, and the Civil Rights Movement*, 219.

36. "Negroes Becoming Too Satisfied," *Omaha World-Herald*, June 13, 1966.

37. "Those Waiting in the Wings Came," *Omaha Star*, July 8, 1966.

38. Marjorie Parham (newspaper publisher, Cincinnati, OH), interview by author, June 2013.

39. "Leadership Sums Up Attitudes of Youth," *North Omaha Sun*, July 14, 1966.

40. Untitled Recount of Riots, July 13, 1967, 2–3, box 7, Mss 901, Robert L. Black Jr. Collection, folder 10, CHRC Meetings 1967, CHS.

41. "The Grassy Side," *Cincinnati Enquirer*, July 2, 1967.

42. "Blacks Miss Black Power Point, Too," *Dundee and West Omaha Sun*, March 14, 1968.

43. Draft—Staff Paper No. 7, 25.

44. Flaming, *Who 'Riots' and Why?*, 29.

45. Draft of speech by McCrackin, undated, 2, box 51, Mss 917, Maurice McCrackin, folder 11, Black Power Mac's Thoughts, CHS.

46. Gurr, *Why Men Rebel*, 92.

47. Confidential Document Outlining the City of Cincinnati to the President's Commission on Civil Disorder, October 12, 1967, in DC, 16, box 10, Mss 901, Robert L. Black Jr. Collection, folder 5, CHRC Rebellion Riots 1967, CHS.

48. "Rights Unit Criticizes City," *Omaha Star*, July 28, 1966.

49. "Negro Need Was Ignored," *Omaha World-Herald*, July 25, 1966.

50. Woodson Howe, "21 at Initial Hearing on Near North Side," *Omaha World-Herald*, July 19, 1966.

51. Le Bon, *The Crowd*.

52. Frank Peak (public health advocate and former Black Panther, Omaha, NE), interview by author, July 2013.

53. William B. Hale, "It's the Poor vs. Rich, Rioter Says," *Milwaukee Journal*, July 31, 1967.

54. Hobsbawm, *Social Bandits*, 110–13. Doug McAdam defines cognitive liberation as the realization of an individual that he or she can change his or her own conditions. McAdam, *Political Process and the Development of Black Political Insurgency*, 48.

55. Saunders, *Negro in Avondale*, 34.

56. Boesel, *Cities Under Siege*, 332–33.

57. Bloom, *Class, Race, and the Civil Rights Movement*, 220.

58. Bennett, "Mood of the Negro," 28.

59. Memorandum RE: Racial Disturbance, Cincinnati, Ohio, June 1967, July 21, 1967, 17, box E32, Series 6: Federal Bureau of Investigation City Reports, folder NACCD—Cincinnati, OH, NACCD, LBJ.

60. Memorandum to David Ginsburg and Victor H. Palmieri from M. C. Miskovsky, Subject: Synopsis of Interim Report for Office of Investigations, December 5, 1967, 2, box E1, Series 1: Office of Investigation General Subject Files, folder Interim Report—Miscellaneous, LBJ.

61. Confidential Document Outlining the City of Cincinnati to the President's Commission on Civil Disorder, 15.

62. "We Demand Rights Now," *Dundee and West Omaha Sun*, March 3, 1966.

63. Letter from Ernest Chambers to the Department of Justice, August 18, 1967, 2, box 5, Series 2: Exhibits to Hearings, August 1–November 10, 1967, folder Exhibit 61, NACCD, LBJ.

64. Tejumola Ologboni (folklorist, Milwaukee, WI), interview by author, August 19, 2014.

65. Paige, "Political Orientation and Riot Participation."

66. H. Edward Ransford defines the concept of powerlessness as the form of alienation dealing with an individual's expectations for control over his or her own destiny and the larger society. Peripherality, in his view, refers to a condition of interracial marginality in which the minority individual is oriented toward the values of the dominant group and toward acceptance in this group. Ransford, "Isolation, Powerlessness, and Violence."

67. Ransford's final sample consisted of 85 respondents before and 312 after the rebellion. Ransford, "Isolation, Powerlessness, and Violence."

68. Boesel, *Cities Under Siege*, 351.

69. Margaret Josten, "Avondale Man Gives Version of 'Why of It,'" *Cincinnati Enquirer*, June 14, 1967.

70. Weber, *Summer Mockery*, 43.

71. Bloom, *Class, Race, and the Civil Rights Movement*, 201.

72. Howard Sibles, "Sobbing Negro Girl Screams Why? Why?," *Omaha World-Herald*, March 5, 1968.

73. Report to Community Action Commission of the Cincinnati Area, Subject: Civil Disorders, from Seven Hills Neighborhood Houses, Inc., undated, 10, box 7, Series 2: Exhibits to Hearings, August 1–November 10, 1967, folder Exhibit 94, NACCD, LBJ.

74. Kohler, *Cincinnati's Black Peoples*.

75. "Negro Cleric Hits at Some Leaders," *Enquirer*, June 14, 1967.

76. James Mimms (bus driver, Cincinnati, OH), interview by author, June 18, 2013.

77. Bloom, *Class, Race, and the Civil Rights Movement*, 203.

78. Report to Community Action Commission of the Cincinnati Area.

79. Memo to staff from Henry B. Taliaferro, subject: "Milwaukee Trip: Monday & Tuesday, 28, 29, August 1967," September 26, 1967, 10, box E24, Series 4: Office of Investigation City Files, Jackson—General to New Brunswick—Newspaper Clippings, folder Milwaukee—General, NACCD, LBJ.

80. Interview with Frank Gimble by Bernard Dobranski and John Boswell, September 29, 1967, no. 32, box E51, Series 10: Field Research Reports and Field Interview Folders, folder Milwaukee—Arrest Data to Milwaukee Reconnaissance Survey—Field Research Report, folder Milwaukee—Team Interview Reports, NACCD, LBJ.

81. Interview with Fr. James Groppi by Charles King, October 26, 1967, 3–4, box E51, Series 10: Field Research Reports and Field Interview Folders, folder Milwaukee—Team Interview Report—Revisit Report, NACCD, LBJ.

82. Jones, *Selma of the North*; and Modlinski, "Commandos."

83. Memorandum to Charles Nelson from John Boswell, Subj: Team Trip to Milwaukee, November 6, 1967, 34, box E51, Series 10: Field Research Reports and Field Interview Folders, folder Milwaukee Arrest Data to Milwaukee Reconnaissance Survey Field Research Report, NACCD, LBJ.

84. Memorandum to Files, RE Milwaukee, Wisconsin, August 1, 1967, 6, box E33, Series 6: Federal Bureau of Investigation City Reports, folder NACCD—Milwaukee, Wisconsin, NACCD, LBJ.

85. Interview with Fr. James Groppi by Charles King, October 26, 1967, 2–3.

86. McLaughlin, *Long, Hot Summer*, 13.

87. Vernon, *Black Ghetto*, 29–30.

CHAPTER 3

1. Transcript from *Crosstalk*, November 27, 1967, box 6, Milwaukee Series 44: Maier, Henry, folder 31, Barbee, Lloyd, 1967–71, UWML.

2. McAdam, "Tactical Innovation."

3. Meeting Notes from Dr. Ralph Turner, Dr. Robert Shellow, and David Boesel, October 19, 1967, 6–9, box E38, Series 8: Material Pulled from Commission Files, Hearing—Transcripts to Staff Meetings (Notes), folder Staff Meetings (Notes), NACCD, LBJ.

4. Governor's Commission on the Los Angeles Riots, *McCone Commission Report*, 4. For Reagan's comment, see Fikes, *Racist and Sexist Quotations*, 83.

5. McAdam, "Tactical Innovation and the Pace of Insurgency," 735–36.

6. Levy, *Great Uprising*, 2.

7. "Safeway Rezone Request Held," *Omaha Star*, February 8, 1963; Dalstrom, *A. V. Sorensen*, 204; "Extra Police on Duty in Wake of Near Riot," *Omaha World-Herald*, July 4, 1966; and "Violence Erupts Third Straight Night," *Omaha World-Herald*, July 5, 1966.

8. "Violence Erupts"; "Guards Used after 3rd Night of Violence," *Omaha World-Herald*, July 5, 1966; Donald Janson, "Riot Duty Troops Gather in Omaha," *New York Times*, July 5, 1966; and "4 Policemen and Unknown Number of Civilians Injured," *Omaha World-Herald*, July 5, 1966.

9. "Mob Tosses Bottles but Few Injured," *Omaha World-Herald*, July 5, 1966; "Police Arrest 78 Adults, 44 Juveniles on North Side," *Omaha World-Herald*, July 5, 1966; and "HQ, Engineering Guards 1st to Get Call for Duty," *Omaha World-Herald*, July 5, 1966.

10. "Violence Erupts"; "Guard Finds Streets Quiet but Tense," *Omaha World-Herald*, July 5, 1966; Larsen and Contrell, *Gate City*, 273; "Police Arrest 78 Adults, 44 Juveniles on North Side"; "Flew Home to Help End Disturbances," *Omaha World-Herald*, July 6, 1966; Dalstrom, *A. V. Sorensen*, 205; and "Officers Get Guard Help in Disorder," *Omaha World-Herald*, July 6, 1966.

11. "More Apps. Than Placement Orders," *Omaha Star*, July 15, 1966 (quote). See also Larsen and Cottrell, *Gate City*, 272; and "Labor Dept. Open North Omaha Office Today," *Omaha World-Herald*, July 9, 1966.

12. "Mayor D_____ling of Riots; Calls for More Action, Less Meetings," *Omaha Star*, July 22, 1966 (title partially obscured on microfilm).

13. "We Demand Rights Now," *Dundee and West Omaha Sun*, March 3, 1966; "Police Arrest 78 Adults, 44 Juveniles on North Side"; "Youth Tell Grievances," *Omaha World-Herald*, July 5, 1966; and "Mayor D_____ling of Riots."

14. "New Demands after Tuesday Meeting."

15. "Mayor D_____ling of Riots"; "Basketball Clinics Start Monday," *Omaha Star*, July 15, 1966; "Announce 5 New Summertime Youth Projects," *Omaha Star*, July 22, 1966; "City Signs 200 Negro Applicants," *Omaha World-Herald*, July 8, 1966; and "Job Corps Center to Expand," *Omaha Star*, July 8, 1966.

16. Draft—Staff Paper No. 7, "Analysis of Cincinnati Disturbance," November 13, 1967, 29, box E67, Series 12: Staff Papers from Office of Assistant Deputy Director, folder Staff Paper No. 7 Cincinnati: Analysis of Cincinnati Disturbance, NACCD, LBJ.

17. Betsy Neel (retired nurse, Cincinnati, OH), interview by author, June 21, 2013.

18. Summary Report, National Guard Assistance to Civil Authorities in Riot Activities, Cincinnati, June 19, 1967, 1, box E21, Series 4: Office of Investigation City Files, folder Cincinnati Miscellaneous Reports, NACCD, LBJ.

19. Kerner Commission, 26.

20. Summary Report, National Guard Assistance, Cincinnati, June 19, 1967, 2.

21. Cincinnati Division of Police, "A Report of the Riot in Cincinnati, Ohio; The Week of June 11, 1967," undated, 23, box E73, Series: Investigations Cincinnati—Depositions to Elizabeth—Newspapers Clippings, folder Cincinnati: Riot, NACCD, LBJ.

22. Memo to Charles Nelson from Ira Simmons, Re: Interview with Dr. Robert Reid, November 9, 1967, 1–2, box E43, Series 10: Field Research Reports and Field Interview Folders, folder Cincinnati—Team Interview Report—2d Trip, NACCD, LBJ.

23. Memorandum to David Ginsburg from M. C. Miskovsky, Subject: Final Report of the Office of Investigations, March 25, 1968, 63, NACCD/E1, LBJ; "Summary Report, National Guard Assistance to Civil Authorities in Riot Activities, Cincinnati, OH, 13–18 June 1967. Sent to Major General Erwin C. Hostetler," NACCD/E21, LBJ, 2; Memo to Charles Nelson from Ira Simmons, 1; and Cincinnati Division of Police, "Report of the Riot in Cincinnati," 17.

24. Cincinnati Division of Police, "Report of the Riot in Cincinnati," 37.

25. "City Acts to Avert New Violence; 24 Avondale Stores Damaged," *Cincinnati Post & Times-Star*, June 13, 1967; and "Summary Report, National Guard Assistance to Civil Authorities in Riot Activities, Cincinnati, OH, 13–18 June 1967, Sent to Major General Erwin C. Hostetler on June 19, 1967," NACCD/E21, LBJ, 2.

26. "FBI Weekly Report—Cincinnati June 23, 1967," NACCD/E21, LBJ, 1; "Memorandum to Major General Erwin C. Hostetler from Clyde E. Gutzwiller on Summary

Report, National Guard Assistance to Civil Authorities in Riot Activities, Cincinnati, OH, 13–18 June 1967," June 19, 1967, 361; and "Final Report Civil Disturbances Cincinnati, OH, 12–18 June 1967 [to Major General Erwin C. Hostetler from Clyde E. Gutzwiller], 1 August 1967," both in box 50, Series 1654, Ohio State Archives, Columbus.

27. "Negroes' Anger Spills Forth in Council Hearing," *Cincinnati Enquirer*, June 14, 1967.

28. Report to Community Action Commission of the Cincinnati Area, Subject: Civil Disorders, from Victory Neighborhood Service, undated, 6, box 7, Series 2: Exhibits to Hearings, August 1–November 10, 1967, folder Exhibit 94, NACCD, LBJ.

29. Cincinnati Division of Police, "Report of the Riot in Cincinnati," 76.

30. FBI Weekly Report—Cincinnati, June 23, 1967, 1, box E21, Series 4: Office of Investigation City Files, folder Cincinnati FBI Reports, NACCD, LBJ.

31. Reconnaissance Survey—Milwaukee, undated, 37, box 51, Series 10: Field Research Reports and Field Interview Folders, folder Milwaukee—Arrest Data to Milwaukee Reconnaissance Survey—Field Research Report, folder Milwaukee Reconnaissance Survey—Field Research Report, NACCD, LBJ.

32. Tejumola Ologboni (folklorist, Milwaukee, WI), interview by author, August 19, 2014.

33. Maier, *Mayor Who Made Milwaukee Famous*, 65.

34. Ologboni, interview; Mutope Johnson (visual artist, Milwaukee, WI), interview by author, August 19, 2014; and Charles Robinson (lawyer, Milwaukee, WI), interview by author, August 20, 2014.

35. Maier, *Mayor Who Made Milwaukee Famous*, 89.

36. James Mimms (bus driver, Cincinnati, OH), interview by author, June 18, 2013.

37. "Riot in Millvale Reaches Threshold of West Hills Area," *Western Hills Press* (Cincinnati), June 15, 1967.

38. Fogelson, *Violence as Protest*, xv.

39. Marvin McClarty (retired police officer, Omaha, NE), interview by author, November 15, 2005.

40. Ologboni, interview.

41. Monti, "Collective Violence in Urban America," 86–88; and Berk, "Role of Ghetto Merchants," 55–56.

42. Rudy Smith (photographer, Omaha, NE), interview by author, July 2013.

43. Central Themes for Cincinnati, undated, 6, box E43, Series 10: Field Research Reports and Field Interview Folders, folder Cincinnati—Central Themes for Cincinnati, LBJ; and Memo to Charles Nelson from Ira Simmons, November 9, 1967, 1–2. FBI Weekly Report—Cincinnati, June 16, 1967, 1, box E21, Series 4: Office of Investigation City Files, folder Cincinnati FBI Reports, NACCD, LBJ.

44. Ologboni, interview.

45. William Haynes (optician, Omaha, NE), interview by author, July 26, 2013.

46. "City Acts to Avert New Violence."

47. Fogelson, *Violence as Protest*, 12.

48. McLaughlin, *Long Hot Summer*, 99.

49. "No Room for Omaha Riots NAACP Chief Declares," *Omaha World-Herald*, August 28, 1965.

50. Prior to becoming mayor, A. V. Sorensen helped build the Gene Eppley Boys' Club in North Omaha in 1962 with a personal donation of $25,000. Many Black citizens felt the establishment of the organization on the Near North Side was merely a campaign ploy. Sorensen responded that those comments hurt him deeply and that he could have been elected without the Black vote. Proving his devotion to the Boys' Club, Sorensen donated his mayoral salary of $17,500 to the Near North Side organization during his mayoral tenure from 1965 to 1969. As a testament to the importance of this organization, the Omaha Boys' Club was never damaged throughout the disturbances. Dalstrom, *A. V. Sorensen*, 119–27.

51. Ernest W. Chambers (barber, activist, and former state senator, Omaha, NE), interview by author, February 28, 2006.

52. McLaughlin, *Long, Hot Summer*, 159–60.

53. "Announce 5 New Summertime Youth Projects," *Omaha Star*, July 22, 1966; "City Opening New Teenage Center on the North Side," *Omaha World-Herald*, July 9, 1966; and "Basketball Clinics Start Monday," *Omaha Star*, July 15, 1966.

54. Dalstrom, *A. V. Sorensen*, 210; Woodson Howe, "21 at Initial Hearing on Near North Side," *Omaha World-Herald*, July 19, 1966; and "Mayor D_____ling of Riots."

55. "Announce 5 New Summertime Youth Projects"; and "Recreation Is Forgotten," *Omaha World-Herald*, July 27, 1966.

56. Dalstrom, *A. V. Sorensen*, 206; "City Must Keep Commitment, Says Cornelius," *Omaha Star*, July 8, 1966; "July 4 Disturbances Leaders Sum It Up," *North Omaha Sun*, July 14, 1966; and "City Signs 200 Negro Applicants," *Omaha World-Herald*, July 8, 1966.

57. "Job Corps Center to Expand"; Larsen and Cottrell, *Gate City*, 255, 274; and "More Apps. Than Placement Orders."

58. Staff Paper No. 7, November 13, 1967, 46–47.

59. "Negroes Give Council List of Demands," *Cincinnati Post & Times-Star*, June 13, 1967.

60. Cincinnati Division of Police, "Report of the Riot in Cincinnati," 42–43; "Community Leaders Invited to Meeting," *Cincinnati Post & Times-Star*, June 14, 1967 (quote); and FBI Weekly Report—Cincinnati, June 16, 1967, 2.

61. Interview with Dr. Bruce Green by Diane Phillips, November 1, 1967, 5, box E43, Series 10: Field Research Reports and Field Interview Folders, folder Cincinnati—Team Interview Report, NACCD, LBJ; and Staff Paper No. 7, November 13, 1967, 46 (quotes).

62. Cincinnati Division of Police, "Report of the Riot in Cincinnati," attachment no. 16.

63. Cincinnati Division of Police, "Report of the Riot in Cincinnati," attachment no. 30, 1–2.

64. Cincinnati Division of Police, "Report of the Riot in Cincinnati," attachment no. 30, 1–2 (emphasis in original).

65. Cincinnati Division of Police, "Report of the Riot in Cincinnati," attachment no. 26, 168.

66. Cincinnati Division of Police, "Report of the Riot in Cincinnati," attachment no. 30.

67. Common View Demands with Mayor's Response, undated, Exhibit 7, box E51, Series 10: Field Research Reports and Field Interview Folders, folder Milwaukee Reconnaissance Survey—Field Research Report (draft), NACCD/E51, LBJ.

68. Common View Demands with Mayor's Response.

69. Memo to staff from Henry B. Taliaferro, subject: "Milwaukee Trip: Monday & Tuesday, 28, 29 August 1967," September 26, 1967, 9, box E24, Series 4: Office of Investigation City Files, Jackson—General to New Brunswick—Newspaper Clippings, folder Milwaukee—General, NACCD, LBJ.

70. Milwaukee, Wisconsin Team Interview Report by Bernard Dobranski, undated, box E51, Series 10: Field Research Reports and Field Interview Folders, folder Milwaukee—Arrest Data to Milwaukee Reconnaissance Survey—Field Research Report, folder Milwaukee—Team Interview Reports, NACCD, LBJ.

71. Maier, *Mayor Who Made Milwaukee Famous*, 73.

72. Maier, *Mayor Who Made Milwaukee Famous*, 74.

73. "60 Inner City Residents, Maier Meet," *Milwaukee Sentinel*, August 5, 1967.

74. Maier, *Mayor Who Made Milwaukee Famous*, 74, 82–83, 87.

75. Maier, *Mayor Who Made Milwaukee Famous*, 79.

76. WTMJ-TV News Film Archive, August 4, 1967, Wisconsin Historical Society, UWML.

77. Memorandum from Police Sergeant Robert G. Johnson, Subj: confidential intelligence in Final Report Civil Disturbances Cincinnati, OH, by Clyde E. Gutzwiller, August 1, 1967," 1–5, box 50, Series 1654: Adjutant General Ohio National Guard After Action Reports 1965–1974, folder 1966 1–1: ONG-Troop Call Outs (Chart of Actions), 1965–73, Ohio State Archives, Columbus.

78. Marian Spencer (activist, former city council member, Cincinnati, OH), interview by author, June 18, 2013.

79. "Police Arrest," *Omaha World-Herald*, July 5, 1966.

80. Chapter II/I Pattern of Violence and Damage, undated, 16, box E37, RG 282, Series 8: Material Pulled from Commission Files, folder Chapter II Supplementary Working Materials: Cities in Which Racial Disorders Have Occurred This Year, vol. 2, NACCD, LBJ.

81. Field Community Tension Data Report—Cincinnati, Ohio, June 30, 1967, 1–2, box E21, Series 4: Office of Investigation City Files, folder Cincinnati Miscellaneous Reports, NACCD, LBJ; and Gene Roberts, "Cincinnati Riots Spread to Prison," *New York Times*, June 16, 1967.

82. Maier, *Mayor Who Made Milwaukee Famous*, 70.

83. "Police Arrest 78 Adults, 44 Juveniles on North Side"; and Arrests Made During Riot—Cincinnati, June 28, 1967, 5, box E37, Series 8: Material Pulled From Commission Files, Chapter II Supplemental Working Arrest Records to Supplemental Working the Background [sic] of Disorder, folder Chapter II Supplementary Working Materials: The Riot Participant: Arrest Records Working File, NACCD, LBJ.

84. Conviction Count—Milwaukee, undated, 1, box E2, Series 1: Office of Investigation General Subject Files, folder Interim Report—Office of Investigations—Reports of Investigators [Cities] New Haven, Milwaukee, Los Angeles, NACCD, LBJ.

85. WTMJ-TV News, July 31, 1967, Film Archive, Wisconsin Historical Society, UWML.

86. Cincinnati Division of Police, "Report of the Riot in Cincinnati," 153.

87. Cincinnati Division of Police, "Report of the Riot in Cincinnati," 155.

88. Felker-Kantor, *Policing Los Angeles*, 20.

89. Larsen and Contrell, *Gate City*, 273.

90. Untitled Recount of Riots, July 13, 1967, 2–3, box 7, Mss 901, Robert L. Black Jr. Collection, folder 10, CHRC Meetings 1967, CHS.

91. Felker-Kantor, *Policing Los Angeles*, 26.

92. Neel, interview.

93. Johnson, interview.

94. Rosalind Baker (former Schuster's model, Milwaukee, WI), interview by author, August 20, 2014.

95. McLaughlin, *Long, Hot Summer*, 115.

96. Felker-Kantor, *Policing Los Angeles*, 30; and Horne, *Fire This Time*, 64.

CHAPTER 4

1. Gene Roberts, "Cincinnati Riots Led to Isolation," *New York Times*, June 18, 1967.

2. Kocolowski, "History of North Avondale," 260.

3. Pauline E. (homemaker, Cincinnati, OH), interview by author, June 2013.

4. White, *The Last Great Strike*; and Irons, *Testing the New Deal*.

5. Bloom, *Class, Race, and the Civil Rights Movement*; and Horne, *Fire This Time*.

6. Gilje, *Rioting in America*, 177; Leinwand, *Riots*, 106; and Lichtenstein, Strasser, and Rosenzweig, *Who Built America*, 112–13.

7. Arrests Made During Riot—Cincinnati, June 28, 1967, 5, box E37, Series 8: Material Pulled from Commission Files, Chapter II Supplemental Working Arrest Records to Supplemental Working the Backgroung [sic] of Disorder, folder Chapter II Supplementary Working Materials: The Riot Participant: Arrest Records Working File, NACCD, LBJ.

8. Margaret Josten, "Did Outsiders Set 'Hour of Agony' Fires?," *Cincinnati Enquirer*, June 14, 1967.

9. Milwaukee Mayor Maier's remarks to the service station awards luncheon of the beautification committee, 12 noon, the Miller Inn, 4000 W. State St. Monday, August 7, 1967, 1, box 148, Milwaukee Series 44: Maier, folder 4, Press Releases and Statements, July–August, 1967, UWML.

10. Mead, *Beyond Entitlement*, 22; and Auletta, *Underclass*, xvi. William Julius Wilson defined underclass as "a massive population at the very bottom of the social ladder plagued by poor education and low-paying jobs." Wilson, *Declining Significance of Race*, ix. Michael Zweig's definition of the underclass as "ruined workers, pushed out of the economy or to its lower reaches" strays from these notions of pathology and is particularly poignant in the context of the Midwest's declining economy. Zweig, *Working-Class Majority*, 91.

11. Flaming, *Who "Riots" and Why?*, ix, 15.

12. 1967 Summer Employment Survey by West End Special Service Project of Hills Neighborhood Houses, Inc., undated, 6, box 12, Mss 901, Robert L. Black Jr. Collection, folder 5 CHRC Task Force on Full Employment 1967, CHS.

13. Flaming, *Who "Riots" and Why?*, 28.

14. Draft copy of Statement of Job Opportunities, June 29, 1967, 1, box 7, Mss 901, Robert L. Black Jr. Collection, folder 10: CHRC Meetings 1967, CHS, 7.

15. Tilly, "Collective Violence," 10; Kerner Commission, 73; Hobsbawm, *Social Bandits*, 110; and Confidential Document Outlining the City of Cincinnati to the President's

Commission on Civil Disorder, October 12, 1967, in DC, 16, box 10, Mss 901, Robert L. Black Jr. Collection, folder 5 CHRC Rebellion Riots 1967, CHS.

16. Text of Speech Presented by Floyd B. McKissick—National Director to the National Conference on Black Power, July 21, 1967, 2, box E3, Series 1: Office of Investigation General Subject Files, folder Liaison FBI Miscellaneous Reports [1964–1967], NACCD, LBJ.

17. Preliminary Draft by Jason I. Newman on Consumer Protection for Low-Income Groups, November 13, 1967, from Statement of OEO before Consumer Subcommittee of House Govt Operations Committee, October 12, 1967, 1, box 1, Series 7: Commission Research Studies, folder Consumer Protection for Low Income Groups, NACCD, LBJ.

18. Berk, "Role of Ghetto Merchants," 48, 53–56, 190.

19. In Cincinnati, Berk and his team of researchers conducted interviews along major commercial throughfares including Reading Road, Burnet Avenue, and Forest Avenue. In Milwaukee, the interviews were conducted along North Third Street and Teutonia Avenue. Berk, "Role of Ghetto Merchants," 48, 190.

20. Berk, "Role of Ghetto Merchants," 179–80, 183; and Peggy A. Murrell, "Rioter Glibly Explains Hatred," *Milwaukee Journal*, August 8, 1967 (quotes).

21. Marjorie Parham (newspaper publisher, Cincinnati, OH), interview by author, June 2013.

22. Geenen, *Schuster's & Gimbels*, 83.

23. Although Price Hill was a suburb of the city, because Cincinnati officers were occupied with the ongoing insurrection, the suburban police responded to the call in the adjacent neighborhood of South Cumminsville. "Riot in Millvale Reaches Threshold of West Hills Area," *Western Hills Press* (Cincinnati), June 15, 1967.

24. Fairbanks, "Cincinnati Blacks and the Irony of Low-Income Housing Reform."

25. Cincinnati Division of Police, "A Report of the Riot in Cincinnati, Ohio; The Week of June 11, 1967," undated, 134, box E73, Series: Investigations Cincinnati—Depositions to Elizabeth—Newspapers Clippings, folder Cincinnati: Riot, NACCD, LBJ.

26. Robert Hoig, "Firemen Bitter: 'Near North Considers Us White Trash,'" *Omaha World-Herald*, June 27, 1969.

27. "Vel Phillips Unable to Quiet Rioters," *Milwaukee Sentinel*, August 1, 1967; Justice Department Weekly Summary—Milwaukee, August 4, 1967, 1, box E33, Series 6: Federal Bureau of Investigation City Reports, folder NACCD-Milwaukee, Wisconsin, NACCD/E33, LBJ; Memo to Director from SAIC Barton—Milwaukee Subj Civil Disturbance—Milwaukee, August 9, 1967, 2, box E24, Series 4: Office of Investigation City Files, Jackson—General to New Brunswick—Newspaper Clippings, folder Milwaukee-Miscellaneous Reports, NACCD, LBJ; and Disturbance in Vicinity of North Third Street, Milwaukee WI, August 1, 1967, 4–5, box E24, Series 4: Office of Investigation City Files, Jackson—General to New Brunswick—Newspaper Clippings, NACCD, LBJ.

28. Pauline E., interview.

29. "City Acts to Avert New Violence; 24 Avondale Stores Damaged," *Cincinnati Post & Times-Star*, June 13, 1967; and "Police, Firemen among Casualties in Rioting," *Cincinnati Post & Times-Star*, June 14, 1967.

30. Parham, interview.

31. McAdam, *Political Process*, 48. See also Hobsbawm, *Social Bandits*, 110–13.

32. 1967 Race Riots Aftermath video, 19:09 MI-96-118 WLWT News Footage, CHS.

33. Draft—Staff Paper No. 7, "Analysis of Cincinnati Disturbance," November 13, 1967, 60, box E67, Series 12: Staff Papers from Office of Assistant Deputy Director, folder Staff Paper No. 7 Cincinnati: Analysis of Cincinnati Disturbance, NACCD, LBJ. See also "Black Middle Class," *Chicago Defender*, August 20, 1966.

34. "Fourteen Ministers Issue Appeal," *Omaha World-Herald*, July 5, 1966.

35. Text of Floyd McKissick speech, July 21, 1967, 1, box E3, Series 1: Office of Investigation General Subject Files, folder Liaison FBI Miscellaneous Reports [1964–1967], NACCD, LBJ.

36. King, "Ghetto Riots and the Employment of Blacks," 136.

37. *Glorifying the Lion*, MI-95-44, WLWT News Footage, CHS.

38. "Those Waiting in the Wings Came," *Omaha Star*, July 8, 1966.

39. Marian Spencer (activist, former city council member, Cincinnati, OH), interview by author, June 18, 2013.

40. Letter to William Wichman from Robert Black, June 13, 1967, 1, box 10, Mss 901, Robert L. Black Jr. Collection, folder 5, CHRC Rebellion—Riots 1967, CHS.

41. Weber, *Summer Mockery*, 19–20.

42. Second Trip Cincinnati—Team Interview Report, undated, 83, box E43, Series 10: Field Research Reports and Field Interview Folders, folder Cincinnati—Team Interview Report—2d Trip, NACCD, LBJ.

43. "Vel Phillips Unable to Quiet Rioters," *Milwaukee Sentinel*, August 1, 1967.

44. Interview with Dr. Bruce Green by Diane Phillips, November 1, 1967, 8 box E43, Series 10: Field Research Reports and Field Interview Folders, folder Cincinnati—Team Interview Report, NACCD, LBJ.

45. "Staff Paper No. 7," November 13, 1967, 79.

46. Central Themes for Cincinnati, undated, 12, box E43, Series 10: Field Research Reports and Field Interview Folders, folder Cincinnati—Central Themes for Cincinnati, NACCD, LBJ.

47. Peter Murrell Sr. (dentist and activist, Milwaukee, WI), interview by author, August 21, 2014.

48. Document, July 31, 1967, box 148, Milwaukee Series 44: Maier, folder 4, Press Releases and Statements, July–August 1967, UWML.

49. Staff Paper No. 7, November 13, 1967, 79.

50. *Glorifying the Lion*, MI-95-44, CHS.

51. "Announce 5 New Summertime Youth Projects," *Omaha Star*, July 22, 1966.

52. Memorandum RE: Racial Disturbance, Cincinnati, Ohio, June 1967, July 21, 1967, 9, box E32, Series 6: Federal Bureau of Investigation City Reports, folder NACCD—Cincinnati, OH, NACCD, LBJ; and Letter from Bailey W. Turner to Friends, June 22, 1967, 1 box, 51, Mss 917, Maurice McCrackin Manuscript Collection, folder 8, Black Community Cincinnati, CHS.

53. "Vivian Strong Memorial Fund Started," *Omaha Star*, July 3, 1969.

54. Ochonicky, *American Midwest in Film and Literature*, 125.

55. Flaming, *Who "Riots" and Why?*, 28, 39, 56.

56. Staff Paper No. 7, November 13, 1967, 77.

57. Ochonicky, *American Midwest in Film and Literature*, 146.

58. Hill and Fogelson, "Study of Arrest Patterns," 43–45.

59. Hill and Fogelson, "Study of Arrest Patterns," 68–69.

60. Memo to staff from Henry B. Taliaferro, subject: "Milwaukee Trip: Monday & Tuesday, 28, 29 August 1967," September 26, 1967, 8, box E24, Series 4: Office of Investigation City Files, Jackson—General to New Brunswick—Newspaper Clippings, folder Milwaukee—General, NACCD, LBJ.

61. White women in this era were by no means apolitical bystanders. Weaponizing both their gender and racial identities, white women employed symbolic motherhood and family in service of racial exclusion. Tom Sugrue wrote that campaigns for open housing in Detroit—specifically, African Americans moving into predominately white neighborhoods—were construed as "a threat to virtuous womanhood, innocent childhood, and the sanctity of the home." Sugrue, "Crabgrass-Roots Politics," 562; see also McRae, *Mothers of Massive Resistance*.

62. Jack McCaslin (activist, Omaha, NE), interview by author, December 5, 2005.

63. Report to Community Action Commission of the Cincinnati Area (CAC) by Legal Aid Society, received October 11, 1967, 16, box 7, RG 282, Series 2: Exhibits to Hearings, August 1–November 10, 1967, folder Exhibit 94, NACCD, LBJ.

64. "Graph of Number of Offenses—Milwaukee Urban League," box E37, Series 8: Material Pulled from Commission Files, Chapter II Supplemental Working Arrest Records to Supplemental Working the Background [sic] of Disorder, folder Chapter II Supplementary Working Materials: The Riot Participant: Arrest Records Working File, LBJ.

65. Interview with Clint Reynolds, in Team Interview Report, November 6, 1967, box E43, Series 10: Field Research Reports and Field Interview Folders, folder Cincinnati—Team Interview Report, NACCD, LBJ.

66. Flaming interview notes, undated, box 22, Milwaukee Mss Ez, Milwaukee, folder 26, Department of Research, "Who Riots and Why?"—Correspondence and Research Materials, 1967–April 1968, University of Wisconsin–Milwaukee Archive, Milwaukee.

67. David Davis (technician, Cincinnati, OH), interview by author, June 20, 2013.

68. "Gun Dealers Report Sales on Increase," *Omaha World-Herald*, March 8, 1968.

69. Eldred A. quoted in Flaming interview notes. See also "Sales of Firearms Curtailed Swiftly," *Milwaukee Sentinel*, August 1, 1967; "Gun Dealers Report Sales on Increase," *Omaha World-Herald*, March 8, 1968; "Dangerous Folly," *Omaha World-Herald*, March 18, 1968.

70. Flaming, *Who "Riots" and Why?*, viii.

71. Staff Paper No. 7, November 13, 1967, 92; and Community Action Commission Report from Memorial Community Center, June 19, 1967, 4, box 7, Series 2: Exhibits to Hearings, August 1–November 10, 1967, box 1–7, folder Exhibit 94, LBJ.

72. Omaha Emergency Call Transcripts, 13. Author received emergency call transcript photocopies from the 1969 uprising from Donald Nichol (retired firefighter) in October 2005.

73. Omaha Emergency Call Transcripts, 17.

74. Sugrue, "Crabgrass-Politics," 552.

75. Memo from Bert, February 2, 1968, box 3, Milwaukee Series 44: Maier, folder 21, Anonymous and Kook Letters, UWML.

76. Memorandum to David Ginsburg from M. C. Miskovsky, Subject: Final Report of the Office of Investigations, March 25, 1968, 12, box E1, Series 1: Office of Investigation General Subject Files, folder Interim Report Office of Investigations Final Report, NACCD, LBJ (all caps in original).

77. Memorandum to David Ginsburg from M. C. Miskovsky, Subject: Final Report of the Office of Investigations, March 25, 1968, 60, box E1, Series 1: Office of Investigation General Subject Files, folder Interim Report Office of Investigations Final Report, NACCD, LBJ.

78. Central Themes for Cincinnati, undated, 12, box E43, Series 10: Field Research Reports and Field Interview Folders, folder Cincinnati—Central Themes for Cincinnati, NACCD, LBJ.

79. Memorandum to M. C. Miskovsky from N. C. Rayford and H. L. Perry, Subject: Organizations in the Negro Community Before, During, and After the Riot—Milwaukee, January 2, 1968, 3, box E2, Series 1: Office of Investigation General Subject Files, folder Interim Report—Office of Investigations—Reports of Investigators [Cities] New Haven, Milwaukee, Los Angeles, NACCD, LBJ; and Memorandum to David Ginsburg from M. C. Miskovsky, Subject: Final Report of the Office of Investigations, March 25, 1968, 84, Attachment Report of the Office of Investigations, box E1, Series 1: Office of Investigation General Subject Files, folder Interim Report Office of Investigations Final Report, NACCD, LBJ. Franklin, *Young Crusaders*, 41.

80. Draft Memorandum to James Madison from Sam Dennis, Subject Milwaukee, Wisc. Addendum Report, Activity Report for Milwaukee, August 30, 1967, 2, box E33, Series 6: Federal Bureau of Investigation City Reports, folder NACCD—Milwaukee, Wisconsin, LBJ; Memorandum to George L. Roberts from Sam Dennis, Subject September 13, Field Day Activity Report for Milwaukee, Wisconsin, September 14, 1967, 1, box E33, Series 6: Federal Bureau of Investigation City Reports, folder NACCD—Milwaukee, Wisconsin, LBJ; Memorandum to James A. Madison from Sam Dennis ATTN: Larry Hoffheimer Subject Field Day Activity Report—Milwaukee, Wisconsin—August 31, 1967, 1, box E33, Series 6: Federal Bureau of Investigation City Reports, folder NACCD—Milwaukee, Wisconsin, LBJ; FBI Memorandum from J. Edgar Hoover to Mr. Milan Miskovsky, Subject: Selected Racial Developments and Disturbances, December 14, 1967, box E1, Series 1: Office of Investigation General Subject Files, folder High Schools—FBI Reports, LBJ; and "Aftermath," undated, box 3, Series 42: Supplemental Working Material To Chapter II of Report, folder The Aftermath of Disorder, LBJ.

81. Milwaukee, Wisconsin Team Interview Reports, undated, box E51, Series 10: Field Research Reports and Field Interview Folders, folder Milwaukee—Arrest Data to Milwaukee Reconnaissance Survey—Field Research Report, NACCD, LBJ.

CHAPTER 5

1. "Contradictory Line Marks Loder Case," *Omaha World-Herald*, November 11, 1969.

2. Edward Poindexter had tried to recruit Peak for years, but he refused until his "breaking point." Frank Peak, interview by Alonzo N. Smith, February 27, 1982, Nebraska Black Oral History Project, Nebraska Historical Society, Lincoln. See also "Negro Girl Killed by a Police Bullet at Housing Project," *Omaha World-Herald*, June 25, 1969; and "Buildings Are Burned as Violence Erupts," *Omaha World-Herald*, June 29, 1969. An after-action report filed by the National Guard stated that 3,000 people gathered near the scene of Vivian's death and listened to two hours of speeches. "After Action Report (AAR)-#7/69," August 12, 1969, 93, box 104, Governor Norbert Tiemann, folder

Adjutant General 1970, Nebraska Historical Society, Lincoln; "Ten Blocks on No. 24th Hit Hardest," *Omaha World-Herald*, June 26, 1969; and "North Side Violence Continues a 3rd Night," *Omaha World-Herald*, June 27, 1969.

3. Lorber, "Social Construction of Gender," 114, 117; and Johnson, "Gender, Race, and Rumors," 252.

4. Moynihan, *Negro Family*, 29; President's Commission on the Status of Women, *Report on Four Consultations*.

5. Moynihan, *Negro Family*, 30. See also Thomas J. Foley, "Racial Unrest Tied to Negro Family Failure," *Los Angeles Times*, August 14, 1965; and Rowland Evans and Robert Novak, "See page of the Moynihan Report," *Los Angeles Times*, August 19, 1965.

6. President's Commission on the Status of Women, *Report on Four Consultations*, 30–31, 37. Although most of the report dealt with poor Black women, most of the board was made up of middle-class Black women, including Cenoria D. Johnson of the National Urban League; Maude Gadsen of the Beauty Owners Association, Gerri Major of Johnson Publications, and Inabel Lindsay of Howard University. "Riot Here Loses Some of Its Force, Credit Goes to Ohio Guardsmen," *Cincinnati Post & Times-Star*, June 15, 1967.

7. President's Commission on the Status of Women, *Report on Four Consultations*, 30, 35.

8. I employ as a starting point scholar Anthony Lemelle's broad definition of masculinity as a set of "socially constructed characteristics that society expects for the male sex." Lemelle, *Black Masculinity and Sexual Politics*, 3 (quote), 7–8, 32–33. Historian Steve Estes describes this "masculinism" as "the notion that men are more powerful than women, that they should have control over their own lives and authority over others." Estes, *I Am a Man!*, 7.

9. Young, quoted in Moynihan, *Negro Family*, 34.

10. Hacker, quoted in Horne, *Fire This Time*, 38.

11. Daniel M. Goodwin, Typewritten report presented to the Police Community Relations Office in North Omaha, February 28, 1969, author obtained a copy from Mr. Goodwin in November 2005.

12. Clipping from *Omaha World-Herald*, September 14, 1967, 1–2, box 5, Series 2: Exhibits to Hearings, August 1–November 10, 1967, folder Exhibit 56, NACCD, LBJ.

13. Justice Department Cincinnati Weekly Summary, July 15, 1966, 1, box E32, Series 6: Federal Bureau of Investigation City Reports, folder NACCD—Cincinnati, OH, LBJ.

14. Community Action Commission Report from Memorial Community Center, June 19, 1967, 4, box 7, Series 2: Exhibits to Hearings, August 1–November 10, 1967, box 1–7, folder Exhibit 94, LBJ.

15. Giddings, *When and Where I Enter*, 315.

16. Historian Lance Hill argues that many working-class Blacks felt that "the nonviolent movement did not rest on male supremacy, physical power, and aggression . . . [reflecting] a growing disillusionment of working-class blacks with the pacifistic, legalistic, and legislative strategies proffered by national organizations." Hill, *Deacons for Defense*, 3, 28.

17. Horne, *Fire This Time*, 207, 185.

18. "Riot Averted: Police Begin Probe of 'Cop' Dogs Biting," *Cincinnati Enquirer*, May 15, 1962.

19. Mississippi Comes to Cincinnati, Join the NAACP Today (flyer), undated, box 5, Mss 774, NAACP, CHS; and Police Dog Incident 1962 testimony, May 13, 1963, 1, box 5, Mss 774, NAACP, CHS.

20. "Guard Sent to Cincinnati after 2 Die," *New York Times*, April 9, 1968.

21. Many members of the Milwaukee chapter of the NAACP insist that the Milwaukee Police Department burned their headquarters down during the uprising. Memorandum to David Ginsburg from M. C. Miskovsky, Subject: Final Report of the Office of Investigations, March 25, 1968, 83, box E1, Series 1: Office of Investigation General Subject Files, folder Interim Report Office of Investigations Final Report, NACCD, LBJ; and "Panthers Defend Black Business," *Omaha World-Herald*, June 26, 1969.

22. Rudy Smith (photographer, Omaha, NE), interview by author, July 2013.

23. Cincinnati Arrest Record (M42110) June 14, 1967, box E43, Series 10: Field Research Reports and Field Interview Folders, folder Cincinnati—Arrest Record, NACCD, LBJ.

24. Carol Brown (retired nurse, Cincinnati, OH), interview by author, June 20, 2013.

25. Ronald Hudson (retired US Navy, Omaha, NE), interview by author July 22, 2013.

26. Report to CAC from Victory Neighborhood Service Agency, undated, 9–10; Cincinnati Arrest Records, June 14–18, 1967, both in box 7, Series 2: Exhibits to Hearings, August 1–November 10, 1967, folder Exhibit 94, NACCD, LBJ; and Deborah DuBose (retiree, Cincinnati, OH), interview by author, June 20, 2013.

27. Damage done by city, undated, 2, box 1, Series 42: Supplemental Working Material to Chapter II of Report, Subgroup: Office of Director of Field Operations, "Introductions and Outline"—"The Riot Participants," folder Chapter II, Background I, The Pattern of Violence and Damage, NACCD, LBJ.

28. James Mimms (bus driver, Cincinnati, OH), interview by author, June 18, 2013.

29. Cincinnati Division of Police, "A Report of the Riot in Cincinnati, Ohio; The Week of June 11, 1967," undated, attachment no. 16, box E73, Series: Investigations Cincinnati—Depositions to Elizabeth—Newspapers Clippings, folder Cincinnati: Riot, NACCD, LBJ.

30. Greenberg, *Or Does It Explode?*, 211; "Angry Crowd Gathers After Fatal Crash," *Chicago Tribune*, August 13, 1965; Horne, *Fire This Time*, 54–55; "Negro Girl Killed by a Police Bullet at Housing Project," *Omaha World-Herald*, July 25, 1969; and Ron Grossman, "The Gin Bottle Race Riot," *Chicago Tribune*, November 25, 2014. For additional examples of race riots with women victims as catalysts, see Stevenson, *Contested Murder of Latasha Harlins*, 290–95.

31. Daniel Goodwin (barber and activist, Omaha, NE), interview by author, November 30, 2005.

32. Della Wells (artist, Milwaukee, WI), interview by author, August 15, 2014.

33. Goodwin, interview.

34. Pauline E. (homemaker, Cincinnati, OH), interview by author, June 2013.

35. Betsy Neel (retired nurse, Cincinnati, OH), interview by author, June 21, 2013.

36. Sugrue, "Crabgrass-Roots Politics," 562.

37. Flaming interview notes, undated, box 22, Milwaukee Mss Ez, Milwaukee, folder 26, Department of Research, "Who Riots and Why?"—Correspondence and Research Materials, 1967–April 1968, University of Wisconsin–Milwaukee Archive, Milwaukee.

38. Gary Allen, "The Plan to Burn Los Angeles," *American Opinion*, May 1966, in Gene Blake, "Watts Riot as Rehearsal for Red Coup Discounted," *Los Angeles Times*, April 28, 1967.

39. Has The Riot Opened Your Eyes? (flyer), undated, 1, box E14, Series 3: Office of Investigation Organizational Files, Black Nationalist Movement—FBI Reports, file no. 3 to Breakthrough—Miscellaneous, folder Breakthrough—Miscellaneous, NACCD, LBJ.

40. Memorandum to David Ginsburg from M. C. Miskovsky, Subject: Final Report of the Office of Investigations, March 25, 1968, 12.

41. Widick, *Detroit*, 189; and Fine, *Violence in the Model City*, 383.

42. Fine, *Violence in the Model City*, 384.

43. Kotz, Hair, and Scales, "Firearms, Violence and Civil Disorders."

44. Neel, interview.

45. Brenda Middlebrook (homemaker, Cincinnati, OH), interview by author, June 21, 2013.

46. Neel, interview.

47. Mimms, interview.

48. Mimms, interview.

49. Mimms, interview; Neel, interview; and Brown, interview.

50. Cincinnati Division of Police, "Report of the Riot in Cincinnati," 52–54, 56, 65, 69, 72.

51. David Davis (technician, Cincinnati, OH), interview by author, June 20, 2013.

52. Pauline E., interview.

53. Flyer in Memorandum to David Ginsburg from M. C. Miskovsky Subject: Final Report of the Office of Investigations, March 25, 1968, box E1, Series 1: Office of Investigation General Subject Files, folder Interim Report Office of Investigations Final Report, NACCD, LBJ; and "Attachment Report of the office of investigations," 15, NACCD/E1, LBJ (emphasis in original).

54. Gregory, "The Gregory Report on Civil Disorders," 68–76.

55. "Ohio Guardsmen Called in as Race Riot Flares Anew," *Cincinnati Enquirer*, June 14, 1967.

56. Flaming, *Who "Riots" and Why?*, 39.

57. Bentley-Edwards et al., "How Does It Feel to Be a Problem?," 34.

58. "Excerpts from a Study to Determine the Characteristics of Negro Rioters," *New York Times*, July 28, 1968; and Kerner Commission, 1, 74, 331.

59. Harris, *Sex Workers, Psychics, and Numbers Runners*, 2016. Crenshaw, "Demarginalizing the Intersection of Race and Sex"; Crenshaw, "Mapping the Margins"; Jones, *End to the Neglect*; Nadasen, *Welfare Warriors*, xvii; and Stevenson, *Contested Murder of Latasha Harlins*, xvi.

60. "Guard Sent to Cincinnati after 2 Die," *New York Times*, April 9, 1968; "Policeman Enters a Plea of Innocent in Shooting of Girl," *Omaha World-Herald*, June 26, 1969; Weber, *Summer Mockery*, 48; Interview with Dr. Bruce Green by Diane Phillips, November 1, 1967, in Team Interview Report, November 6, 1967, 5, box E43, Series 10: Field Research Reports and Field Interview Folders, folder Cincinnati—Team Interview Report, NACCD, LBJ; and Draft—Staff Paper No. 7, "Analysis of Cincinnati Disturbance," November 13, 1967, 46, box E67, Series 12: Staff Papers From Office of

Assistant Deputy Director, folder Staff Paper No. 7 Cincinnati: Analysis of Cincinnati Disturbance, NACCD, LBJ.

61. Cincinnati Arrest Records, June 14–18, 1967, box 7, Series 2: Exhibits to Hearings, August 1–November 10, 1967, folder Exhibit 94, NACCD, LBJ; "Final Report Civil Disturbances Cincinnati, OH, 12–18 June 1967 [to Major General Erwin C. Hostetler from Clyde E. Gutzwiller] 1 August 1967," box 50, Series 1654, Ohio State Archives, Columbus.

62. "Guard Sent to Cincinnati after 2 Die," *New York Times*, April 9, 1968. "Chambers Quiets Milling Pupils," *Omaha World-Herald*, March 9, 1968.

63. Sandra Dickinson (educator, Milwaukee, WI), interview by author, August 13, 2014.

64. DuBose, interview.

65. DuBose, interview.

66. Hunter, *To 'Joy My Freedom*, 60.

67. DuBose, interview.

68. Pauline E., interview.

69. Pauline E., interview.

70. Pauline E., interview.

71. Elaine Davis (former real estate employee, Cincinnati, OH), interview by author, June 20, 2013.

72. Weber, *Summer Mockery*, 53.

73. News Media Study: Special Preliminary Report of Finding for Selected Cities by Dr. Sol Chaneles, November 10, 1967, 5, box 1, Series 12: Office of Information Records: Commission Conference on Media at Poughkeepsie, NY, November 10–12, 1967, folder Commission on Civil Disorders: Complete Record of Materials at Poughkeepsie Conference, November 10–12, 1967, NACCD, LBJ.

74. Flaming interview notes.

75. Flaming interview notes.

76. Wells, interview.

77. "Job Corps Center to Expand," *Omaha Star*, July 8, 1966; Larsen and Cottrell, *Gate City*, 255; and Collins, *Black Feminist Thought*, 284–88.

CHAPTER 6

1. WTMJ-TV News Film Archive, July 31, 1967, tape no. 32, Wisconsin Historical Society, UWML.

2. Memo from Henry B. Taliaferro Jr. to Staff Re: Cincinnati Trip August 30, 1967, September 9, 1967, 3–4, box E21, Series 4: Office of Investigation City Files, Atlanta-General to Dayton-Miscellaneous Reports, folder Cincinnati-General, NACCD, LBJ.

3. Bloom, *Class, Race, and the Civil Rights Movement*, 200.

4. FBI Weekly Report—Cincinnati, June 23, 1967, 1, box E21, Series 4: Office of Investigation City Files, folder Cincinnati FBI Reports, NACCD, LBJ; "Pay for Riot Cost $40,000," *Omaha World-Herald*, July 3, 1969; Report prepared by George Giddings, District 1 Chief "B" Shift, photocopied and given to the author by Donald Nichols, historian for the Omaha Fire Department, October 2005; and Memo to Director from SAIC Barton—Milwaukee Subj Civil Disturbance—Milwaukee, August 9, 1967 2, box E24,

Series 4: Office of Investigation City Files, Jackson—General to New Brunswick—Newspaper Clippings, NACCD, LBJ.

5. "But Blazes, Unrest Seem Less Intense," *Omaha World-Herald*, June 29, 1969.

6. "City May Clean Up the Rubble," *Omaha World-Herald*, August 9, 1969. See also "But Blazes, Unrest Seem Less Intense," *Omaha World-Herald*, June 29, 1969; Affidavit Station WCPO/TV at 11 p.m. on June 19, 1967, box 3, Series 41: Simulmatics Mass Media Study Records Cincinnati—Cleveland, NACCD, LBJ; "17 of 20 Torch Targets White-Owned Business," *Omaha World-Herald*, June 29, 1969; "Owners of Looted Stores Not Sure They Will Re-Open," *Omaha World-Herald*, April 29, 1968; and *Omaha City Directory* (Kansas City, MO: R. L. Polk & Co., 1965), 75–77.

7. "Safeway's Fence Is Up; Gates Will Close Lot," *Omaha World-Herald*, July 24, 1968. In 1967 the city leased the lot from Safeway for $10 a year, allowing the police department to have jurisdiction over the lot to prevent the infringement on property rights. "2 Borrowed Copters Returned to Guard," *Omaha World-Herald*, July 9, 1968; "Mayor Says Store Fence Only Answer," *Omaha World-Herald*, July 22, 1968; and "We Demand Rights Now," *Dundee and West Omaha Sun*, March 3, 1966.

8. "Letter to Unknown Man from Cincinnati Youth Council NAACP (Herb Smith and Bruce Green) 11-28-67," Mss 774 NAACP, box 54, CHS, 2. See also "Disturbances Leaders Sum It Up," *North Omaha Sun*, July 14, 1966; and Milton D. Lewis, "Federal Summer Program Evaluation," undated, 2, box E35, Series 7: Material Received from Other Agencies Equal Employment Opportunity Commission to Justice, Department of Justice, NACCD, LBJ.

9. Niathan Allen, Field Community Tension Factors Report, Cincinnati, OH, July 24, 1967, 1 box E21, Series 4: Office of Investigation City Files, Atlanta—General to Dayton—Miscellaneous Reports, folder Cincinnati—Miscellaneous Reports LBJ.

10. "Memorandum to VP from Larry Countrymen Subj: Visit to Chicago August 21–23 and Milwaukee, Aug 21–25," 3, NACCD/E35, LBJ.

11. Cincinnati, August 25, 1967, FBI report, box E32, Series 6: Federal Bureau of Investigation City Reports, folder NACCD Cincinnati, OH, NACCD, LBJ.

12. Confidential Document Outlining the City of Cincinnati to the President's Commission on Civil Disorder, October 12, 1967, in DC, 18, box 10, Mss 901, Robert L. Black Jr. Collection, folder 5 CHRC Rebellion Riots 1967, CHS; "Cincinnati, FBI report follow-up," August 25, 1967, Memorandum RE: Racial Disturbance, Cincinnati, Ohio, June 1967, July 21, 1967, 10, box E32, Series 6: Federal Bureau of Investigation City Reports, folder NACCD—Cincinnati, OH, NACCD, LBJ; and Schottelkotte News Noon Report, July 26, 1967, box 3, Series 41: Simulmatics Mass Media Study Records Cincinnati—Cleveland, NACCD, LBJ.

13. "July 4 Disturbances Leaders Sum It Up," *North Omaha Sun*, July 14, 1966; "City Signs 200 Negro Applicants," *Omaha World-Herald*, July 8, 1966; Dalstrom, *A. V. Sorensen*, 211; Woodson Howe, "Rec. Groups Hears Needs," *Omaha World-Herald*, July 21, 1966; "Job Corps Center to Expand," *Omaha Star*, July 8, 1966; Larsen and Coltrell, *Gate City*, 255, 724; and "More Apps. Than Placement Orders," *Omaha Star*, July 15, 1966. Mayor A. V. Sorensen and Lt. Gov. Phillip C. Sorensen are of no relation.

14. Mr. Black's "Presentation of the Situation," Presented to the Board of Commissioners, June 22, 1967, box 7, Mss 901, Robert L. Black Jr. Collection, folder 10, CHRC Meetings 1967, CHS.

15. Mutope Johnson (visual artist, Milwaukee, WI), interview by author, August 19, 2014.

16. Status of CCY programs, undated, box 10, Mss 901, Robert L. Black Jr. Collection, folder 1 CHRC Program 1967, 1968, CHS; Confidential Document Outlining the City of Cincinnati to the President's Commission on Civil Disorder, 18; and Affidavit Station WCPO/TV at 6 p.m. on June 2, 1967, box 3, Series 41: Simulmatics Mass Media Study Records Cincinnati—Cleveland, NACCD, LBJ.

17. William Haynes (optician, Omaha, NE), interview by author, July 26, 2013.

18. Marvin McClarty (retired police officer, Omaha, NE), interview by author, November 15, 2005.

19. Confidential Document Outlining the City of Cincinnati to the President's Commission on Civil Disorder, 19; and Cincinnati Questionnaire, undated, box 1, Series 22, Subgroup: Office of Associate Director for Public Safety Series Riot Questionnaires, folder Cincinnati, NACCD, LBJ.

20. Response to Chairman of Community Relations Committee from Brier, undated, box 140, Milwaukee Series 44: Maier, folder 24, Police Department, Community Relations 1968, UWML.

21. 1970 City Council Budget Ledger, Municipal Records, City of Omaha, Located at the Douglas County Courthouse, 1819 Farnam Street; and Mick Road, "Adviser to Urge Deeper Training," *Dundee and West Omaha Sun*, July 2, 1969.

22. Daniel M. Goodwin, typewritten report presented to the Police Community Relations Office in North Omaha, February 28, 1969, author obtained a copy from Mr. Goodwin in November 2005; "Policeman Will Face Manslaughter Charge," *Omaha World-Herald*, June 26, 1969; and "Adviser to Urge Deeper Training," *Dundee and West Omaha Sun*, July 2, 1969.

23. Goodwin, typewritten report; "Policeman Will Face Manslaughter Charge," *Omaha World-Herald*, June 26, 1969; and "Adviser to Urge Deeper Training," *Dundee and West Omaha Sun*, July 2, 1969.

24. "Disorder Reported after Wallace Rally," *Omaha World-Herald*, March 5, 1968; "Window-Breaking Started Vandalism Near 24th, Lake," *Omaha World-Herald*, March 5, 1968; "Why Policeman Had Shotgun Explained," *Omaha World-Herald*, March 7, 1968; Jack McCaslin (activist, Omaha, NE), interview by author, December 5, 2005; "Fire Bombs Are Thrown, Six Arrested," *Omaha World-Herald*, March 6, 1968; Jack Todd, "Omaha, 1968—The Watched Pot Begins to Boil," *Daily Nebraskan* (Lincoln), reprinted in the *Omaha Star*, April 11, 1968; "Mayor Vows Laws to Rule, without Ifs," *Omaha World-Herald*, April 29, 1968; "Was Week-End Rebellion Triggered by 'Appropriate' Police Action?" *Omaha Star*, Clippings File, Douglas County Historical Society, Omaha, NE; "2 Say Police Used Excessive Force," *Omaha World-Herald*, April 30, 1968; "Police Weigh Handbill Case," *Omaha World-Herald*, April 24, 1968; and "Looters on N. 24th Cause Heavy Damage," *Omaha World-Herald*, April 28, 1968.

25. McLaughlin, *Long, Hot Summer*, 146.

26. Felker-Kantor, *Policing Los Angeles*, 20.

27. Aftermath in Milwaukee: Report of phone conversation with Sam Dennis, Community Relations Service, DOF, by Bruce Thomas, Friday, January 12, 1968, 2, box E37, Series 8: Material Pulled from Commission Files, folder Chapter II Supplementary Working Materials: Aftermath: Notes of Conversations with CRS Representatives,

NACCD, LBJ. See also Welch, "Impact of Urban Riots," 757; "Police Ordering Helmets, Mask," *Omaha World-Herald*, July 6, 1966; and To the Governor, ONG or Military Authorities from Mayor Ruehlmann, April 8, 1968, 6:30 p.m., box 50, State Archives Series 1654: Adjutant General Ohio National Guard After Action Reports 1965–1974, folder 1968, 2–14: Cincinnati 1968, Ohio State Archives, Columbus.

28. Johnson, interview.

29. Al Darr, "State Guard Test Reaction to Riots," *Omaha World-Herald*, April 2, 1968; and Schottelkotte News Noon Report, July 26, 1967.

30. "Two Will Attend Riot Conference," *Omaha World-Herald*, January 27, 1968; "City Reviews Riot Control," *Omaha World-Herald*, January 4, 1968; and "3 Riot Ordinances Up for City Council Study," *Cincinnati Post & Times-Star*, October 4, 1967.

31. "3 to Study Riot Controls," *Omaha World-Herald*, February 16, 1968; and David Tishendorf, "Mayor Asks Riot Power," *Omaha World-Herald*, April 19, 1968.

32. Disposition Form by Robert H. Canterbury, April 29, 1968, Subj: Review of After Action Report for Civil Disturbances at Cincinnati, OH, April 8–12, 1968, 4, box 50, State Archives Series 1654: Adjutant General Ohio National Guard After Action Reports 1965–74, folder 1968, 2–14: "Cincinnati 1968" Ohio State Archives, Columbus.

33. Sam Dennis, Field Community Tension Factors Report Milwaukee, Wisconsin, August 21, 1967, box E33, Series 6: Federal Bureau of Investigation City Reports, folder NACCD—Milwaukee, Wisconsin, NACCD, LBJ; and Memorandum to George Roberts from Sam Dennis, Subject Daily Activity Report—Milwaukee, Wisconsin—August 1, 1967, 2, box E33, Series 6: Federal Bureau of Investigation City Reports, folder NACCD—Milwaukee, Wisconsin, NACCD, LBJ.

34. Interview with Clint Reynolds, in Team Interview Report, November 6, 1967, 4, box E43, Series 10: Field Research Reports and Field Interview Folders, folder Cincinnati—Team Interview Report, NACCD, LBJ. See also Memo from Henry B. Taliaferro Jr. to Staff Re: Cincinnati Trip August 30, 1967, September 9, 1967, 2–3, box E21, Series 4: Office of Investigation City Files, Atlanta—General to Dayton—Miscellaneous Reports, folder Cincinnati—General, NACCD, LBJ.

35. Aftermath in Milwaukee: Report of phone conversation with Sam Dennis, Community Relations Service, DOF, by Bruce Thomas, Friday, January 12, 1968, 2, box E37, Series 8: Material Pulled from Commission Files, folder Chapter II Supplementary Working Materials: Aftermath: Notes of Conversations with CRS Representatives, NACCD, LBJ.

36. Affidavit Station WCPO/TV News Noon Report, July 28, 1967, 5, box 3, Series 41: Simulmatics Mass Media Study Records Cincinnati—Cleveland, NACCD, LBJ.

37. McLaughlin, *Long, Hot Summer*, x.

38. FBI Weekly Report—Cincinnati, June 30, 1967, 2, box E21, Series 4: Office of Investigation City Files, folder Cincinnati FBI Reports, NACCD, LBJ.

39. Johnson, *Heartland TV*, 113.

40. Johnson, *Heartland TV*, 115.

41. Johnson, *Heartland TV*, 120 (emphasis in original).

42. Johnson, *Heartland TV*, 116.

43. Johnson, *Heartland TV*, 17.

44. Confidential Document Outlining the City of Cincinnati to the President's Commission on Civil Disorder, Manual of Procedure in Civil Emergencies, July 28, 1966,

box 139, Milwaukee Series 44: Maier, folder 2, Police Department, January–May 1967, UWML.

45. Survey Questionnaire, undated, 3–4, 16, 31, box 7, Mss 901, Robert L. Black Jr. Collection, folder 7, McPheeter's Reports [Black Riots in Cincinnati] 1967, CHS (emphasis in original).

46. Robert Black, Statement about McPheeters Report, October 26, 1967, 1, box 10, Mss 901, Robert L. Black Jr. Collection, folder CHRC Rebellion Riots 1967, CHS.

47. Johnson, interview.

48. Simulmatics News Media Study: Special Preliminary Report of Finding for Selected Cities by Dr. Sol Chaneles, November 10, 1967, 2–3, 14, 17, box 1, Series 12: Office of Information Records: Commission Conference on Media at Poughkeepsie, NY, November 10–12, 1967, folder Commission on Civil Disorders: Complete Record of Materials at Poughkeepsie Conference, November 10–12, 1967, NACCD, LBJ.

49. Simulmatics News Media Study, 18.

50. Guidelines for Covering Civil Disturbances, Omaha, Nebraska, undated, box 1, Series 11, Subgroup: Office of Information Research Data on the Mass media, folder Community Relations Service: Guidelines NACCD, LBJ.

51. Memo to Mayor from Jim, July 26, 1968, box 160, Milwaukee Series 44, Maier, folder 22, Riot Study, 1967–71, UWML.

52. Simulmatics News Media Study, 2–3.

53. Milwaukee, Wisconsin Team Interview Reports, undated, box E51, Series 10: Field Research Reports and Field Interview Folders, folder Milwaukee—Arrest Data to Milwaukee Reconnaissance Survey—Field Research Report, NACCD, LBJ.

54. Hrach, "News Media and the Disorders," 156.

55. Kerner Commission, 207.

56. Gould, *Election That Changed America*, 14.

57. Simulmatics News Media Study, 3, 15.

58. Memorandum to David Ginsburg from M. C. Miskovsky, Subject: Final Report of the Office of Investigations, March 25, 1968, 59, box E1, Series 1: Office of Investigation General Subject Files, folder Interim Report Office of Investigations Final Report, NACCD, LBJ.

59. Avondale Community Council, Annual Report 1967, undated, box 2, Mss 901, Robert L. Black Jr. Collection, folder 9 CHRC Community Organization Avondale Community Center, 1967–70, CHS.

60. James Mimms (bus driver, Cincinnati, OH), interview by author, June 18, 2013.

61. "Guardsmen Quell Riot at Workhouse," *Cincinnati Post & Times-Star*, June 16, 1967.

62. Memorandum to David Ginsburg and Victor H. Palmieri from M. C. Miskovsky, Subject: Synopsis of Interim Report for Office of Investigations, December 5, 1967, 7, box E1, Series 1: Office of Investigation General Subject Files, folder Interim Report—Miscellaneous, LBJ.

63. Disposition Form by Robert H. Canterbury.

64. Draft—Staff Paper No. 7, "Analysis of Cincinnati Disturbance," November 13, 1967, 29, box E67, Series 12: Staff Papers From Office of Assistant Deputy Director, folder Staff Paper No. 7 Cincinnati: Analysis of Cincinnati Disturbance, NACCD, LBJ.

65. Deposition of Reverend Harold Hunt, January 8, 1968, 3, box 2, Series 32: Depositions of Witnesses December 1967–January 1968, Subgroup: Office of General Council Cincinnati Detroit, folder Depositions Cincinnati, NACCD, LBJ.

66. Saunders, *Negro in Avondale*, 34.

67. "Negroes' Anger Spills Forth in Council Hearing," *Enquirer*, June 14, 1967.

68. FBI Dispatch about North Central Regional Action Council Chicago, 100–113, 29, October 4, 1967, 3–4, box E15, Series 3: Office of Investigation Organizational Files, Congress of Racial Equality (CORE) FBI Report to DuBois Clubs of America FBI Reports, file 1, folder Congress of Racial Equality (CORE) FBI Reports, NACCD, LBJ.

69. Congress of Racial Equality (CORE) Report, box E3, Series 1: Office of Investigation General Subject Files, folder Interim Report—Office of Investigations—Reports of Investigators [weapons, fires: 1 of 2] NACCD, LBJ; see also memo to Ginsburg and Palmieri, December 5, 1967.

70. Meeting Notes from Dr. Ralph Turner, Dr. Robert Shellow, and David Boesel, October 19, 1967, 6–9, box E38, Series 8: Material Pulled from Commission Files, Hearing—Transcripts to Staff Meetings (Notes), folder Staff Meetings (Notes), NACCD, LBJ.

71. Notes from Conference with Dr. Turner—David Boesel, Bettsy Jamison and Lock Holmes attending, undated, 5, box E38, Series 8: Material Pulled from Commission Files, Hearing—Transcripts to Staff Meetings (Notes) folder Staff Meetings (Notes) NACCD, LBJ.

72. "*Omaha World-Herald* Centennial Series: Summer of 1966 Was 'Long, Hot' as the Riots Reached Omaha," *Omaha World-Herald*, June 16, 1985; "Official Says 3,500 Miss Class Friday," *Omaha World-Herald*, March 3, 1968; and "Only Third of Students Present at North High," *Omaha World-Herald*, March 8, 1968.

73. "Mayor Vows Laws to Rule, without Ifs," *Omaha World-Herald*, April 29, 1968.

74. Pavel and Gillian had changed parties to Wallace's American Party. "Was Week-End Rebellion Triggered by 'Appropriate' Police Action?" *Omaha Star*, Clippings File, Douglas County Historical Society, Omaha, NE.

75. "2 Say Police Used Excessive Force," *Omaha World-Herald*, April 30, 1968; and "Police Weigh Handbill Case," *Omaha World-Herald*, April 24, 1968.

76. "Looters on N. 24th Cause Heavy Damage," *Omaha World-Herald*, April 28, 1968.

77. "Mayor Vows Laws to Rule, without Ifs."

78. "2 Policemen Off North Side Duty," *Omaha World-Herald*, April 30, 1968.

79. "Police Weigh Handbill Case," *Omaha World-Herald*, April 24, 1968. See also "Was Week-End Rebellion Triggered."

80. John Taylor, "Glass, Food Litter Disorder Area," *Omaha World-Herald*, April 28, 1968.

81. Selected Racial Development and Disturbances Reports, October 17, 1967, October 18, 1967, box E3, Series 1: Office of Investigation General Subject Files, Embargoed, box E3, folder Liaison—FBI—Miscellaneous Reports [October–December 1967], NACCD, LBJ.

82. Larry Parrot, "Negro Students Ask 6 Changes at Central," *Omaha World-Herald*, December 14, 1968; and "Reconciliation Tried at Central High School," *Omaha World-Herald*, December 16, 1968.

83. "What Parents Can Do to Help," undated, 3, box 51, Mss 917, Maurice McCrackin, folder Cincinnati Public School, CHS.

84. Statement issued by Supt. of Schools Paul A. Miller, October 13, 1967, box 2, Mss 901, Robert L. Black Jr. Collection, folder 2: "CHRC Schools 1967," CHS; see also "The Samuel Ach Situation: Preliminary View," undated, box 11, Mss 901, Robert L. Black Jr. Collection, folder 2: "CHRC Schools 1967," CHS.

85. Agenda of the 4 C's meeting May 2, 1968, at Church of Our Savior, 7:30 p.m., box 2, Mss, 901 Robert L. Black Jr. Collection, folder 9, CHRC Community Organization. Avondale Community Center, 1967–1970, CHS; Statement issued by Supt. of Schools Paul A. Miller, October 13, 1967; and "The Samuel Ach Situation," undated.

CONCLUSION

1. Leonard and Leonard, "Historiography of American Violence," 104; and Howard, "American Tradition." See also Eduh Starborn, "They Are Lucky What Black People Are Looking for Is Equality and Not Revenge," June 8, 2020, YouTube, 1:17, https://youtu.be/0xZb026A4Y4.

2. Hofstadter and Wallace, *American Violence*, 7.

3. Howard, "American Tradition."

4. Kerner Commission, 1.

5. McLaughlin, *Long, Hot Summer*, 44.

6. McLaughlin, *Long, Hot Summer*, 58.

7. Gordon, *Race in the Heartland*, 2.

8. Gordon, *Race in the Heartland*, 2.

9. Jeremy Kohler, "Midwest Is One of the Worst Places for African Americans to Live, Report Says," *St. Louis (MO) Dispatch*, October 11, 2019.

10. Gordon, *Race in the Heartland*, 5.

11. John Elgion and Julie Bosman, "How Minneapolis, One of America's Most Liberal Cities, Struggles with Racism," *New York Times*, June 1, 2020, updated July 21, 2020.

12. Elgion and Bosman, "How Minneapolis."

13. Gordon, *Race in the Heartland*, 2.

14. Gordon, *Race in the Heartland*, 2.

15. Logan Sander, "The Politics of Midwestern Identity and Racial Divides," in *The Midstory* (blog), June 3, 2020, www.midstory.org/the-politics-of-midwestern-identity-racial-divides. Specifically, Detroit's population is 77.61 percent Black; Gary, 76.48 percent; Flint, 54.1 percent; and St. Louis, 43.57 percent.

16. Tamara Winfrey-Harris, "Stop Pretending Black Midwesterners Don't Exist," *New York Times*, June 16, 2018.

17. Gordon, *Race in the Heartland*, 4.

18. Gordon, *Race in the Heartland*, 11.

19. Marwa Eltagouri, "For Many Midwestern Cities with Shrinking Populations, Immigration Is a Lifeline," *Chicago Tribune*, September 18, 2017.

20. Longworth, *Caught in the Middle*; and Miraftab, *Global Heartland*.

21. Halvorson and Reno, *Imagining the Heartland*, 110.

22. Alan Feuer, "Fears of White People Losing Out Permeate Capitol Rioters' Towns, Study Finds," *New York Times*, April 6, 2021.

23. Howard, "The Long, Painful History of Racial Unrest."

24. See the evolution of the definition at Mark Liberman, "Flash Mobs," *Language Log* (blog), August 12, 2011, https://languagelog.ldc.upenn.edu/nll/?p=3358; and Kiltz, "Flash Mobs," 6–9.

25. Wasik, "My Crowd."

26. Kiltz, "Flash Mobs," 7.

27. Ashley Fantz, "Police Scramble to Fight Flash-Mob Mayhem," *CNN*, August 18, 2011.

28. Kiltz, "Flash Mobs," 6; Rick Jervis, "Flash Mobs Pose Challenge to Police Tactics," *USA Today*, August 19, 2011; Daniel Denvir, "Are Violent 'Flash Mobs' Really a Trend," *CityLab*, September 26, 2011; Cameron Bird, "Hyper-Networked Protests, Revolts, and Riots: A Timeline," *Wired*, December 16, 2011; Bill Wasik, "#Riot: Self-Organized, Hyper-Networked Revolts—Coming to a City Near You," *Wired*, December 16, 2011; Kevin Sheehan, Natasha Velez, and Natalie O'Neill, "Hundreds of Teens Trash Mall in Wild Flash Mob," *New York Post*, December 27, 2013; Erin Skarda, "Flash Mobs Turned Criminal: The Rise of Flash Robberies," *Time Magazine*, May 12, 2011; and Don Walker, Mike Johnson, and Breann Schossow, "State Fair Produces 11 Injuries, 31 Arrests," *Milwaukee Journal Sentinel*, August 5, 2011.

29. Howard, "Linked Fates."

30. Howard, "The Fight for Racial Justice Is a Movement, not a Moment." Shondaland, July 8, 2020, www.shondaland.com/act/news-politics/a33087030/fight-for-racial-justice-is-a-movement-not-a-moment.

31. Zak Cheney-Rice, "The Rioters Aren't Here to Convince You," *Intelligencer*, June 1, 2020.

32. Howard, "Linked Fates."

33. Danielle Moodie Mills, "OpEd: Are We all Just One Bullet Away from Becoming a Hashtag?," *NBC News*, April 8, 2015, www.nbcnews.com/storyline/walter-scott-shooting/oped-are-we-all-just-one-bullet-away-becoming-hashtag-n338111.

34. Howard, "Fight for Racial Justice." See also Jason Silverstein, "The Global Impact of George Floyd: How Black Lives Matter Protests Shaped Movements around the World," CBS News, June 4, 2021, www.cbsnews.com/news/george-floyd-black-lives-matter-impact.

35. Mary-Elizabeth Murphy, "Black Women Are the Victims of Police Violence, Too," *Washington Post*, July 24, 2020.

36. Jacobs, "Violent State."

37. Brittney Cooper, "Why Are Black Women and Girls Still an Afterthought in Our Outrage over Police Violence?," *Time*, June 4, 2020.

38. Cha-Jua, "New Nadir."

39. Tejumola Ologboni (folklorist, Milwaukee, WI), interview by author, August 19, 2014.

40. Kanye West, "Jesus Walks," recorded 2000–2003, track 4 on *The College Dropout*, Def Jam, compact disc.

41. Miranda Bryant, "'It Was Time to Take Charge': The Black Youth Leading the George Floyd Protests," *The Guardian*, June 15, 2020; and US Census Bureau, *American Community Survey 1-Year Estimates*.

42. Gabriel Elizondo, "Child, Teen Witnesses Relive Trauma of Floyd's Killing in Court," *Al Jazeera*, April 5, 2021, www.aljazeera.com/news/2021/4/5/teens-child-witnesses-relive-trauma-of-floyds-death-in-court.

43. US Census Bureau, *American Community Survey 1-Year Estimates*.

44. Janelle Monáe and Wondaland artist collective, "Hell You Talmbout," recorded 2015, single, Wondaland Records, compact disc.

BIBLIOGRAPHY

PRIMARY SOURCES

Manuscript and Archival Collections

Austin, Texas
   Lyndon Baines Johnson Presidential Library
      National Advisory Commission on Civil Disorders
Cincinnati, Ohio
   Cincinnati Historical Society
      Robert L. Black Jr. Collection
      Bureau of Governmental Research Inc.
      Maurice McCrackin
      NAACP
      Urban League of Greater Cincinnati
      WLWT Collection
   Cincinnati Public Library
      Annual Report of the Division of Police, 1967
   Personal Collection of Della Wells
Columbus, Ohio
   Ohio State Archives
      National Guard Collection
Lincoln, Nebraska
   Nebraska Historical Society
      Governor Norbert Tiemann
      Nebraska Black Oral History Project
         Frank Peak
         David Rice

Madison, Wisconsin
    Spilerman, Seymour. *Governmental Units Analysis Data, 1960: Urban Racial Disorders, 1961–1968* [machine readable data file]. Madison: University of Wisconsin, Data and Information Services Center, 1970.

Milwaukee, Wisconsin
    University of Wisconsin–Milwaukee Libraries, Department of Archives
        Henry Maier
        Milwaukee Urban League
        WTMJ-TV Collection

Omaha, Nebraska
    Personal Collection of Daniel Goodwin Sr.
    Personal Collection of John "Jack" McCaslin
    Personal Collection of Donald Nichols Jr.
    Personal Photo Collection of Rudy Smith

Washington, DC
    Freedom of Information Act
        FBI File 157-403-163, Omaha Black Panther Party

Author-Conducted Interviews

Cincinnati, Ohio
    Carol Brown, June 20, 2013
    Earl Brown, June 21, 2013
    David Davis, June 20, 2013
    Elaine Davis, June 20, 2013
    Deborah DuBose, June 20, 2013
    Pauline E., June 2013
    Brenda Middlebrook, June 21, 2013
    James Mimms, June 18, 2013
    Betsy Neel, June 21, 2013
    Marjorie Parham, June 2013
    Marian Spencer, June 18, 2013
    Morris Williams, June 19, 2013

Milwaukee, Wisconsin
    Rosalind Baker, August 20, 2014
    Sandra Dickinson, August 13, 2014
    Mutope Johnson, August 19, 2014
    Peter Murrell Sr., August 21, 2014
    Tejumola Ologboni, August 19, 2014
    Mary Page, August 18, 2014
    Charles Robinson, August 20, 2014
    Della Wells, August 15, 2014
    Avis Wright, August 15, 2014

Omaha, Nebraska
    John Butler, August 10, 2013

Ernest W. Chambers, February 28, 2006
Daniel Goodwin Sr., November 30, 2005
William Haynes, July 26, 2013
Ronald Hudson, July 22, 2013
Denny King, August 1, 2013
Sandra Matthews, July 31, 2013
John "Jack" McCaslin, December 5, 2005
Marvin McClarty, November 15, 2005
Frank Peak, July 2013
Rudy Smith, July 2013

Newspapers and Periodicals

Black Panther Intercommunal
    News Service
Black Rebellion
Chicago Defender
Chicago Tribune
Cincinnati Enquirer
Cincinnati Herald
Cincinnati Post & Times-Star
City Bulletin (Cincinnati)
CityLab
Daily Nebraskan (Lincoln)
Dundee and West Omaha Sun
Ebony
Echo Magazine
Gateway (Omaha)
Gawker
The Guardian
Intelligencer
Intercept
Jet
Life
Lincoln Evening Journal

Los Angeles Times
Milwaukee Journal
Milwaukee Journal-Sentinel
Milwaukee Sentinel
Milwaukee Star
Monthly Labor Review
Nation
News-Gazette
Newsweek
New York Post
New York Times
North Omaha Sun
Omaha Star
Omaha World-Herald
Slate
St. Louis (MO) Dispatch
Time
USA Today
Washington Post
Western Hills Press (Cincinnati)
Wired

Government Documents

Collins, William J., and Robert A. Margo. "The Labor Market Effects of the 1960s Riots." Working Paper 10243. National Bureau of Economic Research, Cambridge, MA, January 2004.

Department of Labor. *The Detroit Riot: A Profile of 500 Prisoners.* Washington, DC: Government Publishing Office, 1967.

Governor's Commission on the Los Angeles Riots. *McCone Commission Report! Complete and Unabridged Report by the Governor's Commission in the Los Angeles Riot: Plus One Hundred Four Shocking Photographs of the Most Terrifying Riot in History.* Los Angeles: Kimtex, 1965.

Henningson, Durham, and Richardson. *The Omaha, Nebraska, Community Renewal Program.* Omaha, NE: Omaha City Planning Department, 1966.

Hill, Robert B., and Robert M. Fogelson. "A Study of Arrest Patterns in the 1960s Riots." Unpublished paper for the Bureau of Applied Social Research, Columbia University, New York, December 1969.

Johnson, Lyndon. Executive Order 11365—Establishing a National Advisory Commission on Civil Disorders. July 29, 1967. www.presidency.ucsb.edu/documents/executive-order-11365-establishing-national-advisory-commission-civil-disorders.

Kotz, Arnold, Harold Hair, and John K. Scales. "Firearms, Violence and Civil Disorders." Prepared for the National Advisory Commission on Civil Disorders, Washington, DC. SRI Project No. MU-7105. Stanford Research Institute, Menlo Park, CA, July 1968.

McCone, John A. *Governor's Commission on the Los Angeles Riots. Transcripts, Depositions, Consultants Reports, and Selected Documents of the Governor's Commission on the Los Angeles Riots.* Los Angeles: Governor's Commission on the Los Angeles Riots, 1965.

Meranto, Phillip. *The Kerner Report Revisited: Final Report and Background Papers, Assembly on the Kerner Report Revisited.* Institute of Government and Public Affairs, University of Illinois, Urbana, June 1970.

Moynihan, Daniel Patrick. *The Negro Family: The Case for National Action.* Washington, DC: Government Publishing Office, 1965. www.dol.gov/general/aboutdol/history/webid-moynihan.

National Advisory Commission on Civil Disorders. *Report of the National Advisory Commission on Civil Disorders.* Washington, DC: Government Publishing Office, 1968.

Omaha City Directory. Kansas City, MO: R. L. Polk, 1965.

President's Commission on the Status of Women. *Report on Four Consultations.* Washington, DC: Government Publishing Office, 1964.

US Census Bureau. *American Community Survey 1-Year Estimates.* Census Reporter Profile page for the Midwest Region. 2019. http://censusreporter.org/profiles/02000US2-midwest-region.

——. *Census of Population and Housing: Census Tracts: Cincinnati, Ohio-KY-IND (SMSA), 1970.* Washington, DC: Government Publishing Office, 1973.

——. *Census Tracts: Cincinnati, Ohio-KY (SMSA), 1960.* Prepared by the US Department of Commerce in Cooperation with the Housing Division, Bureau of the Census. Washington, DC: Government Publishing Office, 1963.

——. *Characteristics of Housing Units by Tracts, 1960.* Prepared by the United States Department of Commerce, Bureau of the Census. Washington, DC: Government Publishing Office, 1963.

——. *Characteristics of Housing Units by Tracts, 1970.* Prepared by the United States Department of Commerce, Bureau of the Census. Washington, DC: Government Publishing Office, 1972.

——. *Characteristics of the Population.* Vol. 1, Part 1, Sec. 2: "Employment Status by

Race, Sex, and Age for Regions: 1970." Prepared by the Geography Division, Bureau of the Census. Washington, DC: Government Publishing Office, 1973.

———. *Characteristics of the Population.* Vol. 1, Part 1, Sec. 2: "Median School Years Completed and Median Income in 1969 of Persons 18 Years Old and Over with Income by Sex and Race for Standard Metropolitan Statistical Areas of 250,000 or More: 1970." Prepared by the Geography Division, Bureau of the Census. Washington, DC: Government Publishing Office, 1973.

———. *Characteristics of the Population.* Vol. 1, Part 29: *Nebraska.* "Employment Status by Sex, for Areas and Places." Prepared by the Geography Division, Bureau of the Census. Washington, DC: Government Publishing Office, 1974.

———. *Characteristics of the Population.* Vol. 1, Part 29: *Nebraska.* "Occupation and Earnings of the Negro Population for the Negro Population for Areas and Places: 1970." Prepared by the Geography Division, Bureau of the Census. Washington, DC: Government Publishing Office, 1973.

———. *Characteristics of the Population.* Vol. 1, Part 29: *Nebraska.* "Social Characteristics of the Negro Population for Areas and Places." Prepared by the Geography Division, Bureau of the Census. Washington, DC: Government Publishing Office, 1973.

———. *Characteristics of the Population.* Vol. 1, Part 51: *Wisconsin.* "Employment Status by Sex, for Areas and Places: 1970." Prepared by the Geography Division, Bureau of the Census. 19th ed. Washington, DC: Government Publishing Office, 1973.

———. *Characteristics of the Population.* Vol. 1, Part 51: *Wisconsin.* "Social Characteristics of the Negro Population for Areas and Places: 1970." Prepared by the Geography Division, Bureau of the Census. 19th ed. Washington, DC: Government Publishing Office, 1973.

———. *Characteristics of the Population 1970 in Census of Population Housing Tracts.* Prepared by the Geography Division, Bureau of the Census. Washington, DC: Government Publishing Office, 1973.

———. *Employment Status, by Color and Sex, for the State: 1940 to 1960.* Prepared by the Geography Division, Bureau of the Census. Washington, DC: Government Publishing Office, 1961.

———. *Income in 1959 of Families and Unrelated Individuals, by Color for the State Urban and Rural, 1960.* Prepared by the Geography Division, Bureau of the Census. Washington, DC: Government Publishing Office, 1963.

———. *Industry of the Employed by Race and Class of Worker, and of the Experienced Civilian Labor Force by Color, by Sex, for the State and for Standard Metropolitan Statistical Areas of 250,000 or More: 1960.* Prepared by the Geography Division, Bureau of the Census. Washington, DC: Government Publishing Office, 1963.

———. *Labor Force, by Age and Sex, for States, Urban and Rural, 1960 and for the United States, 1950 and 1940.* Prepared by the Geography Division, Bureau of the Census. Washington, DC: Government Publishing Office, 1963.

———. *Labor Force Characteristics of the Population in 1970 Census of the Population Housing Census Tracts.* Prepared by the Geography Division, Bureau of the Census Washington, DC: Government Publishing Office, 1973.

———. *Occupancy and Structural Characteristics of Housing Units by Census Tracts, 1960.* Prepared by the Geography Division in cooperation with the Housing Division, Bureau of the Census. Washington, DC: Government Publishing Office, 1962.

———. "Preliminary Report: Population Counts for the Standard Metropolitan Statistical Area." In *1960 Population of the Census*. 18th ed. Washington, DC: Government Publishing Office, July 1960.

———. *Race by Sex, for the State, Urban and Rural, 1950, and for the State 1880 to 1940*. Prepared by the Geography Division, Bureau of the Census. Washington, DC: Government Publishing Office, 1952.

———. *School Enrollment by Level and Type of School, by Color, for the State, Urban and Rural, 1960*. Prepared by the Geography Division, Bureau of the Census. Washington, DC: Government Publishing Office, 1961.

———. *Statistical Abstract of the United States: 1967* (88th edition). "Labor Union Membership Total and Percent of Non-Agricultural Employment: 1964." Prepared by the Geography Division, Bureau of the Census. Washington, DC: Government Publishing Office, 1967.

———. *Statistical Abstract of the United States: 1968* (89th edition). "No. 28 Population by Race—States: 1940 to 1960." Prepared by the Geography Division, Bureau of the Census. Washington, DC: Government Publishing Office, 1968.

———. *Statistical Abstract of the United States: 1971* (92nd edition). "Table No. 27 Population, by Race—States: 1940 to 1970." Prepared by the Geography Division, Bureau of the Census. Washington, DC: Government Publishing Office, 1971.

———. *US Census of Population, 1960: Tables 77, 78, 115, Nebraska, Ohio, Wisconsin Final Report*. Washington, DC: Government Publishing Office, 1968.

———. *Year Moved into Unit, Automobiles Available, and Value of Rent of Occupied Housing Units, by Census Tracts, 1960*. Prepared by the Geography Division in Cooperation with the Housing Division, Bureau of the Census. Washington, DC: Government Publishing Office, 1962.

US Department of Justice. *Cincinnati: Public Attitudes about Crime: A National Crime Survey Report*. Washington, DC: Government Publishing Office, 1979.

Discography

Monáe, Janelle, and Wondaland artist collective. "Hell You Talmbout." Recorded 2015, single, Wondaland Records, compact disc.

West, Kanye. "Jesus Walks." Recorded 2000–2003, track 4 on *The College Dropout*, Def Jam, compact disc.

SECONDARY SOURCES

Books, Journal Articles, and Chapters

Abu-Lughod, Janet L. *Race, Space, and Riots in Chicago, New York, and Los Angeles*. New York: Oxford University Press, 2007.

Adams, John S. "The Geography of Riots and Civil Disorders in the 1960s Economic Geography." Special issue, *Economic Geography* 48, no. 1 (1972): 24–42.

Allen, Vernon L. "Toward Understanding Riots: Some Perspectives." Special issue, *Journal of Social Issues* 26, no. 1 (1970): 1.

Auletta, Ken. *The Underclass.* New York: Random House, 1982.

Balto, Simon. "'Occupied Territory': Police Repression and Black Resistance in Postwar Milwaukee, 1950–1968." *Journal of African American History* 98, no. 2 (2013): 229–52.

———. *Occupied Territory: Policing Black Chicago from Red Summer to Black Power.* Chapel Hill: University of North Carolina Press, 2019.

Banfield, Edward C. *The Unheavenly City Revisited.* Boston: Little, Brown, 1974.

Barthes, Roland. *Mythologies.* New York: Farrar, Straus and Giroux, 1972.

Baskin, Jane A., Joyce K. Hartweg, Ralph G. Lewis, and Lester W. McCullough Jr. *The Long, Hot Summer? An Analysis of Summer Disorders, 1967–197: Report No.2* Waltham, MA: Brandeis University, 1972.

———. *Race-Related Civil Disorders: 1967–1969.* Waltham, MA: Brandies University Press, 1971.

Bassiouni, M. Cherif, ed. *The Law of Dissent and Riots.* Springfield, IL: Thomas Publisher, 1971.

Batchelder, Alan B. "Decline in the Relative Income of Negro Men." *Quarterly Journal of Economics* 78, no. 4 (1964): 525–48.

Bates, Beth Tompkins. *Pullman Porters and the Rise of Protest Politics in Black America, 1925–1945.* Chapel Hill: University of North Carolina Press, 2003.

Beardwood, Roger. "The New Negro Mood." In *The Negro and the City*, edited by Louis Banks. New York: Time-Life Books, 1968.

Bednarek, Janet R. Daly, *The Changing Image of the City: Planning for Downtown Omaha, 1945–1973.* Lincoln: University of Nebraska Press, 1992.

Bennett, Lerone. "The Mood of the Negro." *Ebony* 13, no. 9 (1963): 27–38.

Bentley-Edwards, Keisha L., Malik Chaka Edwards, Cynthia Neal Spence, William A. Darity, Darrick Hamilton, and Jasson Perez. "How Does It Feel to Be a Problem? The Missing Kerner Commission Report." *Journal of Social Sciences* 4, no. 6 (September 2018): 20–40.

Biggs, Michael. "Size Matters: Quantifying Protest by Counting Participants." *Sociological Methods & Research* 47, no. 3 (2016): 351–83.

Blankenship, Mary, and Richard V. Reeves. "From the George Floyd Moment to a Black Lives Matter Movement, in Tweets." Brookings Institution, July 10, 2020. www.brookings.edu/blog/up-front/2020/07/10/from-the-george-floyd-moment-to-a-black-lives-matter-movement-in-tweets.

Blocker, Jack S. *A Little More Freedom: African Americans Enter the Urban Midwest, 1860–1930.* Columbus: Ohio State University Press, 2020.

Bloom, Jack M. *Class, Race, and the Civil Rights Movement.* Bloomington: Indiana University Press, 1987.

Boesel, David. *Cities Under Siege: An Anatomy of the Ghetto Riots, 1964–1968.* New York: Basic Books, 1971.

Breaux, Richard M. "Maintaining a Home for Girls: The Iowa Federation of Colored Women's Clubs at the University of Iowa, 1919–1950." *Journal of African American History* 87, no. 2 (2002): 236–55.

Brown, Scot. *Fighting for US: Maulana Karenga, the US organization, and Black Cultural Nationalism*. New York: New York University Press, 2003.

Buenker, John. "Cream City Electoral Politics." In *Perspectives on Milwaukee's Past*, edited by Margo Anderson and Victor Green. Urbana: University of Illinois Press, 2009.

Bunch-Lyons, Beverly A. *Contested Terrain: African-American Women Migrate from the South to Cincinnati, Ohio, 1900–1950*. New York: Routledge, 2002.

Burkholder, Zoe. *An African American Dilemma: A History of School Integration and Civil Rights in the North*. Oxford: Oxford University Press, 2021.

Button, James W. *Black Violence: Political Impact of the 1960s Riots*. Princeton, NJ: Princeton University Press, 1978.

Campney, Brent M. S. *Hostile Heartland: Racism, Repression, and Resistance in the Midwest*. Urbana: University of Illinois Press, 2019.

Canetti, Elias. *Crowds and Power*. Translated by Carol Stewart. New York: Seabury Press, 1978.

Capeci, Dominic J., Jr., and Martha Wilkerson. *Layered Violence: The Detroit Rioters, 1943*. Jackson: University Press of Mississippi, 1991.

Caplan, Nathan S., and Jeffrey M. Paige. "A Study of Ghetto Rioters." *Scientific American* 219, no. 2 (1968): 15–21.

Carmichael, Stokely, and Charles V. Hamilton. *Black Power: The Politics of Liberation*. New York: Vintage Books, 1992.

Castagno, Angelina E. *Educated in Whiteness: Good Intentions and Diversity in Schools*. Minneapolis: University of Minnesota Press, 2014.

Cayton, Andrew R. L., and Susan E. Gray, eds. *The American Midwest: Essays on Regional History*. Bloomington: Indiana University Press, 2001.

Cayton, Andrew R. L., and Peter S. Onuf. *The Midwest and the Nation: Rethinking the History of an American Region*. Bloomington: Indiana University Press, 1990.

Cha-Jua, Sundiata. "The New Nadir: The Contemporary Black Racial Formation." *Black Scholar* 40, no. 1 (2015): 38–58.

Cha-Jua, Sundiata, and Clarence Lang. "The 'Long Movement' as Vampire: Temporal and Spatial Fallacies in Recent Freedom Studies." *Journal of African American History* 92, no. 2 (Spring 2007): 265–88.

Christman, Phil. *Midwest Futures*. Cleveland, OH: Belt Publishing, 2022.

Clarke, John Henrik, ed. *Malcolm X: The Man and His Times*. Toronto: Collier, 1979.

Cohen, Lizabeth. *A Consumer's Republic: The Politics of Mass Consumption in Post-War America*. New York: Random House, 2003.

Cohen, Norman S., ed. *Civil Strife in America: A Historical Approach to the Study of Riots in America*. Hinsdale, IL: Dryden Press, 1972.

Collins, Patricia Hill. *Black Feminist Thought: Knowledge, Consciousness, and the Politics of Empowerment*. New York: Routledge, 2008.

———. *Black Sexual Politics: African Americans, Gender, and the New Racism*. New York: Routledge, 2005.

Conant, Ralph. *The Prospects for Revolution: A Study of Riots, Civil Disobedience, and Insurrection in Contemporary America*. New York: Harper's Magazine Press, 1971.

Cooley, Will. *Moving Up, Moving Out: The Rise of the Black Middle Class in Chicago*. DeKalb: Northern Illinois Press, 2020.

Coser, Lewis A. "Some Social Function of Violence." *The Annals* 10 (1966): 362–67.
Countryman, Matthew J. *Up South: Civil Rights and Black Power in Philadelphia*. Philadelphia: University of Pennsylvania Press, 2007.
Crawford, Vicki L., Jacqueline Anne Rouse, and Barbara Woods, eds. *Women in the Civil Rights Movement: Trailblazers and Torchbearers, 1941–1965*. Bloomington: Indiana University Press, 1993.
Crenshaw, Kimberle. "Demarginalizing the Intersection of Race and Sex: A Black Feminist Critique of Antidiscrimination Doctrine, Feminist Theory and Antiracist Politics." In *Feminist Legal Theories*, edited by Karen J. Maschke. New York: Routledge, 2013.
———. "Mapping the Margins: Intersectionality, Identity Politics, and Violence against Women of Color." *Stanford Law Review* 43 (1991): 1241–99.
Dalstrom, Harl A. *A. V. Sorensen and the New Omaha*. Lincoln, NE: Lamplighter, 1988.
Daly, Charles U., ed. *Urban Violence*. Chicago: University of Chicago Press, 1969.
Daly-Bednarek, Janet R. *The Changing Image of the City: Planning for Downtown Omaha, 1945–1973*. Lincoln: University of Nebraska Press, 1992.
Dawson, Michael C. *Black Visions: The Roots of Contemporary African American Political Ideologies*. Chicago: University of Chicago, 2003.
Delinder, Jean Van. *Struggles before Brown: Early Civil Rights Protests and Their Significance Today*. New York: Routledge, 2015.
Dhingra, Pawan. "Introduction to Journal of Asian American Studies, Special Issue on the Midwest." *Journal of Asian American Studies* 12, no. 3 (2009): 239–46.
Dougherty, Jack. *More Than One Struggle: The Evolution of Black School Reform in Milwaukee*. Chapel Hill: University of North Carolina Press, 2004.
Eick, Gretchen Cassel. *Dissent in Wichita: The Civil Rights Movement in the Midwest, 1954–1972*. Urbana: University of Illinois Press, 2001.
Etcheson, Nicole. *The Emerging Midwest: Upland Southerners and the Political Cultures of the Old Northwest, 1787–1861*. Bloomington: Indiana University Press, 1996.
Ervin, Keona K. *Gateway to Equality: Black Women and the Struggle for Economic Justice in St. Louis*. Lexington: University of Kentucky Press, 2019.
Estes, Steve. *I Am a Man! Race, Manhood, and the Civil Rights Movement*. Chapel Hill: University of North Carolina Press, 2005.
Fairbanks, Robert B. "Cincinnati Blacks and the Irony of Low-Income Housing Reform." In *Race and the City: Work, Community, and Protest in Cincinnati, 1820–1970*, edited by Henry Louis Taylor Jr., 193–208. Urbana: University of Illinois Press, 1993.
Feagin, Joe R., and Melvin P. Sikes. *Living with Racism: The Black Middle-Class Experience*. New York: Beacon Press, 1995.
Fehn, Bruce, and Robert Jefferson. "North Side Revolutionaries in the Civil Rights Struggle: The African American Community in Des Moines and the Black Panther Party for Self-Defense, 1948–1970." *Annals of Iowa* 69, no. 1 (Winter 2010): 51–81.
Felker-Kantor, Max. *Policing Los Angeles: Race, Resistance, and the Rise of the LAPD*. Chapel Hill: University of North Carolina Press, 2018.
Fikes, Robert, Jr., ed. *Racist and Sexist Quotations: Some of the Most Outrageous Things Ever Said*. Saratoga, CA: R & E Publishers, 1992.

Fine, Sidney. *Violence in the Model City: The Cavanaugh Administration, Race Relations, and the Detroit Riot of 1967.* East Lansing: Michigan State University Press, 2007.

Flaming, Karl H. *Who "Riots" and Why? Black and White Perspectives in Milwaukee.* Milwaukee, WI: Urban League, 1968.

Flaming, Karl H., and John N. Ong Jr. *A Social Report for Milwaukee, 1970.* Milwaukee, WI: Milwaukee Urban Observatory, Winter 1973.

Fogelson, Robert M. "Violence and Grievances: Reflections on the 1960s Riots." *Journal of Social Issues* 26, no. 1 (1970): 141–43.

———. *Violence as Protest: A Study of Riots and Ghettos.* Garden City, NY: Doubleday, 1971.

Ford, Melissa. *A Brick and a Bible: Black Women's Radical Activism in the Midwest during the Great Depression.* Carbondale: Southern Illinois University Press, 2022.

Foreman, P. Gabrielle, Jim Casey, and Sarah Lynn Patterson, eds. *The Colored Conventions Movement: Black Organizing in the Nineteenth Century.* Chapel Hill: University of North Carolina Press, 2021.

Franklin, V. P. *The Young Crusaders: The Untold Story of the Children and Teenagers Who Galvanized the Civil Rights Movement.* New York: Beacon Press, 2021.

Frazier, Nishani. *Harambee City: The Congress of Racial Equality in Cleveland and the Rise of Black Power Populism.* Fayetteville: University of Arkansas Press, 2017.

Gaines, Kevin. *Uplifting the Race: Black Leadership, Politics, and Culture in the Twentieth Century.* Chapel Hill: University of North Carolina Press, 1996.

Galster, George. *Reality and Research: Social Science and US Urban Policy Since 1960.* Washington, DC: Urban Institute, 1995.

Gamson, William A. "The Success of the Unruly." In *Social Movements: Readings on Their Emergence, Mobilization, and Dynamics,* edited by Doug McAdam and David Snow. New York: Oxford University Press, 1997.

Gates, Henry Louis, and Cornel West. *The African American Century: How Black Americans Have Shaped Our Country.* New York: Free Press, 2000.

Geenen, Paul. *Schuster's & Gimbels: Milwaukee's Beloved Department Stores.* Charleston, SC: History Press, 2019.

Giddings, Paul. *When and Where I Enter: The Impact of Black Women on Race and Sex in America.* New York: Morrow, 1996.

Gilje, Paul A. *Rioting in America.* Bloomington: Indiana University Press, 1996.

Gordon, Colin. *Race in the Heartland.* Washington, DC: Economic Policy Institute, 2019.

Gordon, Linda. *The Second Coming of the KKK: The Ku Klux Kan of the 1920s and the American Political Tradition.* New York: Liveright, 2008.

Gould, Lewis L. *The Election That Changed America.* Chicago: Ivan R. Dee Press, 2010.

Greenberg, Cheryl Lynn. *Or Does It Explode? Black Harlem in the Great Depression.* New York: Oxford University Press, 1991.

Gregory, Dick. "The Gregory Report on Civil Disorders." In *Riots,* edited by Anita Monte and Gerald Leinwand. New York: Washington Square Press, 1970.

Grimshaw, Allen D. "Three Views of Urban Violence: Civil Disturbance, Racial Revolt, Class Assault." In *Rebellions and Rebellions: Civil Violence in the Urban Community,* edited by Louis H. Masotti and Don R. Bowen. Beverly Hills, CA: Sage, 1968.

Gurr, Ted Robert. *Why Men Rebel*. Princeton, NJ: Princeton University Press, 1970.

Halvorson, Britt E., and Joshua O. Reno. *Imagining the Heartland: White Supremacy and the American Midwest*. Oakland: University of California Press, 2022.

Harbour, Jennifer. "'I Earn by My Own Labor from Day to Day': African American Women's Activism in the Wartime Midwest." *Journal of the Illinois State Historical Society* 108, no. 3–4 (2015): 347–48.

Harding, Vincent. "History: White, Negro and Black." In *No More Moanin': Voices of Southern Struggle*, edited by Sue Thrasher. Special issue, *Southern Exposure* 1 (Winter 1974).

Harris, Daryl B. *The Logic of Black Urban Rebellions*. New York: Praeger, 1999.

Harris, LaShawn. *Sex Workers, Psychics, and Numbers Runners: Black Women in New York City's Underground Economy*. Urbana: University of Illinois Press, 2016.

Heaps, Willard A. *Rebellions, U.S.A.: 1765–1960*. New York: Seabury Press, 1970.

Helgeson, Jeffrey. "Politics in the Promised Land: How the Great Migration Shaped the American Midwest." In *Finding a New Midwestern History*, edited by Jon K. Lauck, Gleaves Whitney, and Joseph Hogan. Lincoln: University of Nebraska Press, 2018.

Hendricks, Wanda A. *Gender, Race, and Politics in the Midwest: Black Club Women in Illinois*. Bloomington: Indiana University Press, 1998.

Higbie, Frank Tobias. "Heartland: The Politics of a Regional Signifier." *Middle West Review* 1, no. 1 (Fall 2014): 81–90.

Hill, Lance. *The Deacons for Defense: Armed Resistance and the Civil Rights Movement*. Chapel Hill: University of North Carolina Press, 2004.

Hill, Lena M., and Michael D. Hill, eds. *Invisible Hawkeyes: African Americans at the University of Iowa During the Long Civil Rights Era*. Iowa City: University of Iowa Press, 2016.

Hine, Darlene Clark. "The Housewives' League of Detroit: Black Women and Economic Nationalism." In *Visible Women: New Essays on American Activism*, edited by Nancy A. Hewitt and Suzanne Lebsock. Urbana: University of Illinois Press, 1993.

Hinton, Elizabeth. *America on Fire: The Untold History of Police Violence and Black Rebellion Since the 1960s*. New York: Liveright, 2021.

———. *From the War on Poverty to the War on Crime: The Making of Mass Incarceration in America*. Cambridge, MA: Harvard University Press, 2017.

Hobsbawm, E. J. *Social Bandits and Primitive Rebels: Studies in Archaic Forms of Social Movement in the 19th and 20th Centuries*. Glencoe, IL: Free Press, 1959.

Hofstadter, Richard, and Michael Wallace, eds. *American Violence: A Documentary History*. New York: Random House, 1972.

Hoganson, Kristin L. *The Heartland: An American History*. London: Penguin, 2019.

Horne, Gerald. *Fire This Time: The Watts Uprising and the 1960s*. New York: DaCapo, 1997.

Howard, Ashley. "An American Tradition." *American Historian*, September 2020, 38–46.

———. "Linked Fates: Social Media as a Framing, Tactical, and Witnessing Tool in the Black Lives Matter Movement." In *News of Baltimore*, edited by Linda Steiner and Silvio Waisbord. New York: Routledge, 2017.

———. "The Long, Painful History of Racial Unrest." *Smithsonian Magazine*, August 28, 2020.

———. "What to the 'Other' Is the Midwest?" *Middle West Review* 9, no. 2 (2023): 127–32.
Hunter, Robert. *Violence and the Labor Movement*. New York: Macmillan, 1914.
Hunter, Tera. *To 'Joy My Freedom: Southern Black Women's Lives and Labors after the Civil War*. Cambridge, MA: Harvard University Press, 1997.
Irons, Janet. *Testing the New Deal: The General Textile Strike of 1934 in the American South*. Urbana: University of Illinois Press, 2000.
Jacobs, Michelle S. "The Violent State: Black Women's Invisible Struggle against Police Violence." *William & Mary Journal of Women & Law Enforcement* 24, no. 1 (2017–18): 39–100.
Jacobson, Joann. "The Idea of the Midwest." *Revue française d'études américaines*, no. 48–49 (July 1991): 235–45.
Janowitz, Morris. *Social Control of Escalated Riots*. Chicago: Center for Policy Study, University of Chicago, 1968.
Jay, Mark, and Phillip Conklin. *A People's History of Detroit*. Durham, NC: Duke University Press, 2020.
Jeffries, Judson L., and Jerrell Beckham. "How Whites Shaped the Study of Urban Unrest: A Scholarly Indictment by Two Black Male Scholars." *Spectrum: A Journal on Black Men* 8, no. 2 (Spring 2021): 107–30.
Johnson, Marilynn S. "Gender, Race, and Rumors: Reexamining the 1943 Race Riots." *Gender & History* 10, no. 2 (August 1998): 252–77.
Johnson, Victoria E. *Heartland TV: Prime Time Television and the Struggle for U.S. Identity*. New York: New York University Press, 2008.
Johnson, Walter. *The Broken Heart of America: St. Louis and the Violent History of the United States*. New York: Basic Books, 2021.
Jolly, Kenneth S. *Black Liberation in the Midwest: The Struggle in St. Louis, Missouri, 1963–1970*. New York: Routledge, 2006.
Jones, Claudia. *An End to the Neglect of the Problems of the Negro Woman!* New York: National Women's Commission and CPUSA, 1949.
Jones, Patrick D. *The Selma of the North: Civil Rights Insurgency in Milwaukee*. Cambridge, MA: Harvard University Press, 2009.
Kazyak, Emily. "Midwest or Lesbian? Gender, Rurality, and Sexuality." *Gender & Society* 26, no. 6 (2012): 825–48.
Kiel, Doug. "Untaming the Mild Frontier: In Search of New Midwestern Histories." *Middle West Review* 1, no. 1 (2014): 9–38.
Kiltz, Linda. "Flash Mobs: The Newest Threats to Local Governments." *Public Management Magazine* 93, no. 11 (December 2011): 6–9.
Kishi, Roudabeh, and Sam Jones. *Demonstrations and Political Violence in America: New Data for Summer 2020*. Armed Conflict Location and Event Data Project. 2020. www.jstor.org/stable/resrep26627.
Kohler, Lyle. *Cincinnati's Black Peoples: A Chronology and Bibliography, 1787–1982*. Prepared originally for the Cincinnati Arts Consortium through the Center for Neighborhood and Community Studies, University of Cincinnati. June 1986.
Lang, Clarence. "Black Power on the Ground: Continuity and Rupture in St. Louis." In *Neighborhood Rebels: Black Power at the Local Level*, edited by Peniel Joseph. New York: Palgrave Macmillan, 2010.

———. *Grassroots at the Gateway: Class Politics and Black Freedom Struggle in St. Louis, 1936–75*. Ann Arbor: University of Michigan Press, 2009.

Larsen, Lawrence H., and Barbara J. Cottrell. *The Gate City: A History of Omaha*. Lincoln: University of Nebraska Press, 1997.

Lassiter, Matthew D., and Joseph Crespino. *The Myth of Southern Exceptionalism*. Oxford: Oxford University Press, 2009.

Le Bon, Gustav. *The Crowd: A Study of the Popular Mind*. London: T. Fisher Unwin, 1926.

Lemelle, Anthony J., Jr. *Black Masculinity and Sexual Politics*. New York: Routledge, 2010.

Leonard, Ira M., and Christopher C. Leonard. "The Historiography of American Violence." *Homicide Studies* 7, no. 2 (2003): 99–153.

Lerner, Gilda. "Early Community Work of Black Club Women." *Journal of African American History* 59, no. 2 (1974): 158–67.

Levy, Peter B. *The Great Uprising: Race Riots in Urban American during the 1960s*. Cambridge, MA: Cambridge University Press, 2018.

Lichtenstein, Nelson, Susan Strasser, and Roy Rosenzweig, eds. *Who Built America: Working People and the Nation's Economy, Politics, Culture, and Society, 1877 to the Present*. New York: Worth Publishers, 2000.

Ling, Peter J., and Sharon Monteith, eds. *Gender and the Civil Rights Movement*. Piscataway, NJ: Rutgers University Press, 2004.

Loewen, James W. *Sundown Towns: A Hidden Dimension of American Racism*. New York: New Press, 2005.

Longworth, Richard C. *Caught in the Middle: America's Heartland in the Age of Globalism*. New York: Bloomsbury USA, 2009.

Lorber, Judith. "The Social Construction of Gender." In *Reconstructing Gender: A Multicultural Anthology*, edited by Estelle Disch. New York: McGaw-Hill, 2008.

Lowndes, Joseph E. *From the New Deal to the New Right: Race and the Southern Origins of Modern Conservatism*. New Haven, CT: Yale University Press, 2008.

Maier, Henry. *The Mayor Who Made Milwaukee Famous: An Autobiography*. Madison, WI: Madison Books, 1993.

Manalansan, Martin F., Chantal Nadeau, Richard T. Rodrigues, and Siobhan B. Somerville. "Queering the Middle: Race, Region, and a Queer Midwest." *GLQ: A Journal of Lesbian and Gay Studies* 20, no. 1–2 (2014): 1–12.

Markusen, Ann R., and Virginia Carlson. "Deindustrialization in the American Midwest: Causes and Responses." In *Deindustrialization and Regional Economic Transformation: The Experience of the United States*, edited by Lloyd Rodwin and Hidehiko Sazanami. New York: Routledge, 2017.

Marx, Gary T. *Protest and Prejudice: A Study of Belief in the Black Community*. New York: Harper and Row, 1967.

Massoti, Louis H. "Riots and Change: A Hindsight View of Urban Disorder in the Sixties." In *Political Microviolence: A Series of Original Essays*, edited by Herbert Hirst and David Perry. New York: Harper and Row, 1972.

McAdam, Doug. *Political Process and the Development of Black Political Insurgency*. Chicago: University of Chicago Press, 1982.

———. "Tactical Innovation and the Pace of Insurgency." *American Sociological Review* 48, no. 6 (1983): 735–54.

McDuffie, Erik S. *The Second Battle for Africa: Garveyism, the US Heartland, and Global Black Freedom*. Durham, NC: Duke University Press, 2024.

McLaughlin, Malcolm. *The Long, Hot Summer of 1967: Urban Rebellion in America*. New York: Springer, 2014.

McRae, Elizabeth Gillespie. *Mothers of Massive Resistance: White Women and the Politics of White Supremacy*. Oxford: Oxford University Press, 2018.

Mead, Lawrence M. *Beyond Entitlement: The Social Obligations of Citizenship*. New York: Free Press, 1986.

Michney, Todd M. *Surrogate Suburbs: Black Upward Mobility and Neighborhood Change in Cleveland, 1900–1980*. Chapel Hill: University of North Carolina Press, 2017.

Miller, Abraham H., and Emily Schaen. "Democracy and the Black Rebellions: Rethinking the Meaning of Political Violence in Democracy." In *The Democratic Experience and Political Violence*, edited by David C. Rapoport and Leonard Weinberg. London: Frank Cass, 2001.

Miraftab, Faranak. *Global Heartland: Displaced Labor, Transnational Lives, and Local Placemaking*. Bloomington: Indiana University Press, 2016.

Montes, Anita, and Gerald Leinwand. *Riots*. New York: Washington Square Press, 1970.

Moore, Leonard N. *Black Rage in New Orleans: Police Brutality and African American Activism from World War II to Hurricane Katrina*. Baton Rouge: Louisiana State University Press, 2010.

———. *The Defeat of Black Power: Civil Rights and the National Black Political Convention of 1972*. Baton Rouge: Louisiana State University Press, 2018.

Morgan, William R., and Terry Nichols. "The Causes of Racial Disorders: A Grievance-Level Explanation." *American Sociological Review* 38, no. 5 (October 1973): 611–24.

Moten, Crystal Marie. *Continually Working: Black Women, Community Intellectualism, and Economic Justice in Postwar Milwaukee*. Nashville, TN: Vanderbilt University Press, 2023.

———. "'Kept Right on Fightin'...': African American Women's Economic Activism in Milwaukee." *Journal of Civil and Human Rights* 2, no. 1 (2016): 33–51.

Mumford, Kevin. *Newark: A History of Race, Rights, and Riots in America*. New York: New York University Press, 2008.

Myers, Daniel J., and Beth Schaefer Caniglia. "All the Rioting That's Fit to Print: Selection Effects in National Newspaper Coverage of Civil Disorders, 1968–1969." *American Sociological Review* 69, no. 4 (August 2004): 519–43.

Myrdal, Gunnar. *An American Dilemma*. New York: Harper & Row, 1944.

Nadasen, Premilla. *Welfare Warriors: The Welfare Rights Movement in the United States*. New York: Routledge, 2004.

Nelson, Daniel. *Farm and Factory: Workers in the Midwest, 1880–1990*. Bloomington: Indiana University Press, 1995.

Newburn, Tim. "The Causes and Consequences of Urban Riot and Unrest." *Annual Review of Criminology* 4 (2021): 53–73.

Ochonicky, Adam R. *The American Midwest in Film and Literature: Nostalgia, Violence, and Regionalism*. Bloomington: Indiana University Press, 2020.

———. "The Millennial Midwest: Nostalgic Violence in the Twenty-First Century." *Quarterly Review of Film and Video* 32, no. 2 (2015): 124–40.

Oler, Andy. *Old-Fashioned Modernism: Rural Masculinity and Midwestern Literature*. Baton Rouge: Louisiana State University Press, 2019.

O'Reilly, Charles T., Willard E. Downing, and Steven I. Pflanczer. *The People of the Inner Core-North: A Study of Milwaukee's Negro Community*. New York: LePlay Research, 1965.

Paige, Jeffrey M. "Political Orientation and Riot Participation." *American Sociological Review* 36, no. 5 (1971): 810–20.

Patillo, Mary. *Black Picket Fences: Privilege and Peril among the Black Middle Class*. Chicago: University of Chicago Press, 2013.

Phillips, Kimberley L. *AlabamaNorth: African-American Migrants, Community, and Working-Class Activism in Cleveland, 1915–1945*. Urbana: University of Illinois Press, 1999.

Pierce, Richard B. *Polite Protest: The Political Economy of Race in Indianapolis, 1920–1970*. Bloomington: University of Indiana Press, 2005.

Ransford, H. Edward. "Isolation, Powerlessness, and Violence: A Study of Attitudes and Participation in the Watts Riots." *American Journal of Sociology* 73, no. 5 (1968): 581–91.

Rhodes, Joel P. *The Voice of Violence: Performative Violence as Protest in the Vietnam Era*. Westport, CT: Praeger, 2001.

Robnett, Belinda. *How Long? How Long? African American Women in the Struggle for Civil Rights*. New York: Oxford University Press, 2000.

Ross, Loretta. "Reproductive Justice as Intersectional Feminist Activism." *Souls* 19, no. 3 (2017): 286–314.

Rucker, Walter C., and James Nathaniel Upton. *Encyclopedia of American Race Riots*. 2 Vols. Westport, CT: Greenwood Press, 2006.

Rude, George. *The Crowd in the French Revolution*. Oxford: Oxford University Press, 1967.

———. *Paris and London in the Eighteenth Century: Studies in Popular Protest*. New York: Viking, 1970.

Salert, Barbara, and John Sprague. *The Dynamics of Riots*. Ann Arbor, MI: Inter-University Consortium for Political and Social Research, 1980.

Saunders, Talitha Slaughter. *The Negro in Avondale, Ohio*. New York: Vantage Press, 1970.

Schrotel, Stanley R. "Supervising the Use of Police Authority." *Journal of Criminal Law, Criminology, and Police Science* 47, no. 5 (1957): 589–92.

Sears, David O. "Black Attitudes towards the Political System in the Aftermath of the Watts Insurrection." *Midwest Journal of Political Science* 13, no. 4 (1969): 515–44.

Self, Robert O. *American Babylon: Race and the Struggle for Postwar Oakland*. Princeton, NJ: Princeton University Press, 2003.

Shaw, Stephanie J. "Black Club Women and the Creation of the National Association of Colored Women." *Journal of Women's History* 3, no. 2 (1991): 11–25.

Shortridge, James R. "The Heartland's Role in US Culture: It's 'Main Street.'" *Public Perspective* 9, no. 4 (June–July 1998): 40–42.

———. *The Middle West: Its Meaning in American Culture*. Lawrence: University Press of Kansas, 1989.

Shultz, George P., and Arnold R. Weber. *Strategies for the Displaced Worker: Confronting Economic Change*. New York: Harper and Row, 1966.

Sitkoff, Howard. *The Struggle for Black Equality, 1954–1992*. New York: Hill and Wang, 1998.

Skolnick, Jerome H. *The Politics of Protest*. New York: Ballantine, 1969.

Smelser, Neil J. *Theory of Collective Behavior*. New York: Free Press, 1962.

Smith, Robert C. *Race, Class, and Culture: A Study in Afro-American Mass Opinion*. Albany: State University of New York Press, 1992.

Smolarek, Bailey B., and Giselle Martinez Negrette. "'It's Better Now': How Midwest Niceness Shapes Social Justice Education." In *The Price of Nice: How Good Intentions Maintain Educational Inequity*, edited by Angelina E. Castagno. Minneapolis: University of Minnesota Press, 2019.

Spilerman, Seymour. *The Causes of Racial Disturbances: Tests of a Theory*. Madison: Institute for Research on Poverty, University of Wisconsin, 1969.

Stevenson, Brenda. *The Contested Murder of Latasha Harlins: Justice, Gender, and the L.A. Riots*. Oxford: Oxford University Press, 2013.

Sugrue, Thomas J. "Crabgrass-Roots Politics: Race, Rights, and the Reaction against Liberalism in the Urban North, 1940–1964." *Journal of American History* 82, no. 2 (1995): 551–78.

———. *The Origins of the Urban Crisis*. Princeton, NJ: Princeton University Press, 1996.

———. *Sweet Land of Liberty: The Forgotten Struggle*. New York: Random House, 2009.

Summers, Martin Anthony. *Manliness and Its Discontents: The Black Middle Class and the Transformation of Masculinity, 1900–1930*. Chapel Hill: University of North Carolina Press, 2004.

Taggart, Paul. "Populism and Representative Politics in Contemporary Europe." *Journal of Political Ideologies* 9, no. 3 (2004): 269–88.

Taylor, Henry Louis, Jr., ed. *Race and the City: Work, Community, and Protest in Cincinnati, 1820–1970*. Urbana: University of Illinois Press, 1993.

Taylor, Henry Louis, Jr., and Walter Hill, eds. *Historical Roots of the Urban Crisis: African Americans in the Industrial City, 1900–1950*. New York: Garland, 2000.

Taylor, Keeanga-Yamahtta. *Race for Profit: How Banks and the Real Estate Industry Undermined Black Homeownership*. Chapel Hill: University of North Carolina Press, 2019.

Taylor, Nikki M. *Frontier of Freedom: Cincinnati's Black Community, 1802–1868*. Athens: Ohio University Press, 2005.

Taylor, Quintard. *In Search of the Racial Frontier: African Americans in the American West, 1528–1990*. New York: Norton, 1999.

Teaford, Jon C. *Cities of the Heartland: The Rise and Fall of the Industrial Midwest*. Bloomington: Indiana University Press, 1994.

———. "The Development of Midwestern Cities." In *Finding a New Midwestern History*, edited by Jon K. Lauck, Gleaves Whitney, and Joseph Hogan. Lincoln: University of Nebraska Press, 2020.

Terry, Robert W. *For Whites Only*. Grand Rapids, MI: W. B. Eerdmans, 1970.

Theoharis, Jeanne F. "Hidden in Plain Sight: The Civil Rights Movement Outside the South." In *The Myth of Southern Exceptionalism*, edited by Matthew D. Lassiter and Joseph Crespino. Oxford: Oxford University Press, 2009.

———. "'We Saved the City': Black Struggles for Educational Equality in Boston, 1960–1976." *Radical History Review* 81 (2001): 61–93.

Theoharis, Jeanne F., and Komozi Woodard, eds. *Freedom North: Black Freedom Struggles Outside the South, 1940–1980*. New York: Palgrave Macmillan, 2003.

Theoharis, Jeanne F., Komozi Woodard, and Brian Purnell, eds. *The Strange Career of Jim Crow North: Segregation and Struggle Outside the South*. New York: New York University Press, 2019.

Thompson, Heather Ann. "Understanding Rioting in Postwar Urban America." *Journal of Urban History* 26, no. 3 (2000): 391–402.

———. "Urban Uprisings: Riots or Rebellions." In *The Columbia Guide to American in the 1960s*, edited by David Farber and Beth Bailey. New York: Columbia University Press, 2001.

———. *Whose Detroit? Politics, Labor, and Race in a Modern American City*. Ithaca, NY: Cornell University Press, 2001.

Tilly, Charles. "Collective Violence in European Perspective." In *History of Violence in America*, edited by Hugh Davis Graham and Ted Roberts Gurr. New York: Bantam, 1969.

Toch, Hans. *Violent Men*. Chicago: Aldine, 1980.

Trotter, Joe William, Jr. *Black Milwaukee: The Making of an Industrial Proletariat, 1915–1945*. Urbana: University of Illinois, 2006.

———. "The Historiography of Black Workers in the Urban Midwest: Toward a Regional Synthesis." *Studies in Midwestern History* 4, no. 4 (November 2018). https://scholarworks.gvsu.edu/midwesternhistory/vol4/iss1/4.

———. *Workers on Arrival: Black Labor in the Making of America*. Berkeley: University of California Press, 2021.

Turner, Frederick Jackson. *The Frontier in American History*. New York: Henry Holt, 1920.

———. "The Significance of the Frontier in American History." Paper presented at the Meeting of the American Historical Association, Chicago, July 12, 1893.

Ubbelohde, Carl. "History and the Midwest as Region." *Wisconsin Magazine of History* 78, no. 1 (1994): 35–47.

Upton, James N., Judson L. Jeffries, and Cathy McDaniels-Wilson. "The Politics of Urban Violence: Critiques and Proposals." *Journal of Black Studies* 15, no. 3 (March 1985): 243–58.

———. "The 2001 Cincinnati Uprising." *International Journal of Africana Studies* 13, no. 1 (2007): 1–14.

Vernon, Robert. *The Black Ghetto*. New York: Merit, 1969.

Wasik, Bill. "My Crowd: A Report from the Inventor of the Flash Mob." *Harper's Magazine*, March 2006, 56–66.

Watts, Edward. "The Midwest as Colony: Transnational Regionalism." In *Regionalism and the Humanities*, edited by Timothy R. Mahoney and Wendy Jean Katz. Lincoln: University of Nebraska Press, 2008.

Weber, Helen. *Summer Mockery: Civil Arrest Study*. Shorewood, WI: Aestas, 1986.
Welch, Susan. "The Impact of Urban Riots on Urban Expenditures." *American Journal of Political Science* 19, no. 4 (1975): 741–60.
White, Ahmed. *The Last Great Strike: Little Steel, the CIO, and the Struggle for Labor Rights in New Deal America*. Oakland: University of California Press, 2016.
Widick, B. J. *Detroit: City of Race and Class Violence*. Detroit: Wayne State University Press, 1989.
Wilson, William Julius. *The Declining Significance of Race: Blacks and Changing American Institutions*. Chicago: University of Chicago Press, 1980.
Winfrey-Harris, Tamara. "Stop Pretending Black Midwesterners Don't Exist." In *Black in the Middle: An Anthology of the Black Midwest*, edited by Terrion L. Williamson. Cleveland, OH: Belt Publishing, 2020.
Wolcott, Victoria W. *Race Riots, and Roller Coasters: The Struggle over Segregated Recreation in America*. Philadelphia: University of Pennsylvania Press, 2014.
Woodard, Komozi. "Message from the Grassroots: The Black Power Experiment in Newark, New Jersey." In *Groundwork: Local Black Freedom Movements in America*, edited by Jeanne Theoharis and Komozi Woodard. New York: New York University Press.
Woods, Randall B. *Prisoners of Hope: Lyndon B. Johnson, the Great Society, and the Limits of Liberalism*. New York: Basic Books, 2016.
Wuthnow, Robert. *Remaking the Heartland: Middle America since the 1950s*. Princeton, NJ: Princeton University Press, 2011.
Zweig, Michael. *The Working-Class Majority: America's Best Kept Secret*. Ithaca, NY: ILR Press, 2001.
Zwiers, Maarten. "The Whistles of George Wallace: Gender and Emotions in the 1968 Presidential Campaign." In *Race Matters: 1968 as Living History in the Black Freedom Struggle*. Special issue, *European Journal of American Studies* 14, no. 1 (2019). https://doi.org/10.4000/ejas.14454.

Dissertations and Theses

Abundu, Margaret J. G. "Black Ghetto Violence as Communication: A Case Study in Non-Conventional Political Protest." PhD diss., Indiana University, 1971.
Berk, Richard Alan. "The Role of Ghetto Retail Merchants in Civil Disorders." PhD diss., Johns Hopkins University, 1970.
Carter, Gregg Lee. "Explaining the Severity of the 1960's Black Rioting: A City Level Investigation of Curvilinear and Structural Breaks Hypotheses." PhD diss., Columbia University, 1983.
Danton, Lawrence A. "The Omaha Experiment: A Study of a Community Effort to Cope with Unemployment Resulting from Plant Mechanization." PhD diss., University of Nebraska, 1964.
Firestone, Joseph M. "The Causes of Urban Riots: A New Approach and a Casual Model." Center for Comparative Political Research, State University of New York at Binghamton, November 1971.

Flaming, Karl Henshaw. "The 1967 Milwaukee Riot: A Historical and Comparative Analysis." PhD diss., Syracuse University, 1970.

Freeman, John Esten. "A Social and Demographic Analysis of Urban Racial Violence." PhD diss., University of Colorado, 1969.

Hrach, T. "The News Media and the Disorders: The Kerner Commission's Examination of Race Riots and Civil Disturbances, 1967–1968." PhD diss., Ohio University, 2008.

King, William Melvin. "Ghetto Riots and the Employment of Blacks: An Answer to the Search for Black Political Power?" PhD diss., Syracuse University, 1974.

Kocolowski, Gary P. "The History of North Avondale: A Study of the Effects of Urbanization upon an Urban Locality." Master's thesis, University of Cincinnati, 1971.

Lieske, Joel Allen. "A Comparative Analysis of Urban Civil Violence." PhD diss., University of North Carolina, 1971.

Mason, Thomas David. "Individual Participation in Collective Racial Violence: A Rational Choice Synthesis." PhD diss., University of Georgia, 1982.

McElroy, Jerome Xavier. "The Socio-Economic Contours of Recent Urban Racial Violence." PhD diss., University of Colorado, 1972.

Modlinski, Julius John. "Commandos: A Study of a Black Organization's Transformation from Militant Protest to Social Service." PhD diss., University of Wisconsin–Milwaukee, 1978.

Monti, Daniel Joseph, Jr. "Collective Violence in Urban America, 1964–1969." Master's thesis, University of North Carolina, 1973.

Mueller, Carol Elizabeth. "Riot Negotiations: Conditions of Successful Bargaining in the Urban Riots of 1967 and 1968." PhD diss., Cornell University, 1971.

Paige, Jeffrey Mayford. "Collective Violence and the Culture of Subordination: A Study of Participants in the July 1967 Riots in Newark, NJ and Detroit, MI." PhD diss., University of Michigan, 1968.

Ransford, Harry Edward. "Negro Participation in Civil Rights Activity and Violence." PhD diss., University of California, Los Angeles, 1966.

Seawell, Stephanie. "The Black Freedom Movement and Community Planning in Urban Parks in Cleveland, Ohio, 1945–1977." PhD diss., University of Illinois, 2014.

Skura, Barry R. "The Impact of Collective Racial Violence on Neighborhood Mobilization, 1964–1968." PhD diss., University of Chicago, 1975.

Slesinger, Jonathan. "A Study of Community Opinions Concerning the Summer 1967 Civil Disturbance in Milwaukee." Unpublished manuscript, University of Wisconsin–Milwaukee, April 1, 1968.

Spruill, Denise Lynn Pate. "'From the Tub to the Club': Black Women and Activism in the Midwest, 1890–1920." PhD diss., University of Iowa, 2018.

Sulik, Stephanie Theresa. "Waving the Red, Black, and Green: The Local and Global Visions of the Universal Negro Improvement Association in Akron and Barberton, Ohio." PhD diss., University of Texas–Arlington, 2020.

Sullenger, Glenn. "A Study of Opportunities of Boys in Omaha." Master's thesis, Municipal University of Omaha, 1937.

Tchakirides, William I. "'Accountable to No One': Confronting Police Power in Black Milwaukee." PhD diss., University of Wisconsin–Milwaukee, 2020.

Watson, James Milton. "Violence in the Ghetto: A Critical Comparison of Three Theories of Black Urban Unrest." PhD diss., University of California–Los Angeles, 1973.
Wikstrom, Gunnar, Jr. "Municipal Government Response to Urban Riots." PhD diss., University of Arizona, 1973.
Witt, Andrew Richard. "Self-Help and Self-Defense: A Re-evaluation of the Black Panther Party with Emphasis on the Milwaukee Chapter." Master's thesis, University of Wisconsin–Milwaukee, 1999.

INDEX

Page numbers in italics refer to illustrations.

A., Eldred, 104, 105
A., Jon, 121
Abbot, James, 140–41
Abernathy, James, 26–27
Abu-Lughod, Janet, 13
African Americans. *See* Black people
Alexander, Chaney, 49
Alexander, Ray, 79
Ali, Leila, 163
Allen, Gary, 120; "The Plan to Burn Los Angeles," 120
Allen, Niathan, 138
American Dream, 23, 146, 177n14
Anders, John, 155
Anderson, Palmer, 176n7
Anderson, Richard R., 139, 155
Armed Conflict Location and Event Data project, 8
Associated Press Stylebook, 4, 172n13
Aub, A. Edgar, Jr., 46

B., William, 104
Bachman, William, 65
Bachrach, Walton H., 12, 67, 118
Baker, Rosalind, 38, 84
Ball, Leonard, 67

Balto, Simon, 30
Baraka, Amiri, 44
Barbee, Lloyd, 63
Barnes, Gwendolyn, 114–15
Beasley, John, 155
Beckett, Paul, 77
Bennett, Lerone, 54–55
Berk, Richard Alan, 91; "The Role of Ghetto Retail Merchants in Civil Disorders," 91
Berry, Theodore, 33
Biggs, Michael, 10
Black, Robert L., 139, 147
Black Freedom Movement: approaches of, 60; tactical and strategic shift in, 16, 17; uprisings as bridge between civil rights and Black Power movements, 44–45, 61; uprisings during, 9, 174n41
Black Ghetto (Vernon), 60–61
Black Lives Matter, 8
Black men: arbitrary stop-and-frisk of, 32, 113; emasculation of, 111–14; grievances of, 18; medical record privacy of, 113; and Moynihan report, 18; nonviolent protests and masculinity of, 194n16; as participants in Cincinnati uprising, 89, 151;

Black men (continued)
participation in uprisings as restoration of masculinity of, 18, 115–16, 117; as protectors of Black women, 114, 119, 123

Black middle class: abandonment of Black working class by, 49; adoption of white norms by, 48; and Cincinnati uprising, 67, 87; as counter-rioters, 13–14, 96; as detached from practical needs of Black community, 134; effect of uprisings on, 152; fear of retaliation during and after uprisings of, 98, 99; friction between Black working class and, 48, 49, 57; as liberated by uprisings, 50; loss of status as, 99–100; as main beneficiary of civil rights movement, 47; mirroring of southern civil rights movement by, 61; as participants in uprisings, 18, 100–101, 108, 161; police treatment of, during uprisings, 96; power of, 48; protest standards of, 50; tacit support of youth violence by, 73; treatment of, during uprisings, 97–98; views of uprisings, 94–98, 95; as "whiter than Whitey," 14, 15

"Black Monday," 151–52

Black nationalism: background of, 45–46; and Black Power movement, 59; and Black youth, 56; Brown's demands in Cincinnati after uprising, 75–76; in Milwaukee, 58; violence in rhetoric of, 153

Black people: armed white invasions of communities of, 119–20; as "canaries in the mines" signaling recession, 13; erasure of, in Midwest, 24, 31, 163–64, 169; family structure of, 111; history of activism in Midwest by, 168; as invaders of white neighborhoods, 120–21; "new 'Negro' mood" of, 54–55; political agency of, 18–19; racial disparities as catalyst for uprisings, 32; racial solidarity of, after uprisings, 152; sense of "Selfhood" of, 150–51; tacit condoning of uprisings by, 89; white indifference to structural racism faced by, 17. *See also* Black people, employment of

Black people, employment of: and Black youth in Omaha, 73; demands for, by Cincinnati Black leadership, 74, 75; lack of, 51; in Midwest industries, 2–3, 26, 51; in Milwaukee, 27, 28; as police officers, 30–31; and racism in trade unions, 3, 13, 27; and structural racism, 27; and uprising participants, 89, 90; white beliefs about opportunities for, 39; Black women and, 114

Black people, white views of: as divided into categories, 40; as responsible for socioeconomic disparities, 23, 38–39, 41; as violent, 8, 156

Black Power (Carmichael and Hamilton), 47

Black Power movement: and Black nationalism, 59; in Milwaukee, 58–59; self-determination and control demands of, 75; uprisings and development of, 152–53; urban uprisings as bridge between civil rights movement and, 61; violence in rhetoric of, 153

Black women: activism during Great Depression by, 45; Black men and mainstream devaluation of, 114; Black men as protectors of, 119, 123; depoliticization of issues and grievances of, 111–12; emasculation of Black men by, 111, 113–14; employment of, 114; in Kerner Commission report, 125; in Moynihan report, 18; participation in gender non-normative ways by, 130–31; participation in gender normative ways by, 16, 125–29; police abuse of, 114–15, 167; as responsible for "wild" children, 111; sexual violence against, by white men, 118–19; and uprisings' gains, 131–32; and violent protest, 124, 127

Black working class: and civil rights movement, 13, 43, 44, 47, 48, 118; demands after uprising of, 74–75; frictions between Black middle class and, 48, 49, 57; ineffectiveness of political system for, 14, 15, 36, 175n80, 176n88;

lack of positive changes for, after uprisings, 133–34; as leaders during uprisings, 118; as participants in uprisings, 13–14, 18, 47, 88, 93; vulnerability of, 47
Black youth: arbitrary stop-and-frisk of, 32, 113; and belief in need for violence, 153; and Black nationalism, 56; as leaders in Omaha uprising, 65–66, 71; as leaders of twenty-first-century uprisings, 167–68; as participants in uprisings, 28, 57, 60, 88, 153–56, 154; positive Black identity of, 56, 57
Blocker, Jack S., 181n105
Bloom, Jack, 47
Bloom, William, 31
Boesel, David, 54
Boswell, John, 58
Bowen, William, 36, 100
Bowles, Bryant, 107
Brier, Harold, 98, 140
Brown, Carol, 117, 122
Brown, Cecil, 33, 68
Brown, H. Rap, 4, 74, 75–76
Brown, Mildred, 49–50, 95–96
Buck, Barbara, 126
Bucklew, Henry, 21
Buenker, John, 179n74
Bush, Myron, 97–98

Calloway, Bertha, 53
Caniglia, Beth Schaefer, 7–8
carceral logic, of state, 9, 30, 80–82, 89, 163
Carmichael, Stokely: *Black Power*, 47; on class and protests, 47; as new generation of Black leadership, 55; police at Cincinnati event with, 30, 66; reception in Milwaukee of, 59
Chambers, Ernie, 19, 31, 55, 112–13
Chicago Defender, 48
Cincinnati, OH: Black people in government in, 33; education in, 29; effectiveness of political system for Black people in, 36; housing in, 28, 92; loss of employment possibilities for Black people in, 26; police abuse after uprising in, 139–40; police in, 30, 66, 83; recreational opportunities in, 29, 139
Cincinnati Enquirer, 67, 89
Cincinnati uprising (1967), 12, 66–68; arrests during, 82, 121, 125, 126, 127; average participant in, 88–89; Black grievances dismissed by mayor during, 52–53; Black middle class as aloof to violence in, 87; Black women's participation in, 126–27; challenges to police authority during, 116–17; cost of, 135; demands to municipal government during, 73–76; and effectiveness of nonviolent protests, 44; gender as catalyst for, 115; and high school students, 155, 156; and incarcerated men in workhouse, 152; Kerner Commission classification of, 5; and middle-class Black leadership, 67; municipal government's response to, 71–73, 136–37, 138, 151; and National Guard, 67, 68, 83–84, 121–22, 126; as opportunity for Black men to regain control, 115–16; police abuse before and during, 83; property damage during, 70, 92, 105; as strategic shift, 44–45; violence by youth during, 73; white participation in, 104
Cincinnati uprising (1968), 143
Citizens Coordinating Committee for Civil Liberties (4CL), 34–35
civil disorders: defined, 6; escalation of, 9; flash mobs as, 165–66; framing of, after murder of George Floyd, 8–9; as neutral term, 4; violent, defined, 173n36. *See also* uprisings
civil rights leadership: and Black working class, 43, 44, 47, 48, 118; inability of, to create lasting changes, 48–49; increase in demands made by, 100; in Milwaukee, 58, 59–60; as mirroring of southern civil rights movement, 61; traditional, during uprisings, 96, 98; uprisings and new generation of, 55, 65–66, 71, 81, 98, 118; waning respect for, in Cincinnati, 68

civil rights movement: advances in 1960s of, 1; as affecting just South, 2; Black middle class as beneficiary of, 47; efforts prior to mid-1960s, 45–46, 60; as elite-driven, 17; as middle-class movement, 13; urban uprisings as bridge between Black Power movement and, 61. *See also* Black Freedom Movement

class: as coconspirator with racism, 61; defined, 47; intraracial class antagonisms of uprising participants, 14; and Midwest as "museum-piece," 25; and militancy, 46; and participation in uprisings, 53–54; and targeting during and after uprisings, 98, 99; and trust in political system, 48; uprisings as reaction against, 60–61; violence in US history, 88. *See also* Black middle class; Black working class

cognitive liberation, 53–54, 94, 183n54

collective interest, 14, 15

Collins, Charles, 152

Common View (Milwaukee), 76–77, 78

Cooper, Brittany, 167

CORE, 55, 68, 152–53

Cornelius, Sam, 65, 138

counter-rioters, middle-class Black people as, 14–15, 96

Crespino, Joseph, 10–11

Danner, Edward, 36

Davis, David, 104, 123, 129

Davis, Elaine, 28, 104, 129–30

Davis, Johnny, 91–92

Dawson, Michael, 45, 181n15

Demet, Francis, 39

demonstrations, defined, 172n14, 173n36

Dennis, Sam, 142, 143

Detroit Housewives League, 45

Detroit uprising, 56, 125

Dickerson, Sandra, 127

Dixon, Thomas, 67–68

Dobranski, Bernard, 58, 77

Dolan, Julia, 39

Donaldson, JoAnn, 57

DuBose, Deborah, 117, 127–28

Dundee and West Omaha Sun, 55; political cartoon in, 95

E., Pauline, 93, 119, 123, 128–29

economy of Midwest: and Black neighborhoods after uprisings, 135–36; Black people as "canaries in the mines" for, 13; industrial decline of, 26, 51; recession in Black areas, 13

education in Midwest: and Black educators in public schools, 37; and class assignments, 29; current state of, 163; protests in schools, 9, 153–56, 154; segregation of, 29

Eick, Gretchen Cassel, 11

employment: Black-white gap in Midwest, 163; programs as response to uprisings, 136–39; of uprising participants, 105; of white working-class males, 102

employment, of African Americans. *See* Black people, employment of

Estes, Steve, 194n8

Felker-Kantor, Max, 83, 142

Final Report of the Mayor's Study Committee on Social Problems of the Inner Core Area of the City (Milwaukee), 36, 38

Flaming, Karl L., 90, 124, 131; *Who "Riots" and Why?*, 90

flash mobs, 165–66

Floyd, George, 8

Floyd, Homer C., 50

Ford, Melissa, 45

Fox, Martha, 51

Frakes, Peter, 12, 66, 67, 74

Freedom North (Theoharis and Woodard), 2

Frye, Marquette, 16

Gadsen, Maude, 194n6

Gaines, Kevin, 48

Gardere, Jeff, 165

gender: as catalyst for uprisings, 15–16, 109–10, 115, 118; in media coverage of uprisings, 131; and Midwest as

"museum-piece," 25; in Moynihan report, 18; and research teams, 131; targeted violence, 118–19, 122–33. *See also* Black men; Black people, employment of; Black women; employment; masculinity; white women
Gibson, Kenneth, 44
Gillian, Richard, 154–55
Gimble, Frank, 58
Goodwin, Dan, Sr., 49, 112, 119, 140
Gordon, Colin, 164
Governor's Commission on Human Rights (Nebraska), 53
Graham, Tecumseh X., 100
Great Migration, 28
Green, Bruce, 48, 49, 74, 98, 100
Gregory, Dick, 124; "Gregory Report on Civil Disorders," 124
"Gregory Report on Civil Disorders" (Gregory), 124
Groppi, James, 58, 59–60, 77, 104
Gurr, Ted, 51–52, 172n12

H., Finley, 121
Hacker, Frederick, 112
Hahn, Norman, 72–73
Hall, Joe, 95
Halvorsen, Britt, 164
Hamilton, Charles, 47; *Black Power*, 47
Harding, Vincent, 41
Harlem, NY, uprising (1943), 16
Hayes, Mrs. Thomas, 35
Haynes, William, 71
heartland, as concept: fashioning of, 24; and myth of racial homogeneity, 24, 31, 163–64, 169; and populist politics, 24–25
Heese, David, 136
Height, Dorothy, 110–12; *Report on Four Consultations*, 110–12, 194n6
"Here-Now-All mood," 54–55
Hewitt, Edwin J., 135
Higbie, Tobias, 24
Hill, Lance, 194n16
Hill, Robert, 103
Hinton, Elizabeth, 11

Hobsbawm, Eric, 175n80
housing: in Cincinnati, 92; Common View's demands after Milwaukee uprising, 76; Milwaukee marches for open, 107; open housing as threat to white womanhood, 192n61; open housing ordinance in Omaha, 34–35; and public transportation, 27; and racial covenants or steering, 28; segregation of, in Omaha vs. Birmingham, 29
Housing and Urban Development Act (1965), 28
Hudson, Ronald, 117
Hunt, Harold, 35, 43, 57, 74, 100, 152

immigrants, in Midwest, 164
Inner Core (Milwaukee), 78
institutional racism. *See* structural racism
integrationist civil rights approach, 46, 48
interracial marriage, 36

Jackson, John, 78–79
Jackson, Nelson C., 35
Jarreau, Marshall, 79
Johnson, Calvin, 49
Johnson, Cenoria D., 194n6
Johnson, Lathan, 134
Johnson, Mutope, 40, 84, 139, 142, 147
Johnson, Victoria E., 145–46
Jones, Kelsey, 34–35
Journeyman Union Manpower Program (JUMP), 27

Karenga, Maulana, 44
Kerner, Otto, 2
Kerner Commission, 2, 5; on average uprising participant, 13; on Black leadership in Milwaukee, 59–60; on Black middle class's view of uprisings, 94; Black women in, 125; on changes in Black organizations after uprisings, 152; conclusions of, 2, 162; and dismissal by local officials of Black grievances, 52–53; on employment programs after uprisings, 137, 138; on increase in demands of traditional

Kerner Commission (*continued*)
Black organizations, 100; on intraracial class antagonisms of participants, 14; on legitimization of violence, 55, 153; on Maier, 31, 34, 77; on Milwaukee city government, 33; on nonviolent protests, 44; on police, 30, 142; on possible violence against Black middle class, 98, 99; on property damage, 90; on racial climate in Milwaukee, 58; system for classifying uprisings of, 5; on talk of violence by national organizations, 55; on targets during uprisings, 15; on violence vs. traditional forms of protest, 73; on white beliefs about Black employment, 39; on Young Commandos, 58–59
King, Charles, 58–59
Klein, James, 155
Kopp, George S., Sr., 38–39

L., Roger, 119–20
Lakers, Peter, 53
Lang, Clarence, 11, 32–33
Larkey, Hilda, 59
Larkey, Jay, 59
Laskey, Posteal, 12, 66
Lassiter, Matthew, 10–11
Le Bon, Gustave, 53
Lemberg Center for the Study of Violence (Brandeis University), 5–7
Lemelle, Anthony, 194n8
Levy, Peter, 174n41
Lilligren, Robert, 163
Lindsay, Inabel, 194n6
Loder, James, 109, 140, 141
Los Angeles, 44, 64
Lucas, Robert, 153
Luce Press Clippings, 6, 7
Lynch, Lincoln O., 153

Mackinder, Halford, 24
Maier, Henry, 34; on Black people not participating in uprising, 89; and *Final Report of the Mayor's Study Committee on Social Problems of the Inner Core Area of the City*, 36, 38; and media, 149; meeting with Black leadership, 71; response of, to open housing marches, 107; response of, to uprising, 12, 68, 69, 77, 78–80, 82; as traditional "liberal," 31; and vocation training programs, 27
Major, Gerri, 194n6
Malcolm X, 46
Mallory, William, 100
Marshall, Cleveland, 51
masculinity: defined, 194n8; looting and, 117; markers of, 114; and nonviolent protests, 194n16; participation in uprisings as restoration of Black men's, 18, 115–16, 117; and protection of women, 119, 122–23; and rhetoric during uprisings, 115; of white men as being threatened, 103, 105
Mathews, William H., 81
McAdam, Doug, 94, 183n54
McCaslin, Jack, 32, 104
McClarty, Marvin, 30, 69, 112–13, 139
McCone Commission, 64
McCracken, Maurice, 51
McKissick, Clifford, 69, 77, 142
McKissick, Floyd, 91, 94, 114
McLaughlin, Malcolm, 47, 60, 72, 84
McNair, Rudolph, 34–35
McPheeters, David, 146–47
McVoy, Lawrence W., 35, 49, 71
media: coverage of uprisings by, 7–8, 147–50; framing of collective violence by, 8–9; gender and coverage of uprisings by, 131; Midwest as proxy for imagined America, 145–46, 147; and "Negro revolt," 1–2; racial bias of, 7; social media and primacy of traditional, 166
meritocracy myth, 23, 25, 41, 162
Middlebrook, Brenda, 121, 122
Midwest: as conveyor of US values, 23, 41, 177n14, 181n105; employment of Black people in, 2–3, 26, 51; end of era as industrial powerhouse, 26; erasure of Black people in, 24, 31, 163–64, 168–69; foundational identity of, 23, 24; history of Black activism in, 168;

immigrants in, 164; as industrial, 2; informal "Jim Crow" in, 117; as media proxy for imagined America, 145–46, 147; as "museum-piece," 25; 1967 uprisings in, 3, 23; as providing cover for white supremacy, capitalism, and paternalism, 23–24; white indifference to structural racism in, 17

midwestern myth, 17, 23, 177n14; American dream as alive in, 146; and Black youth, 56; denial of structural racism in, 40, 169; frontier in, 120, 177n14; hard work as rewarded in, 28, 31, 51, 90; of meritocracy, 23, 25, 41, 162; as national ethos, 162; persistence of, 19; of racial homogeneity, 24, 31, 163–64, 169; vs. realities of Black life, 31, 163; region as insulated from racial friction in, 40–41; use of violence to maintain, 102; and Wallace-initiated civil disorders, 22

militant civil rights approach, 45–46

Miller, Paul, 156

Milwaukee, WI: Black leadership in, 58, 59–60; Black nationalism in, 58; Black people in government in, 32–34, 179n74; Black Power movement in, 58–59; education in, 29; employment of Black police in, 140; housing in, 27; Neighborhood Youth Corps and Youth Council Operation jobs, 28; open housing marches, 107; police abuse in, 10, 12, 83, 97; public transportation in, 27; racial climate in, 58

Milwaukee uprising (July 30–August 4, 1967), 12, 68–69, 84; arrests during, 82–83; Black women's participation in, 125–26; and Common View's demands, 76–77; as continuation of protests ignored by government, 76; fatalities and injuries during, 92; Kerner Commission classification of, 5; media collaboration with local government during, 149; "Milwaukee's Marshall Plan," 79; municipal government's response to, 71, 78–80, 137, 140; and National Guard, 12, 68–69, 79, 82, 84, 126; participants in, 28, 124; police abuse during, 97; property damage during, 92; white participation in, 102, 104. *See also* Maier, Henry

Mimms, James, 57, 69, 121–22, 151

Minneapolis, MN, 163

Minutemen, 107

Miskovsky, M. C., 55, 150, 153

Modlinski, Julius, 77

Monáe, Janelle, 169

Morrison, Frank, 65–66

Moss, Otis, Jr., 152

Moynihan, Daniel Patrick, 18; *The Negro Family*, 18

Moynihan, Paul, 77

Murrell, Peter, 99

Myers, Daniel J., 7–8

myths: of American innocence, 162; of meritocracy, 23, 25, 41, 162; midwestern (*see* midwestern myth); of racial homogeneity of heartland, 24, 31, 163–64, 169

National Advisory Committee on Civil Disorders. *See* Kerner Commission

National Association for the Advancement of Colored People (NAACP): burning of Milwaukee headquarters of, 116, 195n21; conservatism of, 49; on Executive Code of Fair Practices, 31; and Omaha uprising, 65–66; picketing by, 52; Young Commandos, 12, 58–59

National Association for the Advancement of White People, 107

National Guard: in Cincinnati, 67, 68, 83–84, 121–22, 126; in Milwaukee, 12, 68–69, 79, 82, 84, 126; in Omaha, 65, 116; training, 142; as ultimate culmination of state power, 83, 84–85; use of, as strategic political tool, 80

Nebraska: Black grievances dismissed by government in, 53; Black people in government in, 32–33, 36; interracial marriage in, 36

Neel, Betsy, 66, 83–84, 119, 121

Negro Family, The (Moynihan), 18
"negro history," 41
Negro in Avondale, The (Saunders), 54
Newark, NJ, uprising, 56
Newburn, Tim, 9
New Right backlash, 64
New York Times, 7–8, 79–80, 87, 125
nonviolent protests, 52; effectiveness of, 44–45, 51, 56, 60, 96; leadership in Milwaukee of, 58; and masculinity, 194n16; Omaha Black boycott, 10

Ochonicky, Adam, 102, 103
Ohio Executive Code of Fair Practices (1963), 31
Ologboni, Tejumola: and housing segregation, 28; on ineffectiveness of peaceful protests, 55–56; on Milwaukee uprising as preplanned, 68; on racism in Midwest vs. in South, 38; on targets of uprisings, 69–71; on violence as language of America, 167
Omaha, NE: Black boycott in, 10; Black educators in public schools in, 37; Black people in government in, 32–33, 34; Boys' Club in, 187n50; death of teenager in police custody in, 55; housing in, 28; loss of employment for Black people in, 26; municipal government's response to uprisings in, 66, 71–73, 136–37, 138, 139; new charter in, 34; open housing ordinance in, 34–35; police-community relations in, 140–41; police in, 30, 109; vs. segregation in Birmingham, 29; Wallace in, 21–22, 140–41, 176n4, 176n7
Omaha Star, 15, 19, 49, 95, 100–101, 116
Omaha uprising (July 2–5, 1966), 11–12, 64–66; arrests during, 82; Black grievances dismissed by government and, 52–53; Black youth as leaders in, 65–66, 71; gender as catalyst for, 16; Kerner Commission classification of, 5; media collaboration with local government during, 148–49; and National Guard, 65, 116; taunting of police during, 83; white participation in, 104. *See also* Sorenson, A. V.
Omaha uprisings: 1968, 140–41, *141*, 153–56, *154*; 1969, 100–101, 109–10, 116, 117, 135–36, 198n7
Omaha World-Herald, 69–70, 176n7

Paige, Jeffrey, 14, 56
Palin, Sarah, 24
Parchia, Earl, 78
Parham, Marjorie, 36, 50, 92, 93
Pavel, Duane, 154–55
Peak, Frank, 53, 110, 193n2
peripherality, 56, 183n66
Phillips, Diane, 98
Phillips, Vel, 92, 97, 98, 133–34
Pierce, Richard, 31
"Plan to Burn Los Angeles, The" (Allen), 120
Poindexter, Frank, 193n2
police: arrests during uprisings by, 81–82, 121, 125, 126, 127, 130–31; and Black women in non-normative roles, 130–31; challenges to authority of, during Cincinnati uprising, 116–17; and Common View's demands, 77; community relations after uprisings, 139–42, 156–57; discrimination in hiring officers in Cincinnati, 30; disrespect of Black officers by, 112–13; increase in armed, after uprisings, 141–42, 156–57; middle-class Cincinnati Black leadership request for increased, 67; and Milwaukee uprising, 68–69; training of, after uprisings, 142; treatment of Black middle class during uprisings by, 96; whites' call for increased, 32
police abuse: arbitrary stop-and-frisk of Black men, 32, 113; of Black women, 114–15; as catalysts for uprisings, 16, 109–10, 118; Cincinnati uprising and, 12, 66, 67, 83, 139–40; and Common View's demands, 77; as complaint before and after uprisings, 30; death of teenagers in Omaha, 55, 100–101,

109–10, 140; during 2020 uprisings, 168; invisibility of, 167; in Milwaukee, 10, 12, 83, 97; in Omaha, 140–41; race and, 30

political system: and accommodation, 49; Black grievances dismissed by, 52–53; and Black political agency, 18–19; Black politicians in, 44, 49; class and trust in, 48; increase in clout of Black people, 151; ineffectiveness of, for Black working class, 14, 15, 36, 175n80, 176n88; and law and order agenda, 8; in Milwaukee, 58; piecemeal solutions after uprisings by, 133–34; response to uprisings of, 133–34, 145–50; tokenism in, 31–32, 54, 55; unresponsiveness of, to nonviolent protests, 44–45, 51, 56, 60, 96; uprising activists attempts to coerce, 64; and uprisings as calculated strategy, 3, 4; use of civil rights committees by, 35; use of traditional civil rights leadership during uprisings by, 96, 98; voting as leading to power in, 32–34, 179n74

Poole, John, 67–68

Popp, Tom, 39, 59

populist politics, and heartland concept, 24–25

powerlessness, feelings of, 56, 57, 183n66

Price, Rena, 16

property damage, during uprisings, 10, 69–71, 70, 90–92, 93, 101, 105, 174n44

protests, defined, 172n14

Pschachler, Hubert, 68

Purnell, Brian, 2; *The Strange Careers of the Jim Crow North*, 2

R., Willie, 121

race: makeup of Midwest, 24, 163–64; media coverage of, during uprisings, 7–8; and Midwest as "museum-piece," 25; of participants in uprisings, 8, 9; and police departments, 30; relations as well-managed, 35–36; in US history narrative, 162; and view of catalysts for uprisings, 32

racism: as coconspirator with class, 61; and federal programs and enforcement of laws, 26–27; in media, 7; in police departments, 112–13; by trade unions, 3, 13, 27; uprisings as reaction against, 60. *See also* racism, in Midwest

racism, in Midwest: and erasure of Black people, 13, 168–69; and midwestern myth, 40–41; and myth of racial homogeneity of heartland, 24, 31, 163–64, 169; as part of foundational identity, 23, 24; vs. in South, 13, 29, 36, 38

Radical Information Project (University of Michigan), 9

Ransford, H. Edward, 183n66

Reagan, Ronald, 64

rebellions, 4, 5. *See also* uprisings

rebels, use of term, 5

recreational facilities, 29

Reid, Robert, 70, 100

Reno, Joshua, 164

Report on Four Consultations (Height), 110–12, 194n6

revolts, 5, 172n14. *See also* uprisings

Revolutionary Action Movement, 55

Reynolds, Clint, 36, 104

Rhodes, Jim, 31

Riot Data Review (Lemberg Center), 5–7

riots: grievances underlying, 172n13; as response to unmet demands, 14, 15, 175n80; US Criminal Code definition of, 9

Roberts, Gene, 87

"Role of Ghetto Retail Merchants in Civil Disorders, The" (Berk), 91

Rucker, Carl Edward, 154–55

Saunders, Talitha, 54; *The Negro in Avondale*, 54

schools, uprisings in, 9, 153–56

Schott, Jacob, 83, 151

Schrempp, Mrs. Warren, 35

Schrotel, Stanley, 30

segregation, 29, 40

Seitz, Ed, 40–41

Shellow, Robert, 153

Index 235

Shuttlesworth, Fred, 68
Smith, James W., 109
Smith, Rudy, 69–70, 116
social media, 166–67; vs. traditional media, 166
Sorensen, A. V., 116; creation of Mayor's Patrol by, 73; demands presented to, after 1966 uprising, 11; meeting with teenage rebels, 65–66, 71; and National Guard, 65; and Omaha Boys' Club, 187n50; and Omaha charter, 34; and recreational and jobs programs, 72, 138, 139; reinforcement of fissures within Black community by, 81
Sorensen, Phillip C., 65
South: civil rights movement as only in, 2; civil rights movement in Midwest vs. in, 61; racism in Midwest vs. in, 13, 29, 36, 38, 117
Spencer, Donald, 74, 101, 139
Spencer, Floyd, 67
Spencer, Marian, 43, 80–81, 96
Spilerman, Seymour, 174n41
Stahmer, David, 36
state, definition of uprisings by, 9
Stevenson, Howard, 140–41, 141
Stokes, Elvin, 176n7
Strange Careers of the Jim Crow North, The (Theoharis, Woodard, and Purnell), 2
Strong, Vivian, 100–101, 140
structural racism: and employment, 27; and midwestern myth, 40, 169; and myth of racial homogeneity of heartland, 24, 31, 163–64, 169; and working-class activism, 176n88
Student Nonviolent Coordinating Committee (SNCC), 55, 75, 153
Studt, George, 151
Sugrue, Thomas, 4, 192n61
Super. B. D., 105
Sykes, J. G., 63

T., Willie, 131
Taggart, Paul, 24
tangible gain, 14, 15
Taylor, Eloise, 39

Taylor, Keeanga-Yamahtta, 28
Teaford, John C., 2
terminology: and carceral logic of state, 9; Kerner Commission classification, 5; naming mass demonstrations, 4, 172nn13–14; for "uprising," 5, 9, 172nn13–14; US Criminal Code definition of "riots," 9
Terry, Robert, 39–40
Theoharis, Jeanne, 2; *Freedom North*, 2; *The Strange Careers of the Jim Crow North*, 2
Tilly, Charles, 15
trade unions: racism by, 3, 13, 27; and working-class activism, 176n88
Truth About Civil Turmoil, 120
Tucker, Sterling, 15
Tucker, Walter, 101
Turner, Bailey W., 74, 100, 150
Turner, Frederick Jackson, 120, 177n14
Turner, Ralph, 153

underclass, defined, 189n10
United Brothers, 44
United Negro Improvement Association, 45
uprisings: Black middle class as liberated by, 50; Black middle class views of, 94–98, 95; Black physical violence against whites during, 117, 127; as bridge between civil rights movement and Black Power movement, 61; as calculated political strategy, 3, 4; categorization of seriousness of, 5–7, 172n23; change in norms as purpose of, 71; civil rights committees and, 35; as consumer revolts, 91; deaths during, 10; disruption of functioning of cities by, 64; and effectiveness of nonviolent protests, 44–45, 51, 56, 60, 96; foundation for, 17, 51; geographic breadth of, 11; and intraracial class antagonisms, 14, 15; as last resort to address grievances, 38, 52; as logical extension of civil rights demonstrations, 54; looting during, 71, 117,

127–28; and matriarchal structure of Black families, 111; media coverage of, 7–8, 147–50; and new generation of Black leadership, 55, 65–66, 71, 81, 98, 118; as opportunities for Black men to regain control, 115–16; police abuse during, 97; political system's use of traditional civil rights leadership during, 96, 98; property damage during, 10, 69–71, 70, 90–92, 93, 101, 174n44; as reaction against the "system," 60; as rehearsals for a Communist revolution, 120; rhetoric during, 115, 123–24; in schools, 9, 153–56, 154; since 1960s, 160; statistics of, 3, 9, 10, 23, 174n41, 174n45; as symbolic weapons, 75–76; tacit condoning of, by Black people, 89; terminology, 4, 5, 9, 172nn13–14; as transitional moment within Black Freedom Movement, 44–45, 61; twenty-first century, 19, 165, 166–68; whites' call for increased police during, 32; and working class, 13–14. *See also names of specific rebellions*

uprisings, catalysts for: gender, 15–16, 109–10, 118; police abuse, 109–10, 118; racial disparities, 32; Wallace appearance, 21–22, 140–41, 154, 154–55, 176n7

uprisings, effects of: Black people viewed as violent criminals, 156; in Cincinnati, 71–72, 136–37, 138, 139, 151; creation of "blue-ribbon investigative committees," 146–47; creation of employment programs, 136–39, 140; diminishing political returns of, 17, 64; excising urban places, 145–46; gender and gains from, 131–32; increased cooperation among civil rights groups, 150, 151, 152–53; increase in clout of Black people, 151; in Milwaukee, 71, 78–80, 137, 140; New Right backlash, 64; in Omaha, 66, 71–73, 136–37, 138; on police-community relations, 139–42, 156–57; on recreational opportunities, 139; renewed sense of racial solidarity, 152; sense of "Selfhood," 150–51; solutions as piecemeal, 133–34

uprisings, participants in, 14, 124; arrests of, 81–82, 121, 125, 126, 127, 130–31; average, 88–89; Black men as, 18, 89, 151; Black middle class as, 18, 100–101, 108, 161; Black working class as, 13–14, 18, 47, 88, 93; Black women as, 16, 18, 125–29, 130–31; Black youth as, 28, 57, 60, 88, 153–56, 154; class of, 53–54; comparison of white and Black, 103; as criminals, 81; employment status of, 89, 105; feelings of powerlessness and levels of trust of, 56, 57, 183n66; hostility toward white and middle-class Black people of, 46; and masculinity of Black men, 18; positive Black identity of, 56; race of, 8, 9; roles of, 165; whites as, 161; white working-class males as, 18, 93, 102–5

uprisings, targets during, 15; Black middle class as, 97–98; class position and, 99; employment centers as, 105; individuals perceived as not belonging in community as, 92–93; white-owned businesses as, 90–92; wives of police as, 122–33

Upton, James, 14

Urban League and Omaha uprising (1966), 65

US Capitol, January 6, 2021, assault on, 164

US organization, 44

Vaughan, Lenford, 109

Vernon, Robert, 60; *Black Ghetto*, 60–61

Vinegar, Clyde, 29, 67, 68, 74, 139

violence: and arming of whites, 105, 107, 121; Black belief in necessity of, 124, 153; and Black Nationalist and Black Power rhetoric, 153; by Black women, 127; and civil disorders, 9; collective, by whites, 8; conditions for collective, 52; as definitional component of riot, 9; and firearms during uprisings, 103–5; as fixture of US life, 8, 167; historical perpetrators of, 172n12; instead

violence (*continued*)
of more traditional forms of protest, 73; interpersonal, during uprisings, 92–93; as justifiable protest tactic, 161; and law and order agenda, 8; media framing of, 8–9; and myth of American innocence, 162; and new generation of Black leadership, 55; as part of Midwest's founding, 23; use of, to maintain midwestern myth, 102; white perception of Black predilection toward, 8. *See also* uprisings

Virgin, John A., 114–15

voting: as leading to political power, 32–34, 179n74; rights, 38, 46

Voting Rights Act (1965), 1

W. Jessie, 121

W., Mary, 131

Wallace, George, 1968 presidential campaign, 20, 21–22, 140–41, 176n4, 176n7

Wallace, Ruth, *126*

Ward, Adolphus, *101*

Washington, Charles, 72

Washington, Robert, 56

Washington Post, 7–8

Watts, CA, uprising: Allen's "The Plan to Burn Los Angeles," 120; gender as catalyst for, 16; increase in armed police presence in, 142; matriarchal structure of Black families as cause of, 111; and US organization, 44

Weaver, Robert, 74

white people: arming of, 105, 107, 121; belief in absence of discrimination in Midwest, 13; belief in race relations as well-managed, 35; Black grievances and lived experiences ignored by, 32; Black middle class's adoption of norms of, 48; Black physical violence against, during uprisings, 117, 127; Black political agency and retrenchment of power of, 18–19; businesses of, as targets, 15, 90–92; call for increased police during uprisings by, 32; catalysts for uprisings according to, 32; civil rights movement leadership's adoption of norms of, 54; collective violence by, 8; excising urban places of uprisings by, 145–46; fear of loss of rights to minorities, 164; fear of invasion of neighborhoods by Black people, 120–21; indifference of, to structural racism, 17; invasion of Black communities by armed, 119–20; masculinity of, as threatened, 103, 105; and media portrayal of uprisings, 147–50; and midwestern myth, 17, 23, 25; as Midwest's only racial group, 24, 31, 163–64, 169; as participants in uprisings, 8, 9, 161; sexual violence against Black women by, 118–19; uprisings and growth of vigilante groups among, 19, 107, 120–21; working-class, as participants in uprisings, 18, 93, 102–5. *See also* Black people, white views of; white women

white women: normative participation in uprisings of, 129–30; open house as threat to, 192n61; use of symbolic motherhood by, 192n61

Who "Riots" and Why? (Flaming), 90

Wichita, KS, drug store sit-in (1958), 10

Wichman, William, 67

Wilson, Larry, 176n7

Wilson, William Julius, 189n10

Winfrey-Harris, Tamara, 24, 164

Woodard, Komozi, 2; *Freedom North*, 2; *The Strange Careers of the Jim Crow North*, 2

Woods, Reverend General, 136

Wright, Noel, 127

Yarnell, Harold E., Jr., 120

Young, Whitney, 112

Young Commandos, 12, 58–59

Zeidler, Frank, 36

Zweig, Michael, 47, 189n10

www.ingramcontent.com/pod-product-compliance
Lightning Source LLC
Chambersburg PA
CBHW021900230426
43671CB00006B/464